Gibson, Paul,
    1936-

Bear trap.

$21.50

DATE			

BEAR
TRAP

BEAR TRAP

WHY WALL STREET DOESN'T WORK

PAUL GIBSON

THE ATLANTIC MONTHLY PRESS
NEW YORK
♦

Published simultaneously in Canada
Printed in the United States of America

Library of Congress Cataloging-in-Publication Data

Gibson, Paul R.
    Bear trap: why Wall Street doesn't work / Paul Gibson.
    Includes index.
    ISBN 0-87113-534-5
    1. Wall Street—History. 2. Securities industry—United States—History. 3. Stock-brokers—United States. 4. New York Stock Exchange—History. I. Title.
    HG4572.G47 1993   332.64′273—dc20   92-43735

Design by Laura Hough

The Atlantic Monthly Press
19 Union Square West
New York, NY 10003

First printing

TO DOROTHY, SUZANNA,

ROSALIND, JULIET, AND JOHN

ACKNOWLEDGMENTS

THE BANE OF BEAT REPORTERS COVERING Wall Street's daily activities is their lack of time and opportunity to step back and contemplate the significance of those events. This book attempts to create a cohesive narrative that explains what's happening in the world of finance by tying together hundreds of discrete events. I am indebted to the journalists who uncovered the stories of Wall Street that I have drawn upon and to the numerous Wall Streeters who gave generously of their time and helped me to understand their business.

I am thankful for the wisdom offered by Alvin Butkus, James Flanigan, James Michaels, Allan Sloan, Geoffrey Smith, Howard Rudnitsky, and David Warsh, all of whom have guided my thinking for this book and for stories written when we were colleagues at *Forbes* magazine.

At Atlantic Monthly Press, I am indebted to publisher Morgan Entrekin, who matches insight with enthusiasm, and to his staff. I also thank the librarians at Drew University and in Morris County, New Jersey, who aided my research.

This book would have remained a dream, but for the loving support extended to me by my wife, Dorothy, my daughters Rosalind Gibson and Suzanna Narducci, Suzanna's husband, John, and by my family across the Atlantic. I have drawn deeply on their love, help, insights, and guidance.

Chatham, New Jersey
January 1993

CONTENTS

CONTENTS

CHAPTER ONE

Bear Trap

GREED AND SCANDAL ALMOST RUINED WALL
Street in the eighties. Technology and the lightning-fast movement
of money around the globe are combining to complete the job in the
nineties.

Hear the alarming views of some industry leaders.

Richard Fisher can pinpoint the time and place when he confronted the new reality. It was in 1989, not long before the urbane
Fisher took over as chairman of Morgan Stanley, perhaps the most
technologically advanced and globally minded investment house in
the business. Fisher was doing a walk-around at his midtown Manhattan headquarters, checking on his troops and boosting morale. He
had arrived at the Treasury desk in the cavernous trading room
where Morgan Stanley routinely handles billions of dollars' worth of
transactions for its own and its clients' accounts.

A trader was peering anxiously at a bank of computer screens
that resembled mission control for a space launch, only these were
flashing tidbits of information about government securities, interest
rates, and currencies from around the world. An impressive sight.

"I said, 'Gee, that's terrific,' " recalls Fisher. The trader replied, "No, it's not. I've got eleven screens and the customer has twelve."

Here's Morgan Stanley spending a fortune on communications. Tens of millions each year so that the firm can know in an instant every jiggle in the world's financial markets and plot the prices of God knows how many different securities and their derivatives. And this trader is telling Fisher that's not enough. The customer he's selling knows more about the markets than he does.

That's a power shift, and Fisher winced at what he was hearing. As a top gun and the person soon to have in his hands the ultimate responsibility to shareholders for the firm's well-being, Fisher knew he was in a bind.

Every day the deals handled by youthful traders grow in complexity, size, and speed. This is delegation of responsibility at its most awesome. Only later, after the traders have made those multi-million-dollar commitments, can they pause and tell their bosses what they've done. By then it may be too late. One miscalculated bet and much of the firm's capital could be gone.

Still, Fisher could live with that. The heads of all investment banks learn to suffer through sleepless nights, praying the young techies fresh from grad school with their high-powered computers won't blow up the markets. But now this trader was telling Fisher something more disturbing. Morgan Stanley had lost its edge.

Today one customer. Tomorrow, how many pension managers and mutual fund clients will know what Morgan Stanley knows and maybe even more?

For years, Wall Street had made its money buying at one price and selling at another. Stocks. Bonds. Treasuries. Deutsche marks. Collateralized mortgage obligations. It didn't matter what you called the merchandise. All that counted was the spread. The less the customers knew, the wider the spread and the more money for the house.

No wonder Fisher's jaw dropped. This was the end of the game. And as we move into the nineties the final moments are upon us. Those spreads will shrink to the vanishing point once customers have access to the same information as their bankers and brokers. No more easy profits from acting as a middleman.

The old Wall Street is dying.

The world's financial capital, grossly mismanaged, overweight, and sclerotic, is caught in a trap. Whether it will escape without being mortally wounded is doubtful.

External forces are squeezing the profitability—and the life—out of traditional Wall Street. Global money, computers, and instantly available information plus arcane changes in regulation and taxation are making it impossible to earn profits the old-fashioned way in underwriting or in selling stocks and bonds.

Worse, the new ethic sweeping the land will not tolerate self-dealing and fraud of the kind the financial community practiced in the 1980s.

Fused together, these forces add up to one chilling prospect: Wall Street, as we know it, won't work anymore.

As much as anything, Wall Street was built on the idea that the little guy could go there with his savings and make a few bucks. Simply put, Wall Street's role was that of middleman. It took those tiny streams and channeled them into bigger pools of capital that would finance the growth of the nation. No more. Wall Street is playing a different game.

How capital gets raised and where money is invested are the central questions of a modern economy. Upon the answers depend such mundane but important items as how often we work, the price of a suit or a slice of pizza, and how much change the Bill Clinton administration will indeed achieve in the coming years.

An equally important question is, What will take the place of the Wall Street we know? Socialized capitalism? Industrial planning? The allocation of funds by central bankers? Before we can answer those questions we must look first at how Wall Street is changing.

What ails Wall Street are seven major maladies:

Aging. Like autos and textiles, financial services is now a mature business, with scant differences between the services or products various companies offer. Proprietary products? They're gone. Protection doesn't exist on Wall Street. Knockoffs and copies abound.

Overweight. There are too many overpaid bankers and brokers, too many expensive offices for a market whose golden days lie behind it. Excess capacity abounds. If tomorrow morning the houses cut head count, office space, and communications gear by a quarter, it probably wouldn't be enough to make every house profitable.

The volume increases that were a feature of the ebullient eighties—revenues almost tripled to $60 billion—aren't likely to be repeated in the parsimonious nineties. Yet the firms, with hardly any exceptions, keep expanding and remain volume oriented. Small wonder then that the money they make on what they stake has slumped in a decade from a rich 31 percent average return on equity to 9 percent, a ridiculous level for such a risky business.

This is a labor-intensive, high-pay, and inefficient business where costs are deemed less important than revenues. Nearly two-thirds of the employees work in Wall Street's back offices and don't generate income.

Competition. Commercial bankers, industrialists, and retailers are swarming over Wall Street's turf. Former clients duplicate brokers' services. Nearly everywhere you look the financial community has problems.

Consider some recent trends. Fidelity Investments, the mutual fund giant, now runs an internal stock exchange, where it executes trades for its own accounts and those of dozens of small brokers. Discounter Charles Schwab gains business by paying his brokers one-third the $98,401 taken home by the average broker on Wall Street.

Commissions, which accounted for a quarter of each revenue dollar a decade ago, now produce barely seventeen cents. Few houses now make money in underwriting and most give away research and equipment worth millions of dollars in a desperate and often futile attempt to woo institutional clients.

Power loss. As Fisher has learned, clients are as savvy as their investment bankers and need Wall Street less and less.

Haphazard regulation. Washington's rule makers have spent years chipping away at the foundations of the securities industry. Needless, and frequently conflicting, rule changes have reduced the opportunities for making money safely. The burden of regulation adds to operating costs.

Obstinacy. Much of the industry ignores the evidence of change and disputes its need for new management strategies to replace those that keep getting them into trouble.

Excessive information. This should be a plus, but isn't. Rapid communications and a surfeit of computer power enable the houses to duplicate each other's hot products and turn them into low-profit commodities. "Product life cycles are accelerating," says Jean-Louis Lelogeais, who studies this business for Booz, Allen and Hamilton, the consultants. It took fifteen years for paper issued by the federal government's mortgage agency to become a commodity, but only two years before spreads on the newer asset-backed securities collapsed.

The spread is the gap between what a buyer will willingly pay and a seller insists on receiving. When the gap narrows, as new products turn into commodities, profit opportunities vanish. Making and trading financial products is much like producing computers. Cutthroat competition and cloning are rampant. The newest generation of products rarely, if ever, matches the profitability of those it replaces.

Wall Street made a new game plan to compensate. During the 1980s, in a calculated move, every major house switched strategy. They changed from being solely or primarily agents to acting largely as principals in a desperate bid to enhance profits. Today the trading and investing of funds for their own accounts ranks far higher in importance than the making of markets for clients and the collecting of commissions and fees. The game plan is going badly awry.

The ramifications here are enormous. So are the increased risks. Wall Street is now in competition with its former clients for investment opportunities. "Corporate customers are pissed off with Wall Street," says Lelogeais. "They say Wall Street is a pain in the neck, a bunch of crooks and let's do away with them." Close relationships built over the years between investment bankers and clients have vanished as Wall Streeters pushed their own interests first. And the proliferation of workstations, personal computers, and smart, easy-to-use software threatens thousands of white-collar jobs on Wall Street.

Putting your own funds into a deal rather than those of your customers is great if it works. Too often it doesn't. Look at the record. In an outburst of competitive folly, the Wall Street firms tried to outdo each other by staking their own and borrowed funds in bridge loans, junk bonds, the aiding of raiders, and—in the 1990s—in the rigging of markets and in currency speculations. At Salomon Brothers and Merrill Lynch, to cite but two examples in an industry-wide binge, long-term debts soared in less than five years from under $800 million apiece to over $5 billion each. Excessive use of leverage resulted in the disastrous collapse of Drexel Burnham Lambert and pushed First Boston, Shearson Lehman Hutton, and Prudential-Bache to the brink. Salomon, the pacesetter in trading for itself, produced the first major scandal of the nineties, by attempting to corner the world's largest securities market, the U.S. Treasury auction.

Critics fume about Wall Street's greed and regale their audiences with stories of its criminals, from Michael Milken on down. What isn't explained is the desperation that lies behind the financial community's apparent disdain for morality and regulation. In a business of such intense competition, only brave managers stick to principles. The rest succumb to their fears of less scrupulous competitors edging ahead.

Wall Street bends rules and goes to extremes because its conservative, traditional ways of making money no longer work. Faced with slumping profitability, managers get caught up in sanctioning bigger and riskier deals they believe will yield higher profits. To protect themselves, they invent intricate and obscure hedging devices. Within this context, both foolishness and wrongdoing thrive.

This is a story of Wall Street against Washington and the world. Of how three decades of change that began when President John F. Kennedy altered the rules of investment are shifting power and letting other financial institutions and money centers challenge Wall Street's and New York's supremacy. Not since Washington arbitrarily kicked J. Pierpont Morgan out of investment banking has there been such turmoil in the financial community.

This turmoil causes concern among the more thoughtful of its leaders, such as Frank Zarb. His days on Wall Street stretch back to the fifties, when a different culture was in place. Today he is head man at Smith Barney, which as a midsize firm is more money manager than investment banker. Ask Zarb about what has happened on Wall Street and he replies, "It wasn't anybody's fault, any individual's fault. It was a wave that carried away the community and that was a mistake."

Or ask Frederick Joseph, the former boss of Drexel Burnham. "Management planning and Wall Street? That's an oxymoron, isn't it?" he responds. Fittingly, Joseph, who sometimes claims credit for promoting his firm's role in the junk-bond business, condemned himself and his peers at a conference on bankruptcy.

"Anyone acquainted with the top bankers of our day, or the leading financial geniuses of Wall Street, or our large corporations," says economist John Kenneth Galbraith, "knows that you can encounter some of the most limited men to be found anywhere."[1]

Galbraith can be a curmudgeon but he has put his finger on part of the problem. The sums being invested keep getting larger, but the acumen of the participants doesn't. John Gutfreund had admitted as much long before his ignominious exit from Salomon. "Our problem is symptomatic of Wall Street's problem. The business has grown faster than our ability to manage it," Gutfreund said four years before his firm was caught rigging the Treasury auctions.[2]

Listen to Robin Stainer, another veteran industry watcher. "It's a fairly heretical thing to say, but a lot of the market comprises smart people convincing less smart people that an activity is in their common interest when often it is not," says Stainer, a partner with consultants Arthur Andersen in London. You might say that in financial circles the art of the con flourishes.

Today, the leading firms are using their own funds to take huge positions in complicated deals involving interest rates, currencies, and esoteric securities that aren't fully regulated or documented. Federal regulators fear any of these could collapse one day soon and send all securities markets tumbling along with many of the nation's banks and other financial institutions, which also are in over their heads.

With the evolution of global money, Wall Street has leveraged itself from cottage industry into freewheeling worldwide business, in which billions of dollars in obligations go unrecorded in private pacts and where one misstep could trigger economic meltdown.

This isn't a business the public can ignore blithely. The financial community's transactions in dollar terms are equal to about one-fifth of the gross national product. What happens there can—and does—leave the rest of the nation shaking in its boots for months. Thanks to electronics, nearly $2 trillion moves around the world each day in search of investment opportunities. To put that in perspective: If you put almost four million dollars into a pile every minute, day and night, including Sundays and holidays, it would take a year to get to $2 trillion.

In this rising tide of global money, simple stocks and bonds—the bedrock of traditional investing—are being swept aside. Usurping their place are chains of interlinked investments. Dangerous? You bet.

Robert Glauber is now at Harvard, but he was a senior Treasury official and director on the Brady commission, which probed the 1987 crash. Still a worried man, what alarms him now are the elaborate hedging devices put in place by the big-league investors. "Are they making the same erroneous assumptions made by so many portfolio insurers?" Glauber wonders.

Ah, portfolio insurance. That was the elaborate hedging strategy the smart money operators thought would get them safely out ahead of the crowd if the stock market turned down. Wrong. In October 1987 the insurance strategies blew up. Today we have intricate daisy chains—often referred to as *swaps*—that now link virtually all types of financial instruments and players to each other. Their aim, as we will see in detail in chapter 6, is to custom design investments that aren't as dangerous as bread-and-butter stocks and bonds. Perhaps that's possible. Glauber has his doubts. He wonders whether these newer hedging devices will prove any more reliable than their predecessors in the event of another sudden downdraft in the markets. As he says, will the hedgers be able to cover themselves "with a few deft trades on the futures or the stock exchanges?"[3]

Among those who share Glauber's concern is Paul Volcker. The former Federal Reserve chairman bluntly contends that "the financial system as a whole, and individual institutions within it, can't be effectively hedged against the failure of large numbers of important clients."[4]

Here's another scary thought. The laws that govern the business of finance were born in the Depression. Written for a bygone era, they don't cover today's investing strategies or needs. Nor can they cope with interlocked, global markets. Securities firms, thrifts, commercial banks, commodity brokers, and pension funds each have their own regulators and separate sets of rules. Those regulators, as often as not, report to different committees in Congress. Plenty of cracks for the wily to slip through. The Bank of Credit and Commerce International demonstrated how wide are the gaps between global regulators. Futurists such as Alvin Toffler say volatility in the financial markets is only going to get worse. "Old safety mechanisms, designed to maintain financial stability in a world of relatively closed national economies," says Toffler, "are as obsolete as the rust-belt world they were designed to protect."[5]

Another part of the problem here is technology. It breeds conformity. Money managers spend their days staring at information-filled screens and reach almost identical conclusions about the economic outlook. Conformity is fine until it translates into the madness of crowds and creates panic in the markets. Traders say currency moves that used to take six months to a year now occur in weeks or hours. The rest of the world can only watch and hold its breath, as it did during the Maastricht mayhem.

In the stock market, months of boredom are punctuated by hours and days of terror. With the arrival of autumn, investors bite their nails. October has become the scariest of months, with its record of one megacollapse, two minicrashes, and a global currency crisis in three of the last five years. Throw in the plunges that came with the Kuwait invasion, the Soviet coup, and the credit card scare in 1991 and you begin to see why individuals are reluctant investors.

Tucked in the back of many investors' minds is the warning uttered by former chairman of the New York Stock Exchange, John J. Phelan, Jr. Sometime in the nineties, he predicted, we could have a horrendous crash. "The granddaddy of all granddaddies," said

Phelan, so bad that "1,000 points will look like a pretty mild day."[6] You might ask, But wouldn't the exchange stop trading? Yes, but what about all the transactions that take place away from the Big Board and beyond the control of the regulators?

Among students of long-term business cycles, plenty see all the private and public debts and deficits pointing toward a gloomy future. Goodness knows what will happen to the markets and Wall Street if they're right.

From the perspective of many customers, Wall Street has brought about its own demise. The disenchanted are legion. Individual investors, long-suffering victims of dubious advice, are turning their backs on Wall Street and handing their investments over to professional managers of pension and mutual funds. Or quitting entirely. In turn, vast pools of capital in those funds are bypassing Wall Street.

Pension funds, insurance companies, and even manufacturing firms are taking the management of their assets away from Wall Street and handling them in-house. It's cheaper and the results thus far are no worse. Increasingly, these institutions, armed with their own computers and advisors, trade among themselves and avoid public stock exchanges whenever they can. Only 10 percent of the trading of major index funds goes through an exchange. The rest is handled by internal transactions or through off-exchange systems. The professionals would do their darnedest to ensure this trading wouldn't stop in the event of a precipitous drop in the Dow.

Meanwhile, corporate treasurers find common cause with fund executives in forcing the Wall Street houses to lower the fees they charge for dealmaking, underwriting and trading securities. More and more, corporate America avoids consulting Wall Street. Many large companies such as International Business Machines, Philip Morris, and Du Pont employ their own staffs to handle the financing of acquisition deals and the issuing of commercial paper. IBM even runs a money fund, and in Switzerland Dow Chemical owns a bank. Less work and less profit for Wall Street.

* * *

Some predictions. Before Wall Street finds a cure for its ailments, thousands of high-paid investment bankers and brokers, along with many of the clerks, lawyers, printers, journalists, publicists, bartenders, and limousine drivers who make their living off financial services, will join the jobless.

Before this decade ends, the final closing bell will sound for floor traders at the New York Stock Exchange as they are replaced by electronics and automated markets. New York's once-bustling financial district will become a litter-strewn ghost canyon.

Sounds farfetched? Take a walk around lower Manhattan today. Already this area is filled with real estate white elephants, vacant office buildings that few want to rent at any price. Shuttered, too, are Tequila Willies and other once-favored watering holes.

A couple of years back, Burton Resnick, a New York developer, bought 40 Wall at auction for $77 million with a loan from Citicorp. Resnick's aim was to restore the structure to its former glory as one of *the* business addresses in Manhattan. What happened? Resnick cut his rents from thirty dollars a square foot to twenty and still couldn't find tenants. Citicorp has foreclosed on its loan and today might accept a *$10 million* bid to get the office block off its hands.[7]

An exodus from Wall Street is under way. Some of the jobs are going across the Hudson River to cheaper locations in New Jersey, where First Chicago sent a thousand of its employees. Others go further afield, to Florida, for instance, where Salomon now operates its back office. Still others just disappear. This is bleak news for a city where until recently financial services supplied four out of ten new jobs and where the equivalent of twenty Empire State Buildings stand vacant.[8]

Here's a point to ponder. Across the country, Wall Street's top clients, the five hundred largest financial institutions, employ some 8,180 portfolio managers, roughly 16 apiece, according to Michael Goldstein, investment strategist at Sanford C. Bernstein. Wall Street itself has an institutional work force that tops 50,000, including support staff. That's six sellers for every buyer. Even swank hotels in Singapore and Hong Kong, with the advantage of cheaper labor, don't assign that many workers to each guest.

Some more predictions. In the 1990s there will be plenty of candidates among the financial community to join Drexel Burnham in oblivion and only three or four hot favorites to make the winner's circle.

The rich fees charged by money managers will come under attack. Customers tolerated a 3 percent charge while the custodians of their money produced double-digit returns. Few expect high returns for stocks, bonds, or money funds this decade. In fact, after adjusting for inflation, plenty of investors may receive less back from their managed accounts than they pay to their advisors.

Securities and investment instruments will grow in complexity. As stocks and bonds are cast aside as old-fashioned, so futures and options will also get relegated to backwaters by yet fancier substitutes. The quantitative analysts—"quants," in trade slang—and their computers will take charge of the business of finance, creating more products, but riskier and less profitable ones. Market liquidity will shrink and volatility rise as professional investors move funds into private rather than public exchanges. We are witnessing the beginning of segregated investment markets, one for amateurs and another for professionals. As this trend accelerates, securities will trade in multitiered markets, which offer different prices. As part of this divergence, the institutions will develop a private trading system beyond the reach of the present regulatory bodies. In time, trading in private markets could become more important than public ones.

New York's preeminence as the world's financial capital will come under attack. London and Tokyo will recover from recent blunders to make the world of finance a three-zone affair. Other cities, from Frankfurt and Paris to Hong Kong and Shanghai, also will gain in importance as money centers. For the moment, London has something of an edge in convenience and culture. When its traders arrive at work, the Tokyo markets are still operating. Before they go home, New York and Chicago are open for business. That's useful if you're running a global portfolio. A couple of other pluses for London: it's less violent than New York and less xenophobic than Tokyo.

Yet, paradoxically, geography and place will become *less* important as global communications shrink time and distance. Already an investor from his perch in a condo on top of a Colorado mountain can hook up to an electronic marketplace almost as easily as someone in a Manhattan office, and at a fraction of the price. Before the decade ends, it will be nearly impossible to find a corner of the earth that cannot be reached by fax or phone. Armed with a notebook computer and a cellular phone, an investor will be able to go on safari in remote Kenya, confident of never losing touch with the current state of the markets. And trade her investments, whatever the time of day or night.

Another paradox. The more that people can be in touch, the less they will choose to be. Regulatory curbs can only do so much to control volatility in public markets, and even less in private ones. As markets continue to roil—stocks one day, currencies the next—more individuals will quit trying to beat the markets on their own and instead place their cash with professional money managers. For brokers this is a double blow. Fewer commissions for Wall Street translates into greater power in the hands of institutional customers.

Wall Street itself is becoming less of a place and more of a concept, a diffuse one at that. Keeping track isn't easy when the roles change from moment to moment. In what other business do firms buy and sell each other's products or participate as partners in deals while simultaneously competing for other transactions with the same partners?

At a casual glance, Wall Street appears to be prospering, with record earnings in 1991 and again in 1992. Regard this as a respite before the storm. The red ink that flooded the Street in 1990 is likely to be the accounting color of the decade.

What's happening here is more than the hollowing out of a major service industry. If spending on technology guaranteed prosperity, Wall Street could look ahead with confidence. Vendors of computers, software, and other communications gear say Wall Street has spent $19 billion in recent years on technology. No firm on the Street lacks for the latest in equipment or programming. Yet that spending doesn't solve the problem, it only exacerbates it.

As microchips and electronics change the way information and money flow, much of what's involved in the business of money becomes redundant. To compensate, Wall Street has only one choice. Raise the level of risk taking.

Wall Street has always been a hazardous business. But in the past, safe bread-and-butter endeavors—the collecting of fees for raising capital and selling securities—compensated for those risks most of the time. No more.

This is indeed a beleaguered business. Thirty years of regulatory, ethical, and technological changes have taken their toll. A close examination of this cumulative effect, as we will see in the next chapter, reveals that Wall Street's future is anything but golden.

CHAPTER TWO

The Winds of Change

POPULAR LORE IS ABOUT A QUARTER RIGHT when it traces Wall Street's woes back to May Day 1975.

True, that was the day the Justice Department broke the cartel of fixed commission rates for securities, and it ranks in the annals of the Street as a day of infamy. Yet one day, or a single event, cannot explain all of the problems in the financial community. The troubles for the financial community started earlier and would get worse with time. The odds are high that the worst is yet to come.

Still, May Day is as good a time as any to start exploring why a passel of legislative and regulatory changes in the past three decades—some complex, some simple—will limit the Street's ability to make money in the 1990s.

On that particular May Day the clouds hanging over Wall Street obscured more than the immediate view. "Brokers had a feeling of not really knowing what perils lurked ahead," commented an observer at the time.[1] The gung-ho crowd, which had its many members, predicted it would be a nonevent. The more sanguine figured the abolition of industry-wide rates for commissions wouldn't be too much of a problem. Competition for business would intensify, to be sure. But brokers planned to recoup any revenues lost on institutional transactions by raising commission charges for individual investors. So what if individual customers complained? Their choices were limited. At this point, a discount brokerage was barely more than an untested idea in Charles Schwab's mind.

That any investor—big or small—could negotiate a lower charge for trading stocks was something of a miracle. For years, the brokerage community had stubbornly resisted change and defied its critics. In 1968, lawyers at the U.S. Department of Justice had written a brief in which they said fixed commissions were contrary to investor interests and government policies.[2] The Securities and Exchange Commission (SEC) had weighed in with accusations of "conflicts of interest and inefficiencies."[3] Now at last, the wheels were about to come off the gravy train.

On the last day of April 1975, the listed charge for commissions for institutions trading at Goldman, Sachs had ranged as high as forty-four cents a share.[4] Urged on by Washington, the institutions now went shopping like a bunch of determined housewives, demanding cuts of between 40 percent and 60 percent. Wall Street resisted, but the siege was on.

Within three years, the charge to most institutions had dropped to around twenty-six cents a share and would keep falling.[5] Today brokers on Wall Street *pay* the institutions to get some of their business, so intense is the competition. Now even individual investors can phone a discount broker and trade for as little as three cents a share. Although most small investors pay far more than that, the days of easy money for brokers are over. Already their pain is apparent. Before the unfixing, every second dollar of revenue on Wall Street came from commissions. Today, fewer than one in five does.

As bad as May Day 1975 was, it wasn't the start of Wall Street's misery. For that we need to go back another dozen years. To July 17, 1963. On that soggy summer day in Washington, D.C., President Kennedy threw a curve ball that an unprepared Wall Street couldn't handle.

Kennedy was facing what's become a perennial problem for U.S. presidents—the U.S. balance of payments deficit was growing uncomfortably large. Worse, the nation's gold stocks had fallen to their lowest level in almost a quarter century. Gold still mattered since foreigners could present their dollars and get gold instead. Funds were flowing out of the country as European and Canadian firms flocked to the United States to raise money they couldn't get in their own cash-starved domestic markets. Looking for a politically dramatic solution, Kennedy asked Congress to impose a tax on Americans who purchased foreign securities.

As new taxes go, this was a whopper. By imposing a 15 percent levy, Kennedy wanted to make borrowing in the United States prohibitively expensive for foreigners.

Global reaction varied from deep concern in London and full-scale panic in Toronto to complete indifference in New York. Wall Street should have paid more attention to what became known as Kennedy's Interest Equalization Tax.

Kennedy didn't know it, but unwittingly he was hastening the era of global money and weakening America's clout within the financial system. His levy did more than keep foreign borrowers out of the U.S. capital markets. It helped build a viable alternative marketplace for foreigners and U.S. investors alike. New York's reign as the unchallenged center of world finance was ending.

The new challenger: the London-based Euromarket, which by the mid-1980s would expand sufficiently to claim the title of the world's largest debt market. London also would become in time the hub for currency trading, particularly for dollars.

"That tax cost us a fortune," says Allan Roth, who teaches finance at Rutgers University and at the time was a staffer at the Securities and Exchange Commission. "It pushed money offshore and created competition for the investment banking industry in the United States," says Roth, who had lobbied against the tax with only modest support from the financial community. Thus was born what became the Eurodollar market.

Curiously enough, a precedent already had been set because of the Cold War. Even before the Kennedy tax some dollars had stayed abroad. In the 1950s, the Soviet bloc governments figured it was

1 7

safer to keep their dollar deposits in London than in New York. That way the Russians could transact business in Europe and avoid the risk of the United States freezing those deposits as part of a political confrontation. Moscow wasn't alone in worrying about the xenophobic actions of a cash-strapped Washington. U.S. firms operating abroad also took to keeping their dollars in London, where there was a ready demand for them.[6]

New York probably could have shrugged off the pesky new competition coming out of London but for an odd coincidence of timing. The Mideast oil crises of the 1970s erupted just when borrowers and lenders alike were beginning to appreciate the bifurcation of the greenback. A fresh flow of dollars cascaded around the globe, and the fledgling and freewheeling Euromarket became the perfect conduit. When they weren't expanding their opulent desert palaces and buying armaments, Saudi Arabia, Kuwait, and the other oil-rich countries, including Iraq, put their surplus dollars to work via the Euromarket.

To be sure, the New York bankers participated in some of this international growth, but only slowly. In the first year after Kennedy put in his tax, the two top U.S. bankers in London were Kuhn, Loeb and White Weld, both of whom would shortly disappear in takeovers.[7] After that, the New Yorkers were always playing catch-up. It would take almost two decades before the transatlantic movement reached its zenith, with New York investment bankers keeping the Concorde filled and building fancy offices in London. By then, the American bankers not only had to contend with Europe's universal banks, which handle both commercial and investment transactions, but also faced stiff competition from the Japanese.

In global finance there are more twists and turns than in any Robert Ludlum thriller. You never know where the money will go or to what uses it will be put. In the mid-1980s the Euromarkets became a crucial source of funding for Japan's bubble economy. By issuing bonds with strippable warrants, Japanese firms could fund all manner of projects at almost no cost. In effect, the Japanese companies were playing upon investors' greed by issuing two securities in one—a bond with an absurdly low rate of interest plus a warrant that entitled the holder to buy shares at a special price at a future time. Investors gave up current yield in the hope of buying stocks on the cheap. Most misjudged their bets. Later, when the Japanese stock market crashed, many investors found their warrants worthless. But for the companies that had issued the bonds there were oodles of cheap funds. Japan Inc., with its access to cheap funding via the Euromarket, flooded the world with computers, cars, and stereos. Thus London's revival as a financial hub came at New York's expense and contributed to the decline of America's industrial power.

Banking in London had a singular advantage over New York. It was beyond the reach of the regulation-happy and conservatively run Federal Reserve. In the United States, the Fed kept a tight lid on interest rate ceilings and imposed stringent reserve requirements, crimping bank profits. In Europe, regulators weren't nearly so fussy. And the local governments, for the most part, resisted the temptation to slap on levies that might have dried up this gusher of dollars. If they had, their own economies would have slumped. As one commentator described it during the heyday in the mid-1980s, "The Euromarket was a bit like Oz, a land of wealth where your wishes come true." Assets were liquid, anonymity reasonably sure, and returns high.[8]

As events turned out, Kennedy's IET only exacerbated the financial woes of the United States and its financiers. Jacques Attali, who runs the European Bank for Reconstruction and Development, ties all those dollars abroad to the expansion of U.S. deficits. The dollar, he says, "remained king, but its preeminence rested on its contraband circulation and no longer in the guarantee of the ruling economy, which until then it had reflected."[9]

Now step back to 1974 and a scene in the Rose Garden at the White House. It was, said President Gerald Ford, "really an historic Labor Day." Flanked by labor leaders, Ford was signing into law the country's biggest reform of pension plans. Few could argue against the need to put some controls into the managing of pensions after nearly a third of their value had disappeared in the early 1970s bear market. Yet few foresaw the effect this legislation would have on Wall Street.

The Employee Retirement Income Security Act, said Ford, would give workers more benefits and rights "than almost anything in the history of the country."[10] Ford was only telling the half of it.

The legislation that became known as ERISA would, in fact, change the whole shape of investing. Two decades ago, everyone would have laughed at the suggestion that the $200 billion then in private pension assets would mushroom to today's $2 trillion or so. Less still did Ford realize he was launching a new era for institutional investing.

Boiled to its essence, ERISA promoted two investment themes—prudence and diversification. Although Congress didn't bother to spell out exactly what was meant by either term, corporate pension managers soon figured they could be responsible for any losses. Initially this meant moving funds out of stocks and into safer bonds. Later it meant indexing.

ERISA achieved its purpose and triggered an increase in the value of pension funds. But by altering the rules for money management, ERISA would subtly shift into new hands the power that control of money brings. Probably no one in the Rose Garden that day realized what was afoot. Control over the single largest source of investable funds would shift from the sell side—Wall Street—to the buy side—the managers of the institutions with moneys to invest. No longer would all the great investment ideas—and plenty of dumb ones, too—emanate from Wall Street. The pension fund managers, aided by an army of advisors, would become almost as knowledgeable as the gurus of high finance in lower Manhattan.

Today thousands of financial advisors earn their living by feeding investment ideas to pension managers and monitoring their performance. Most operate far from Wall Street, which historically would have grabbed the lion's share of this business.

Still, that's today. In the years immediately following the reforms, ERISA was manna from heaven for Wall Street and would become a catalyst for much of the takeover craze of the 1980s. The arrival of the new rules for pension funds had coincided with the start of a rally in both stocks and bonds. Rising prices meant pension plans soon had surpluses that exceeded the levels set under the ERISA rules. Had the politicians and the labor leaders made too much of their worries about workers retiring with insufficient funds? It certainly looked that way to a bunch of corporate raiders.

By the mid-1980s, the wealth of pension funds had climbed to the point where they represented well over a quarter of all corporate assets. An irresistible target. Abetted by their investment bankers, raiders soon learned the knack of using those pension surpluses to pay for their highly leveraged acquisitions and of covering the interest payments by reducing pension payments. A friendly actuary could always be found to confirm that there was no point in giving the retirees money before they needed it. Unethical? Perhaps. Still, few in financial or political circles appeared to care much about ethics in the 1980s, and, if they did, their voices went largely unheard.

Here Wall Street was guilty of myopia. While it lasted, the takeover boom made raiders rich and filled the bankers' coffers with outrageously large fees. When the inevitable end of dealmaking came, Wall Street had to face ERISA's darker side, the power shift to the buy side.

Pension funds are the Fort Knoxes of the investment world. By the end of the 1990s, pension funds, growing twice as fast as the gross national product, could reach $3.5 trillion. That's roughly double their level in 1988 and seventeen times larger than when ERISA became law.

Already pension fund managers control every second share traded on the New York Stock Exchange and two-thirds of those issued by the top five hundred companies. When the next century begins, pension funds probably will control every second *dollar* invested in the stock market.[11]

This isn't a rich business for Wall Street.

The essence of ERISA's many mandates is prudence in investing. Fund managers fret about suits. In practice, prudent investing boils down to managers paying minimal commissions and following the herd. The favored strategy is indexing.

We will look at the indexing phenomenon in detail in chapter 7.

For the moment, ignore the complexities and the dangers to investors. Just take it that indexing is an easy way for professional managers to match the stock market's performance while avoiding the need to pay brokers a lot of money. Vastly oversimplifying, the pros replicate the market through an index such as the Standard and Poor's 500 instead of picking individual stocks. Investing by index might be dull, but it makes for a safer life. When it comes to preserving their jobs, the pros know they're less likely to get fired by indexing and matching the market—even if it's collapsing—than by losing the retirees' nest eggs with a portfolio of stalled highfliers. Their acts of self-preservation translate into much less money for brokers and fewer jobs. A stock picker might pay a lofty commission, knowing it helps support research that will yield investment ideas. A fund manager won't bother, if he's trading stocks by the basketload. A quarter century ago, when President Ford took ERISA into the Rose Garden, this was one trend neither the lawmakers nor the financial community expected.

The combination of ERISA and May Day has proven brutal on commissions. Yet there was more pain to come from Washington.

"I took all the flack," says Lee Spencer. He's recalling the furor that erupted late in 1982 when Morgan Stanley belatedly realized the profits were going to vanish from its underwriting business.

Spencer was point man at the Securities and Exchange Commission and in Morgan Stanley's eyes the villain of the piece because he was crafting a rule change to stimulate competition. Where May Day, Kennedy's IET, and Ford's ERISA had only crimped margins, Spencer's rewriting of the rules would all but obliterate them. Wall Street was about to walk into a buzz saw wielded by the Reaganite free marketeers.

In December 1982, the SEC introduced what became known as its Rule 415. Overnight, the gentlemanly process of negotiated prices, the hallmark of underwriting among the elite firms, vanished. So did the fat fees. At a stroke, 415 turned underwriting into a cutthroat bidding auction with the lowest offer getting the deal.

Morgan Stanley was the first investment banker to cry foul.[12]

"At the eleventh hour the underwriters realized 415 would work to increase competition and lower spreads," recalls Spencer, who now practices law on Wall Street. "Before the rule change the pace was leisurely, the fees very thick."

Until this point, underwriting had been an orderly affair with the top bankers enjoying all the perks of an oligopoly. A compliant SEC had tilted the rules in their favor to such an extent that borrowers filing with the agency had to name the four or five underwriters they would use and stick with them. No shopping around for a better deal. An underwriting took months to pass through the Washington labyrinth, with the bankers' meters always ticking.

Spencer's new rule allowed corporations to take a shortcut through the tedious and costly registration process of issuing stocks and bonds. Now a borrower could zip through the process in a day, offering the deal to the hungriest banker for a razor-thin fee. No longer would an Exxon or a Ford need to register each time it wanted to issue bonds. Instead, firms could go to the SEC with a single, monster filing saying merely that they would raise a set sum—often in the billions of dollars—one that they could tap into months or even years hence. This was all part of the Reagan-era drive to lessen bureaucratic form filing and beef up competition. As conditions warranted, the firms would issue small tranches, or segments, from their monster filings until they had raised the total amount originally registered.

The trade calls these *shelf registrations.* Less paperwork, less time wasted, and, in addition to lower fees, one massive advantage came with this change. By altering the rules, the SEC had implicitly acknowledged the importance of time when measured in money terms.

When Spencer crafted 415, rampant inflation and volatile interest rates were combining to turn a corporate treasurer's job into a nightmare. As the 1970s ended, the Federal Reserve had made one of its periodic switches in policy. The monetarists, with Paul Volcker as their banner carrier, had taken charge. By regulating the money flow and letting interest rates fluctuate, they hoped to regain control over inflation. Volcker's new policy became a Catch-22.

Those bouncing interest rates might one day improve the economy and drive out inflation, but for corporate America, raising money had become devilishly tricky. When interest rates spurted during the lengthy underwriting process, companies found themselves paying more than they expected. For the bigger firms there was a simple solution: go to the less bureaucratic Euromarket, where, thanks to Kennedy's IET, funds were plentiful, delays minimal, and underwriters more obliging than in New York.

Roy C. Smith ran Goldman, Sachs's operations in London before becoming a professor at New York University and knows as much about the financial markets as most. "No single event in the postwar period," says Smith, "contributed more to the volatility of interest and foreign exchange rates than did this action by the Fed."[13]

Judged by the explosion in the Euromoney market, Smith has a point. Euromarket underwritings expanded seven times faster in the early 1980s than they had in the late 1970s. The peak came in 1986 at $190 billion, a higher level than the U.S. capital markets had reached for public corporate underwritings until that point.[14]

There's an ironic twist in all this. Price wars in underwriting began because finance had become a global business. The arrival of hordes of American bankers in London intensified the bidding in that market. Suddenly the corporations, the issuers of stocks and bonds, were on top. Underwriting fees plummeted both there and at home as bankers, almost for the first time in their lives, scrambled to compete.

If anything, the SEC was more aware of what was happening in the marketplace than were the bankers. The agency had scant choice but to change the rules. The alternative was to watch sizable chunks of U.S. underwriting business go overseas into the less regulated Euromarket. Call it self-preservation by the bureaucrats, if you like. Better to loosen a few rules through shelf registrations than lose most of the underwriting market to foreigners. Without 415, who knows what might have happened. Issues of any size would have found underwriters in London, or in the even less regulated Luxembourg market, rather than on Wall Street.

Here's another way the screw has tightened. As competition for business intensified in Europe, securities firms ruthlessly outbid each other to guarantee the complete offering. In trade parlance these are *done deals.* If the gamble works and the underwriter can sell the whole deal, the rewards go into one pocket. But guess wrongly and all those unsold stocks or bonds get stuffed into the house's own portfolio, where they stay until the markets improve. It takes huge amounts of capital for underwriters to fly solo, and the costs of tying up so much of a firm's capital with inventories of unwanted securities are enormous. Like a flu bug, done deals and intense competition would spread from London to New York.

To appreciate how competitive this business of underwriting is, look at what happened in 1991. This was a memorable year for new issues. The number of new financings soared to more than five thousand. This was almost twice the level achieved in 1986, a year when underwriting revenues had reached the then staggering level of $5.9 billion. So how much more did Wall Street book in fees in 1991 on nearly double the volume? Exactly one hundred and thirty-four million extra dollars. A pitiful 2 percent gain, and that's not even accounting for inflation.

Martin Lipton, the takeover guru, was among the first to spot what was happening. With unusual prescience, Lipton told the *New York Times* early in 1982, "We are going from a 'relationship genera-tion' to a 'transactional generation' and that will be intensified."[15]

Lipton was right. What began as a Katy-bar-the-door movement at the SEC would launch the biggest change in relationships in decades between the Street and its clients and also among the houses themselves. Old-timers recall with nostalgia when partici-pating in a syndication meant "putting on your hat and going to meetings." Nowadays the deal gets put on the computer screen and anyone can participate, with equal access and knowledge inevitably producing lower rewards for all.

Before the technology revolution, the pecking order among underwriters meant everything. Firms lived or died by their position on the tombstone ads that announced the successful underwriting of an issue of bonds or stocks. Being asked to join a syndicate was as much an event for some firms as a sophomore's getting an invitation to a prom. With reason. Besides the prestige of being part of the club, syndicate members collected handsome fees, and the closer to the top, the greater the fees and the profits.

It's doubtful if many realized it at the time, but Morgan Stanley gave a hint about what was to come in underwriting three years before Spencer wrote his rule. In a show of righteous indignation, Morgan Stanley walked out of an offering for International Business Machines rather than comanage the issue with Salomon as IBM insisted. The cost to Morgan Stanley was steep. For years, IBM didn't give the firm any underwriting business. Had Morgan Stanley erred by being so stubborn? Later some executives confessed they had, but what alternative was there? Morgan Stanley was already acknowledging that underwriting had become an all-or-nothing business.[16]

Much more than in the past, the Wall Street houses began making conscious choices about where they would compete. In the year before 415's debut, Morgan Stanley and Salomon had dominated underwriting. Between them the pair handled almost as many issues as the next four houses—Merrill Lynch, Goldman, First Boston, and Lehman—combined.[17] In time, Goldman and, to an even greater extent, Merrill began muscling their way to the top of the underwriting league tables, particularly for negotiated corporate debt offerings. In fact, by the early 1990s, Merrill, in a show of overachievement, had taken the lead in eight of the seventeen fee-earning business lines for which tallies are kept.[18]

Rather than compete in debt underwritings whose fees had become as thin as shadows, Morgan Stanley and Salomon, for their part, would decide there were better uses of their capital elsewhere—in cornering the Treasury markets, for example, in the latter's case.

The true legacy of Rule 415? That's hard to estimate. The aftershocks are still causing damage. Clearly, since losing their fees, Wall Streeters have increased their tolerance for risk. Sure, the firms will still handle plain vanilla underwritings, but they would far rather hawk exotic combinations. The flavors of the day are fixed- and floating-rate securities issued in one currency and then immediately swapped into another. Maybe as much as $3 trillion worth of contracts tied to these new securities now snake around the globe.

The regulators are worried and are starting to admit it. At the Federal Reserve Bank of New York, President E. Gerald Corrigan and his colleagues are sounding the alarm bells. In a tart note to banks, the New York Fed has warned that if they don't put in better controls, they will be "vulnerable to financial loss, fraud, and damage to their reputation and market standing."[19]

What worries Corrigan is why we need all this financial engineering and interest-rate and currency swapping. Why, he wants to know, do so many holders of securities carrying fixed interest rates want variable ones, and vice versa? "Since I have a great deal of difficulty in answering that question," says Corrigan in measured tones, "I then have to ask myself whether some of the specific purposes for which swaps are now being used may be quite at odds with an appropriately conservative view of the purpose of a swap, thereby introducing new elements of risk or distortion into the marketplace." That's a mouthful. In plain words, Corrigan thinks swaps are unnecessarily risky and he's scared of the consequences.

Rocket scientists and mathematical geniuses among the traders may know what's going on. Chances are many of their gray-haired bosses, educated precomputer, don't. As Corrigan contends, "High-tech banking and finance has its place, but it's not all that it's cracked up to be."[20]

CHAPTER THREE

A Question of Ethics

"The bells of hell go ting-a-ling for you, but not for me"
—Sung by British fighter pilots in World War II

WALL STREETERS LIVE ON THE KNIFE'S EDGE.
They face down the odds against their own mortality, reveling in the wealth that dealmaking, or junk bonds, or currency trading brings.

The knife is starting to cut.

With rare prescience, investment banker Felix Rohatyn, financial guru to the Clinton camp in the 1992 presidential contest, heralded what was to come. Late in 1986 he had predicted, "The political consequences will be determined in the next recession. If overleveraged companies fail and unemployment increases, if people get hurt and the banks get in trouble, there will be a major backlash."[1]

Indeed, the 1990s will become like the 1930s, a period of recriminations, ethical changes, and new rules to curb excesses. As the debts of the past decade come due, the pressures for reform are mounting much as they did following the 1929 crash. With the Clinton administration settled into the White House, reform-minded, populist politicians in Washington are more than ever determined to overcome industry resistance to altering the rules that govern financial conduct.

The excesses of Wall Street don't sit well with a society that's learning to make do with less. The era of Gatsby-style conspicuous consumption is over. People are questioning why a high-school teacher with twenty years' experience in Tulsa, Oklahoma, earns thirty-four thousand dollars while an investment banker three years out of college gets ten times that amount.

Shortly after the collapse of Drexel Burnham, a group of its eleven thousand former employees appeared on a television talk show. If they expected sympathy, host Phil Donahue didn't supply it. "You not only were arrogant, you were snobbish, and in a lot of ways, very impolite and mean," said Donahue. "Nobody likes you. You're Wall Street yuppies and you've got a bad image."[2]

In this atmosphere, conspiracy theorists could claim to see an evil empire at work manipulating the markets. Or as a couple of critics once put it, "Dennis Levine in mergers and acquisitions leads to Ivan Boesky in stock arbitrage. Boesky leads to Drexel Burnham in corporate dealmaking. And Drexel Burnham leads to Michael Milken, the king of junk bonds."[3]

It scarcely matters that prosecutors had a hard time proving the existence of such a cabal let alone in assessing its influence. The impression left with the public is that within the financial community, peer pressure is as prevalent as in any school playground. As another knowledgeable critic told Congress, "What at first may be considered unethical practices becomes, after experimentation, occasional use, then common use almost universally accepted." Literally universal.

No sooner had Judge Kimba Wood sentenced Michael Milken than the Salomon affair erupted. Abroad, gory tales of looting workers' savings and rigging stock prices filled the British tabloids for months as the pension fund looting by media mogul Robert Maxwell and the Blue Arrow stock manipulation case unfolded. In Japan, Nomura, the world's largest securities house, was entangled in share dealings with gangsters.

Headhunters say Wall Street changed significantly after the insider trading scandals, by spending heavily for hiring senior compliance officers. "Every firm is looking to protect itself from regulators, lawsuits, and serious losses," says Gary Goldstein, a recruiter.

As someone once said of Anglophones singing in a German opera, the words sound fine, but do you think they know what they mean? Too often, top brass in all the financial centers find complying with regulators not to their taste. "There is nobody I know who wouldn't rather be doing a deal," Thomas W. Strauss once admitted when he was running Salomon Brothers.[4] "A lot of management issues are the sheer drudgery of running a business."

Reformation doesn't come easily. Consider the mundane question of research reports. Publication of a buy recommendation—Wall Street rarely says sell—can move the price of a stock several points in a volatile market. Should a brokerage house buy shares ahead of a report that touts a particular company? The ethical response is obvious to outsiders. Yet in March 1991, the New York Stock Exchange's Board of Governors felt sufficiently concerned about firms filling their own inventories with stocks they hoped to unload at a higher price after their research reports appeared that it had a memo issued on the matter. "Such conduct," the governors reminded the heads of member firms, "would not be in keeping with just and equitable principles of trade."[5]

Sixteen months after that memo, the *Wall Street Journal* turned up another, equally embarrassing piece of internal correspondence. This memo, surfacing from Morgan Stanley, showed how the firm was suppressing bad research reports that might affect its underwriting business. Written by its head equity underwriter, it spelled out the firm's policy that researchers should not issue "negative or controversial comments about our clients as a matter of sound business practice."[6] Morgan Stanley insists the mandate never went into effect. Still, investors could draw their own conclusions, as they also could from Merrill Lynch's conduct in an appeals court in St. Paul, Minnesota.

Merrill was trying to overturn charges that it had bilked an aged widow by excessively trading her $144,000 account. In its defense, Merrill's lawyers argued that the trading—no fewer than 141 trades totaling $2 million—made money for the widow. The appeals court, in upholding a $2 million punitive damage award, tartly observed, "The gravity of the wrong committed by Merrill Lynch is not mitigated by the fact that the account was nevertheless profitable." As the lawyer for the widow's estate said, "You can't rob a bank and then, if they catch you, just give the money back and everyone's even."[7]

Don McCabe teaches ethics and business at Rutgers. He wanted to know if moral values were changing. In 1990, he conducted a study of six thousand undergraduate students at thirty-one top colleges. The basic finding: those majoring in business admitted to more cheating than any other group. "The scary thing," says McCabe, "is that the cheaters were the cream of the student crop. They represent a disproportionate share of our future CEOs, lawyers, and investment bankers."

If anything, McCabe sees moral values in business declining. For this, he blames the impersonal atmosphere that comes through the wider use of computers and electronic communications. "Already the view is, 'It's me versus the rest of the world and I'll make more money by screwing others,'" says McCabe. "With computers they no longer need look each other in the face. It can only get more impersonal as a business."

In fact, according to Thomas J. Jordan, a consultant on technology on Wall Street, the fashionable sin is cheating. Firms are letting staffers copy and pirate computer programs to avoid paying fees and royalties. This is happening even at reputable houses. "It's illegal. It's immoral. Big dollars are involved," says Jordan. This isn't small beer he's talking about. The Software Publishers Association reckons copyright dodgers avoid paying $3 billion annually. A crackdown could be coming. "It's going to be like Watergate," Jordan is telling his clients. "When the probes begin you will be asked, what did you know about the cheating and when did you know about it? It's getting to be a very serious problem."

Jack Casey occupies an unusual position. He is an ethical ombudsman at Scudder, Stevens and Clark, the money managers. Casey doesn't blame his colleagues for inventing junk bonds or other risky products. In his view, these financial wizards are no more guilty than is the inventor of the chain saw for the chain saw murders. "The blame rests," Casey says, "with the professional advisor, who gave the high-risk securities to the investor looking for low-risk." Adds Casey, "Salesmen are like litigation lawyers. They tell one part of the story. The part that favors the sale. There isn't a lot of warning about the risks involved."

Ethically speaking, most of us are at fault here. We were so busy coining money in the 1980s, we didn't want any reminders about risk. Leverage was going to make us all rich, wasn't it?

James Grant, the witty newsletter writer, once observed, "The 1980s are to debt what the 1960s were to sex." Grant has a point. Everyone went crazy on debt. In 1990, consumers owed almost one dollar for each dollar of disposable income. The federal debt has quadrupled in two decades. Probably no industry accepted the merits of debt more wholeheartedly than Wall Street. For the whole securities industry, bank borrowing ballooned nearly fiftyfold to well above a third of a trillion dollars in the space of sixteen years.

Such an orgy inevitably carries an aftermath. The United States and the industrialized world have paid some of the price with a couple of years of global recession. For Wall Street, the pruning knife has yet to cut. It will.

First though we need to understand how the cult of leverage took over our lives. Step back a couple of decades to a time when money was almost immobile. Then a lunch on Wall Street meant leisurely conversations over lamb chops and a bottle of Margaux, not pizza and Pepsi on the run as it does today. The mahogany dining rooms weren't frills. This was an era when novel ideas on funding were rare. Investment bankers needed to be politely respectful to their clients, who could as easily raise funds from their commercial bankers. Unlike today, commercial banks were glad to make loans.

In that era, too, the Federal Reserve decreed the level of interest paid by banks and thrifts, not competition or inflation. Through its obscure but powerful Regulation Q, the Fed kept rates low, believing this would make for strong banks and a robust economy. Similarly, the federal government—and its counterparts abroad—restricted the movement of capital around the globe through various exchange controls, including keeping the dollar pegged to gold.

All this changed in August 1971 when President Richard Nixon attempted to solve a minor fiscal crisis by abruptly suspending gold payments. Two years later the exchange rate system that had governed money since the free world's money experts had met in Bretton Woods, New Hampshire, in 1944 was history. Those in the financial business had a new game to play: "What's this currency worth?" From almost nothing, the changing of currencies for profit soared to a $750 billion-a-day business. Everywhere money was on the move.

In their ivory towers, scholars and market watchers endlessly debate a chicken-and-egg question. Do markets change with the lifting of regulations? Or does market competition force the regulators to change? At the Federal Reserve of New York, the latter view prevails. According to Fed officials, competitive pressures impinging upon the banking franchise are the "catalyst for change"[8]—and require their intervention.

Sounds fine until you stop to consider how bureaucratic inertia slows the process. It took the Penn Central Transportation Company collapse in 1970 and a full-blown crisis in the commercial paper market before the Fed moved tentatively toward removing interest rate ceilings. Arguably, the Fed's slowness in reacting to competitive pressures in the financial markets helped set the stage for the money troubles of the 1980s. The last of the Regulation Q restraints that put the thrifts at a disadvantage in attracting deposits didn't disappear until 1986. This was far too late to avert the S&L crisis. By the time the Fed did lift Q, the creators of the money market mutual funds had a hammerlock on the flow of funds. Money market funds were around for much of the 1970s but attracted only modest amounts of cash until 1978. As inflation soared, the thrifts could no longer compete with the higher yields offered by the money funds. A glance at the arithmetic shows why.

A typical bank or thrift needs about $4.50 in income for every $100.00 it puts on the books.[9] Three bucks of that goes for operations; the rest gets eaten up by insurance and regulatory costs. In contrast, a money market mutual fund spends no more than seventy-five cents collecting funds from individuals. In the wooing game, the banks and thrifts alike lost out badly to firms such as Merrill Lynch, with its cash management accounts. After 1978, the value of deposits in the money funds soared almost tenfold to above $230 billion in 1982.[10] The latter date is significant. That year, lobbyists for the thrifts succeeded in getting Congress to ratify what many consider the worst-conceived piece of legislation in a generation, the Garn–St Germain Depository Institutions Act.

Ostensibly, Garn–St Germain would deregulate deposit pricing and revitalize the thrifts by expanding their mandate. Expectations were high. "It attempts," said a thrift regulator at the time, "to remove artificial regulatory constraints that have prevented thrift institutions from serving the public and profiting from that service to the greatest degree possible."[11] So much for intent. To put it simply, the legislation took the distortions created by Regulation Q and made them worse. The process took a few years, but the result was a financial misadventure of epic proportions. By April 1986, Washington had lifted the last restrictions on savings deposit rates. By then the thrifts were going full bore, pumping those deposits into real estate and other follies. Unfortunately, Congress had listened to the lobbyists and had left intact the insurance on depositors' accounts. The final cost to taxpayers of the thrift debacle could reach $600 billion, by some estimates.

On Wall Street, Garn–St Germain was a godsend. Tucked among the fine print were some rule changes that didn't sound like much, but in Wall Street's hands would radically alter the flow of funds into and out of the thrifts. For example, out went the restriction that said a thrift couldn't receive any more than 5 percent of its deposits in one chunk from a single source. Wall Street went into high gear, scooping up funds from big investors and passing them along to the thrifts that promised the highest yields. A legal loophole let these "brokered funds" qualify for the federal government's generous insurance program that was meant only to apply to deposits of less than $100,000. Taxpayers will pay for this loophole exploitation for years to come. For their part, the thrifts gobbled up the brokered deposits that came from Wall Street and then dutifully returned the money for investing in junk bonds and mortgage-backed securities or real estate deals. No group of clients was ever more pliant or accepting of Wall Street's belief in the merits of grossly leveraged balance sheets. By tapping this rich vein, Wall Street could overlook and, in some cases, blithely ignore what Rule 415 and excessive competition were doing to its own margins.

Sorting out the blame for the thrift crisis is almost an exercise in futility. But Congress certainly made things worse when, in yet another rule change, it effectively barred the thrifts from holding junk bonds. Its action sent all junk bonds into a tailspin even though the thrifts held only about 7 percent of all the junk issues. The biggest holders were the mutual and pension funds plus the insurance companies. Between them they held 75 percent of the market, with the rest in the hands of individual investors. All of these investors paid for Washington's misguided rush to get the thrifts out of junk bonds.[12]

It would take four years for the junk market to make a semblance of recovery and in the process would try the patience of innocent investors caught up in the midst of congressional folly.

It's unlikely we will ever know the full extent of what Wall Street did to the thrifts. At one point, prosecutors claimed Michael Milken and his cohorts had used more than four hundred partnerships to manipulate, bribe, and coerce the thrifts into buying junk bonds that ended up costing them billions in losses.[13]

The arithmetic so embarrasses people connected to Washington or Wall Street that they lapse into obfuscation when they discuss the matter. For example, you need to read deeply between the lines in a lengthy essay penned by former Federal Reserve Chairman Paul Volcker that set out to assess what happened. Writing in the *Wall Street Journal,* Volcker concluded, "Those rewards were, in fact, often largest for those acting primarily as middle men in arranging financing, leaving most of the credit risk to others."[14]

The Resolution Trust Corporation, the government's thrift bailout agency, is only a tad more forthcoming. In the spring of 1992 the RTC presented to Congress its report card on the 632 thrifts then under its control.[15] Again the details were skimpy, but unbelievably, no fewer than 238 of those thrifts had managed to lose money in investments based on the most liquid market in the world—U.S. Treasuries. As one would-be reformer in Washington describes it, "You had the guys with computers selling to the guys adding with their fingers. The thrifts thought they were buying government-insured securities and instead got securities of securities of securities." What he means is, the Wall Street techies with their souped-up computers could chop safe government securities into little pieces and create booby traps for the unwary. Never again, if some reformers have their way, although that's not too likely. In modern finance the guys with the computers are always one step ahead of those creating the rules.

The debt binge owes as much to Washington as it does to Wall Street, and plenty to our own changing mores. In 1978, Congress rewrote the bankruptcy code and the stigma of bankruptcy, like that of divorce, vanished. Three decades earlier, in 1946, only nine thousand people had filed for bankruptcy. By 1988 that many were filing every week.

What's true of people is equally so of firms. In the eighties there was a fiftyfold increase in the value of the assets belonging to firms filing for bankruptcy. Unfortunately, most had allowed their debts to climb even faster.[16]

The federal tax code encourages debt at the expense of equity. Interest payments get deducted from taxable income, unlike dividends, which come from after-tax profits. By one calculation, the overall tax on the return from an equity investment can amount to at least 62 percent. Small wonder then that in the 1980s, owners retired no less than $47 billion worth of equities from the system and replaced much of it with new debt.

In the pursuit of fairness, Congress has twice attempted to rewrite the tax code—in 1981 with the Economic Recovery Tax Act and again with the 1986 Tax Reform Act. Legislators then spent the years in between and afterwards trying to unfix what they had wrought. What any of that did for the level of debt, Wall Street, or investors is difficult to fathom.

The cognoscenti spoke of the importance of reform moves such as the repeal in 1986 of the general-utilities doctrine, and how this prevented corporate reorganizers from avoiding taxes. Perhaps it did. Yet at the end of the day it was hard for laypeople to see how all this tinkering really furthered fairness, American competitiveness, the economy, or longer-term investing.

If anything, congressional maneuvering over taxes stimulated excessive borrowing and the investment splurge that produced a surfeit of office blocks, shopping malls, and even houses while fostering investor disillusionment. For example, by reversing the rules on passive income, Congress knocked the wind out of limited partnerships, one of the Street's hottest products for middle-class investors.

Still, say this for congressional tax meddling: It keeps an army of lawyers occupied and produces intriguing countermoves from the febrile minds of investment bankers. Out of the 1986 tax reform, for example, came securitization. That's an ugly word for turning loans on any lender's balance sheet into marketable securities. This is where the guys with computers come into their own. Literally trillions of dollars are now tied up in this process. As the thrift debacle revealed, when it comes to trading in newfangled financial instruments, not everyone knows what's happening.

Securitization is an antidote to the Internal Revenue Service's speeding tax collections on unrepaid loans. Until 1986, lenders paid taxes only on funds actually received back each month from their customers. Then Congress changed the rules and removed the tax deferrals. With the Internal Revenue Service hammering on their doors, banks and finance companies no longer could afford to hold on their books a fistful of outstanding installment loans—for everything from credit cards, to car and boat loans, to house mortgages. The Wall Street solution: turn the loans into securities. Investors buy them by the carload, figuring these securities are a safe bet since they're backed by the cash from borrowers repaying the original loans. Maybe.

In modern finance nothing stays simple for long. The Wall Street wizards quickly manipulate these new securities. Securitization ties into what's known in the jargon of the trade as interest-rate and currency swapping, another big, complex, and risky business.

These days securitized funds cross national borders at a rate of $12 trillion a year. Initially, underwriters collected handsome fees in the conversion process and then made more money by trading the newfangled securities. Some still do, but competition is reducing profits, if not the risks.

To get back to the debt orgy. Even Japanese competition played a part in the piling up of debt by U.S. corporations. Japanese industrialists had a triple advantage in raising money cheaply. Unlike their U.S. competitors, they could tap their own equity market, issuing stock with sky-high price-to-earnings multiples. In the debt market, the big Japanese firms paid about 3 percent to raise fresh capital, one-fourth the rate U.S. firms often paid. The Japanese raised even cheaper money out of the Euromarket by issuing bonds with warrants that could be stripped for resale on the Tokyo and Osaka stock exchanges while the Nikkei was flying high. Those warrants will make good wallpaper unless the Tokyo stock market recovers.

Now look at the cost of capital in the 1980s from the perspective of an American business. The U.S. tax code and the soggy state of the market for equity offerings made it hard for firms to raise money cheaply or keep shareholders happy. No matter how much fat the firms trimmed, no matter how many thousands of workers lost jobs, Corporate America still couldn't match Japan Inc. What counted more than all the downsizing was the cost of borrowing. Productivity among U.S. workers might rise, but the Japanese always had the edge. A Sony or a Hitachi could afford to buy the latest equipment and erect new plants; U.S. firms couldn't. And didn't.

The popular, but often misguided, solution was to arrange a merger or a reorganization funded by ersatz equity, a.k.a. junk bonds.

While it lasted, the debt-funded craze for mergers and buyouts was wonderful for the investment bankers. One and a half trillion dollars' worth of deals consummated in a decade, according to one estimate, producing in excess of $15 billion in fees. Rarely has the gravy train run so richly. This was a business where every marginal dollar dropped to the bottom line. Collect $80 million in fees, pay out $3 million or so in salaries, and there was plenty left over for bonuses. No wonder the bankers peddled the virtues of deals so forcefully to their clients.

Now came retribution. In a *Fortune* magazine poll in 1991 more than two-thirds of U.S. executives blamed the nation's economic woes on leveraged buyouts. Richard A. Bernstein, top man at Western Publishing Group, was talking for many when he said, "To me it was the worst disaster since the Great Depression. It became an evil game in and of itself, inhabited by people who added nothing to the economy."[17]

Viewed from Main Street, the work of Wall Street has often appeared remote and peculiar. The man in the street at a pinch could understand the role of stocks and even bonds in the raising of capital. But who understands high-tech investing in indexes of indexes, circus swaps, and spiders?

Even within the financial community, Wall Street gives the appearance of being built upon hollow ground. Its profits are extracted from dangerous pursuits—outrageous leveraging and merging and acquiring in the 1980s, followed by rampant speculation in interest rates and currencies in the 1990s. Can it last? Almost certainly not for most firms. What Wall Streeters are doing is indulging in a souped-up version of the pass-the-parcel game children play. Somebody is bound to get caught when the music stops.

Wits say that if you want to know whether earnings at the brokerage houses will rise or fall in the next quarter, don't bother with complicated tools such as regression analysis. Toss a coin instead. You will have as much chance of being right.

Behind the volatile swings of recent years from unprecedented losses to record profits, however, lurks a depressing trend of declining profitability. This is a business running out of control, where the risk taking exceeds the bounds of prudence and where uncertainty abounds.

For example, late in 1990, Alan "Ace" Greenberg, one of the Street's shrewdest traders and head of Bear, Stearns, confessed, "I'm shocked. I have never seen problems like this."[18]

Gripped by fear and with several firms on the verge of bankruptcy, Wall Street was closing the books on its worst year on record. The seven largest brokers faced almost $700 million in losses, of which nearly a third came from the soon-to-be-dismantled Pru-Bache. Merchant banking, the creator of extraordinary wealth a few years earlier, wasn't even firing on one cylinder. The famed dealmakers, whose phone calls once sent shivers down the spines of corporate chairmen, now couldn't get their calls returned.

A sign of the depths of this fear and pessimism: the price of a seat on the New York Stock Exchange fell from a million dollars to below three hundred thousand. At that level the value was less than half of a McDonald's franchise. Amidst the gloom, a contrite Wall Street pledged to mend its ways. The houses fired enough of their high-priced help to more than fill Giants Stadium in the Meadowlands.

"People are scared," said Greenberg. "It's like walking through a minefield."

Yet within weeks the gloom had vanished, burned away like mist on a summer morning. Optimism returned and 1991—the year that everyone thought would be a horror—produced nearly $6 billion in profits, becoming the best ever until 1992 surpassed that result. A measure of prosperity's return came from Goldman, Sachs, whose profits are still divided among its partners. Its 142 partners in its fiscal year ended in November 1991 shared more than $1 billion.[19]

Unfortunately, 1991 and 1992 were flukes. Their bountiful profits will not come along again anytime soon. If future generations on Wall Street remember these years, it will be in the manner that Bordeaux châteaux owners recall the wines of 1978, or better still 1949. These were the years when almost everything in the investment business went right.

Money poured out of low-yielding bank CDs into brokers' coffers. Merrill alone was taking in $275 million a day and steering every third dollar it received into stocks. A rally in stocks boosted the market for new equity issues. Morgan Stanley even found sufficient investors to put a couple of billion dollars into that tired old war-horse General Motors. Governments from Warsaw to Mexico City to Washington, D.C., wanted help privatizing their state-owned companies or in funding their deficits, or both.

Amidst such a gusher of business, who on Wall Street didn't

want to expand? Breathes there a merchant banker who didn't push to open an office in central Europe when the Berlin Wall fell? "Firms are being persuaded that opening an office in Frankfurt with six kids from Wharton is the best thing since Campbell soup," says Frank Zarb at Smith Barney. "It's a repeat of a lot of the mistakes made in past years by our industry."

At home, Shearson Lehman led the way, as it had done in the eighties. Checkbook in hand, Shearson offered sign-up bonuses to its competitors' brokers, whose customers also were suitable for poaching. Such generosity could again prove as premature as the Street's last expansion binge, which began with the Reagan bull market.

At the start of the 1980s, the firms hired by the thousands and spent heavily for new computers and communications gear. According to the trade body, the National Association of Securities Dealers, its members started the 1980s with fewer than 7,000 branches and ended it with more than 24,000. Wall Street firms were determined not to get swamped by paperwork as they had in the mid-1970s. That had been a dreadful period and an odd one. Back then the houses had an abundance of customers' orders and salesmen, but no money. Also missing was modern technology. The New York Stock Exchange was closing one day a week to process paperwork, and a Texas billionaire, H. Ross Perot, thought he could put Wall Street to rights and revive an old-line banker, duPont Glore Forgan. Perot's game plan, as ever, was simple. If he could use computers to sort out the paper mess at one brokerage, orders would stream in from others for his Electronic Data Systems. Better still, he would reap a huge return on his investment in what was then the third-largest brokerage house.

When his grandiose plans faltered and Wall Street began a period of massive closures and consolidations, Perot retreated. Among those to fold was duPont.

This time around no firm wanted to get caught flat-footed and miss the business revival. The industry's tab for renting space plus communications gear jumped from around $1 billion in 1980 to over $6 billion eight years later.

Initially, adding a new clerk, secretary, trader, or salesman did bring in more money, often as much as $15,000 to $20,000 for each addition. But not for long. Soon costs were climbing faster than revenues. How skewed were the salaries on Wall Street? In a rare moment of candor a chief executive once confessed his approach to salary negotiations. Said he, "I figure out what somebody is worth and then add a zero."[20] Houses paid rookies $70,000 plus a $50,000 bonus that was guaranteed. Your thirtysomething, standard-issue, double-degreed banker with four years' service picked up bonuses that ran into the hundreds of thousands. Most managing directors pocketed $1 million or more, virtually all of it in bonus payments.

Outsiders are perplexed by such lavishness. Vincent Perro, a compensation specialist, offers an unusual explanation. Feudalism, he says, didn't die in 1485 with England's King Richard III, as historians like to say. It survives on Wall Street. Protection in exchange for personal loyalty is the ruling order here, and the effects are as debilitating as they were five hundred years ago.

If you doubt this, says Perro, watch the infighting at bonus time. Or ponder the difficulties investment houses encounter when they seek to reorganize their operations for the common good.

On Wall Street, youthful managing directors rule their departments like medieval baronies. All-powerful in their domains, they build exclusive loyalties, much as warlords did with their vassals. Today in the financial services arena, bosses and workers are mutually dependent for personal survival. There's a shared obligation to take care of each other, particularly when the spoils of war are divvied up.

Within these latter-day baronies, local concerns outweigh those of the kingdoms to which they ostensibly belong. And there lies the danger.

The inflation of compensation was matched over the years by a deflation of skills and abilities. Greenhorns rose beyond their capabilities. "We took a head count of five thousand people operating two hundred firms and made them operate five hundred firms," says Bryan Cavill, a trader turned information vendor. Cavill was talking of London, but his point was as valid in New York. Never has the Peter Principle, that managers rise to the level of their incompetence, been more apparent than in financial services. The expansion of firms into the London market meant no one made money. In a four-year period ending in 1991, the industry there lost $1.5 billion. In the United States, by March 1992 there were 1,456 fewer investment firms than before the 1987 crash. What matters more is how many didn't quit. Fully 2,333 more firms still vie for business than existed in 1980, a four-fifths increase. "A business that had been great for most of the broker dealers in the 1960s, and very good for some of them in the 1970s, became unprofitable for most of them in the 1980s," says Charles D. Ellis, a consultant. Even in profitable times, more than a quarter of all securities firms lose money.

Zarb fears another downdraft is about to blow. If he is right, shutting rather than opening offices might be wiser. The early 1990s boomlet in brokerage house profits could fade. Already the surge in new stock offerings has cooled. The stock market looks good only by default.

The hustlers may never admit this, but the reality is quite terrifying. Virtually every group of investors has an overabundance of stocks, and would like less. The retail customer is in the stock market only by default, a temporary victim of low-yielding money funds. Householders in three decades have gone from owning four out of every five shares issued to less than one in two. Worse, they account for less than a third of all trade in equities.

For a while, the pension plans took up the slack and became big buyers of stocks. But lately the public funds have bought only one-third the amount they were purchasing six years earlier. That only leaves the insurance companies and mutual funds. The former never were big buyers of stocks, and the latter increasingly choose indexing ahead of stock picking. Put bluntly, investors—professional and amateur alike—regard equities as uncomfortably treacherous.

The problems keep mounting. Virtually all the operating expenses are far out of line for such a cutthroat business. If Wall Street's cost of borrowing hadn't dropped—down by almost a quarter since 1989—many firms would still be in dire trouble. Cheaper money is a godsend when you have huge inventories of swaps, derivatives, and other exotic instruments to finance. The manner in which interest rates fell is unlikely to be repeated in a hurry. The houses earned incredible returns by playing the yield curve. From early in 1990, the yield gap between the thirty-year Treasury bond and the two-year note kept getting wider with almost every passing week. By borrowing short and investing at the long end of the yield curve, the firms made fortunes when trading for their own accounts.

You didn't need to be overly smart to win in this game. All it took was money, lots of it. What happens when the yield curve takes on another shape? Rising interest rates coupled with escalating operating costs could bring red ink flowing down the Street.

By any yardstick, the securities industry isn't an easy place to make money. For the past half-dozen years, its pretax profitability has lagged that of the average manufacturing company.[21] In almost any other industry, the constant spending on technology, as like as not, would have raised both productivity and profitability.

Here you need to think of technology as an Indian giver. Computers and electronics do raise productivity, but the costs savings aren't enough to keep pace with the price cutting on services that technology also brings. Without computers we wouldn't have indexing and derivatives and couldn't turn mortgages into securities. But computers produce global competition, narrow spreads, and a rapid copying of products that turns every Wall Street invention into a commodity.

Baron Paul Julius von Reuter, with his carrier pigeons, started the craze for real-time financial information. The birds ferried financial news back and forth between Brussels and Aachen in 1850.[22] Today an amateur investor can sit at home and know the state of the stock market almost as quickly as the professionals. All that's needed is a personal computer, a modem, and a handful of dollars. The time lag is a mere thirty seconds. Half a minute after a stock trades on the New York Stock Exchange, the information is beaming into homes across America.

An optimist might feel encouraged that Sears, Roebuck's Prodigy offers such a service for a handful of dollars a month. More stock watchers means more trades and more commissions. Except that isn't the likely outcome.

Even before Sears honed its delivery system, a longtime market watcher had shrewdly seen technology's power. "The sense of the market, the commodity that had for so long made the investment banker invaluable to princes, prime ministers and corporate moguls," he said, "was being let out of the bag."[23]

When technology combines with information you get what people in the business call *transparent markets.* All this means is that everyone sees what's happening, which is good in terms of fairness and lousy for profits. Much is made of the U.S. markets being the most efficient, most liquid, and fairest in the world. What's talked about less is the effect that efficiency has on profitability. Making real-time market information available to all investors sounds wonderful but not for the middlemen who live off the spreads between sellers and buyers. Analysts at Booz, Allen and Hamilton have studied the problem. They found that the bid-and-asked spreads in 1989 were one-quarter as wide as they had been in 1980 for long government bonds, one-fifth as wide for interest-rate swaps, and one-tenth what they were for collateralized mortgage obligations. A tough way to make a living.

Paradoxically, fully transparent markets, with their narrow spreads, aren't enticing to professional money managers. They can make better profits elsewhere. Increasingly, pension funds are pumping billions of dollars into privately negotiated investments. Such private deals often are risky but offer the prospect of greater rewards since fewer firms are competing.

Every fortune ever made in finance has rested on a simple premise. Those with the most information make the most money. That edge, knowing what others don't, is priceless. Pursuing information illegally put the likes of Ivan Boesky, Dennis Levine, and Martin Siegel behind bars.

"Today access to information is almost unlimited," says Joellin Comerford, a consultant. "There is almost nothing anyone can't know or find out." That's troublesome for anyone whose money comes from spotting the quirks that make prices in one market higher than in another. Already arbitrage opportunities are fifty times fewer than they were ten years ago, and they are in danger of vanishing in the foreign exchange markets.

Outsiders are often surprised when they learn how Wall Street makes its money. For instance, among the richest sources of profits are the customers' margin accounts. Every firm makes money on these accounts and for some this is the single largest contributor to profits. Arbitrage is another rich vein. Sometimes, a house makes more by playing the interest-rate spreads on short-term borrowings and lendings than it gets from dealmaking, underwritings, or commissions.

Part of this arbitraging involves *repos* and *reverse repos.* That's trade jargon for repurchase agreements. The mechanics are often complex. What's important is this. On any given night, Wall Streeters are betting $200 billion or more of borrowed money on the direction of interest rates. The money comes from pension and insurance funds, whose managers, presumably, figure they know less about interest rates than do their brokers. Or maybe they are just smart enough to accept a smaller but guaranteed return on their money rather than indulge in Wall Street's hazardous game.

The amounts Wall Street gambles are enormous and a stark reminder of how little firms earn by working for their customers. This, of course, is the essence of another dilemma. This surfeit of capital creates too much competition. About the only way to boost margins is to ratchet up the risks.

Here's another risky part of the investment business that's mushroomed—the swapping among investors of payment obligations. For example, the exchanging of fixed-rate for floating-rate interest payments.

The swapping of contractual agreements on interest rates, currencies, and a slew of esoteric financial instruments and indexes requires incredible leverage. For each dollar of equity, Salomon may have two hundred dollars' worth of these swaps, while Merrill Lynch and Morgan Stanley have a hundred dollars or so apiece. Merrill's total off-balance-sheet contracts topped $446 billion recently.[24] That's the gross, or notional, amount, and company officials claim the exposure to risk is much less.

There's the rub. The firms—and all the big ones are playing this game—enter into private contracts far away from the prying eyes of regulators. No one knows for sure just how much risk is involved, a scary thought when markets are uncertain and volatile. Could swaps unravel in the nineties as bridge loans did in the eighties? No one dismisses the thought lightly.

In the new era of finance, the lesson is obvious. The customers count for less on Wall Street. Morgan Stanley and Bear, Stearns now trade 40 percent of the time for their own accounts. Before Salomon's bubble burst, four dollars in five of the firm's net revenues came from this type of business. At the start of the 1990s, risk-based revenues were two-thirds of the securities industry's total revenues. The fallout from three decades of regulatory change is clear. So are the effects on margins. Underwriting profits by 1990 were only one-tenth of what they had been five years earlier.

You might think that with all the difficulties in making money the old-fashioned way, few firms would be willing to throw their hats into this ring. But no. Outsiders still want in, notably the commercial bankers. Thanks to pliant legislators, the artificial barriers that kept them out in the past will become less of an obstacle.

Before the decade ends, Washington will rewrite the Glass-Steagall law that separates commercial and investment banking, or see the marketplace do the job for it.

A legacy of both the 1929 crash and the Depression, Glass-Steagall prevents most banks from offering real estate, insurance, and securities services. Author Ron Chernow, the biographer of the House of Morgan, has assessed the damage. "The American banking system," he says, "has become the Chernobyl of international finance, a ghastly disaster area boycotted by most investors."[25]

Hyperbole apart, the U.S. commercial banking system looks neither as powerful nor as safe when matched against Europe's or even Japan's. Abroad, a mixture of regulation and custom has led to domination by a relative few well-capitalized companies. To varying degrees in those countries, commercial banks can participate in the securities business and have used that advantage to participate globally in all aspects of finance. European banks have sizable securities businesses, and want to expand. Already Credit Suisse owns First Boston and rival Swiss Bank Corporation has acquired a top Chicago commodities trader. Britain's National Westminster gobbled up large parts of Drexel Burnham when it went under.

In contrast, both the banking and the securities industries within the United States are considerably more fragmented.

A couple of years ago, the New York Fed's E. Gerald Corrigan told the Senate Banking Committee, "We see a U.S. banking and financial system characterized by the dual conditions of recurring bouts of instability and competitive slippage both at home and abroad."[26] Lifting Glass-Steagall could change that although not necessarily for everyone's benefit.

Albert Wojnilower is hardly the first to say the small quasi monopolies into which we divided financial services have gone forever. Wojnilower, an economist at First Boston, says it more wittily than most, comparing the old financial system to an orderly zoo.

The different animals—the banks, securities dealers, and insurance companies—were kept and fed in separate cages, segregated by function and geographical scope. Bars prohibited predatory raidings. Within each cage there was competition and a pecking order. "Now this tranquil order has disintegrated," says Wojnilower. The global economy, electronics, and the ethos of the "now" generation, he says, have led to "animals, keepers and public alike shedding their traditional restraints."

In Wojnilower's view the animals have escaped. Predators abound and the regulators don't know how to put the bars back up. Where there was once sufficient food for all the species in this financial zoo, some will starve.

Rebuilding the zoo is impossible. "The enormous potential of modern technology won't permit it," says Paul Volcker. "The fact is, we cannot turn the clock back to compartmentalization of financial institutions and credit and interest-rate ceilings," says the former Fed chairman, who is now an investment banker.[27]

Yet every time Washington moves to rewrite the legislation and regain some advantages for the U.S. firms, up pops a crisis. Out goes valor, in comes discretion. The most recent attempts to alter the rules fizzled in 1992. The Bush administration introduced a reform package thick enough to rival the Washington, D.C., phone book but never had its heart behind the idea of letting well-capitalized banks own securities, mutual funds, and insurance affiliates. Neither did Congress, with the S&L debacle still fresh in everyone's mind.

Economist David Hale believes another reason lies behind the foot-dragging in congressional committees. "Some of their members were able to attract huge campaign contributions by keeping everyone uncertain about their future," says Hale. Even sixty years ago, Congress wasn't eager to reform the securities and banking businesses until Ferdinand Pecora, a publicity-hungry U.S. district attorney, homed in on corrupt bankers. His hearings in January 1933 uncovered such hair-curling stories that Washington rushed bankers out of the securities business.

Congressional procrastination may not count for much in the future. The Federal Reserve under Chairman Alan Greenspan is permitting certain banks to go into debt and equity underwriting. For example, J. P. Morgan can now do almost as much in issuing securities as Morgan Stanley. Sensible pragmatism at work? Perhaps, but the Fed approach isn't without its critics. "Such selective repeal by regulatory fiat," says Chernow, "is obviously the least equitable way to make public policy."

Nonetheless, pressure is mounting for Congress to sweep away the final restraints. Among the advocates of change is John Burton, respected former dean of Columbia University Graduate School of Business and former chief accountant for the SEC. "We might as well finish the job," he says, "as cause people to go through legal hoops to accomplish the same thing."

Free marketeers will rejoice, but the ensuing shakeout promises to be bloody as investment and commercial bankers travel on a collision course. "The volume of business will not grow quickly enough to satisfy all the banks and securities houses," warns Rainer Gut, chairman at Credit Suisse. The banks and securities firms face a frightening prospect as they grope to reevaluate their franchises. Listen again to Gut as he says, "The chaff will have to be separated from the wheat at both national and international levels and the process of natural selection will accelerate." Welcome to financial Darwinism.

Customer migration is at the heart of modern-day financial struggles. By one estimate, banks will lose some $300 billion in deposits during the course of the decade and have that much less to lend to small businesses and consumers. Here's another indication that commercial banks are forsaking their traditional operations. For the first time in recent memory, U.S. banks had less money out in loans in 1992 than they had staked in U.S. Treasuries.[28]

Who will survive in the new competitive arena? "I hate to say the banks are better managed, but at least they are managed," says Lowell Bryan, who studies banking at management consultants McKinsey. In Bryan's view, investment bankers don't think strategically. They don't look at product life cycles, he says. This is ironic. Bryan is flunking Wall Street for what should be its greatest strength, its ability to analyze business situations. "They understand the revenues, but they don't understand what costs go with the revenues," he says.

In one study conducted by Perro's firm, a third of the firms admitted they allocated costs arbitrarily. Another third said they were working toward a system. The final third said they weren't even bothering.

Any way you look at it, there are more financial institutions than there is business. In the early 1990s, a vintage time on Wall Street, a quarter of all the brokerage houses still were losing money. To them the cup of celebration tasted like vinegar.

CHAPTER FOUR

Michael Milken's Legacy

HERE'S A CONUNDRUM. AS THE 1990S BEGAN, the United States was mired in a recession caused, in large part, by Wall Street's love affair with debt and leverage.

It was as if the national economy were entering a death spiral. Believing they lacked money, consumers and companies alike stopped spending. The less people spent, the more precarious their jobs became and, in turn, the greater their reluctance to open their wallets. Across the land the complaint was universal, "We're strapped for capital."

Everywhere, that is, except on Wall Street.

Paradoxically, the investment bankers, the very people whose self-serving deals had helped to trigger the worst recession since the Great Depression, were sitting on more capital than they could handle.

"I'll pay you a lot of money to find ways to use my capital judiciously," says Nathan Gantcher ruefully as he sits in his paneled conference room at the World Financial Center in lower Manhattan.

Gantcher is a veteran of the investment business. Since he quit a job in advertising twenty-five years ago to come to Wall Street, Gantcher has faced all manner of markets and problems. Never has he confronted such an excess of money as Wall Street now faces.

Today Gantcher runs Oppenheimer and Company, a midsize investment house with a reputation for solid management and protecting its clients' money—yes, there are some who still do this. He is painfully aware of what the capital surfeit is doing to his company's prospects for long-term prosperity. Gantcher puts the industry's problem in perspective when he succinctly states, "We are overcapitalized."

The figures tell part of the story behind this anomaly. At the start of the 1980s, the broker-dealer and investment-banking community had around $7 billion in capital on which it could draw. Three years later the capital in the business had doubled, and would double again in the next three before peaking at $39 billion as the decade ended.[1] The bigger part of the story concerns the source of all this capital and why an excess of money rather than a shortage will put a blight on Wall Street's future profitability.

Wall Street is overpopulated with sugar daddies. It is beset by the Deeper Pockets Syndrome. These latter-day Daddy Warbuckses are the cash-rich firms who bought their way into the business in the 1980s—banks, insurance and industrial companies, even Sears, Roebuck, the retailer.

These newcomers threw money around in amounts never seen before. They arrived in the heyday of dealmaking. Not smart or nimble enough to leave before that party ended, most are stuck and impatiently await the return of the good times. An exhausted Sears did throw in the towel in the fall of 1992, hoping to ward off a shareholder revolt after its basic business wilted. So did Travelers, the insurance giant. But most other outsiders continue to wait, praying for the day when they can get a respectable enough return on their investment to save face. That wait could seem like an eternity.

Put bluntly, the profit gusher expected by the outsiders had turned into an embarrassingly obvious dry hole. When billionaire Warren Buffett is away from the media spotlight, does he rue the day he became the white knight who stopped another billionaire, Ronald Perelman, the cosmetics king, from acquiring Salomon Brothers? You bet. Ringing in his ears are the words he penned in 1988 to the shareholders at Berkshire Hathaway, whose funds went into Solly. "We have no special insights regarding the direction or future profitability of investment banking," wrote Buffett. "What we do have a strong feeling about is the ability and integrity of John Gutfreund, CEO of Salomon, Inc."[2]

James D. Robinson III also must lament American Express's entanglement with Shearson Lehman when he was riding high as AmEx's boss. If Robinson's experiences with Shearson hadn't proven so expensive and embarrassing, he might have appreciated the irony. The media pundits lauded him at first for a low-cost purchase, saying it would add street smarts to American Express's civilized corporate culture.[3] Later Robinson would say, "In hindsight, knowing what we know, we probably wouldn't have done the Shearson deal." By then he was facing billions in losses.

General Electric has spent five frustrating years trying to extricate itself from Kidder, Peabody. Almost as soon as Jack Welch, chairman at GE, sanctioned the $700 million acquisition, he had regrets. The Marty Siegel insider-trading scandal burst into the open only days after the acquisition, tarnishing reputations and reducing the value of the investment. In private, Welch confessed he'd had no idea what was lurking in the closets at Kidder. "We would never have touched Kidder, Peabody if we knew there was a skunk in the place."

This chapter will explore the forces that brought these firms to Wall Street and why their continued presence and the ongoing glut of capital are putting a lid on future profits. It also will examine how the financial community is coping as it reaps the sullied harvest sown by Michael Milken. His legacy is huge and will affect how Wall Street conducts its business for years to come.

Forget for a moment the debate about jailing the man with the messianic voice and strange toupee. Forget, too, about the hundreds of millions of dollars he must repay to society. Instead think of Michael Milken the catalyst.

Milken fanned the winds of change that began blowing when

the rule makers threw out fixed commissions and allowed "shelf registrations" of new bond and stock issues. It was Milken who goaded investment bankers into becoming principals in deals and into dropping their time-honored roles as intermediaries and agents.

Most of Milken's competitors knew investing their firm's funds meant competing with clients and doing senseless deals, but in their minds there was always the greater fear. If they didn't switch strategies, Milken and Drexel might walk away with even more business. The sugar daddies or the public stood ready and willing to abet them. By the middle of the decade, the capital at Salomon, Merrill, and Shearson was heading toward $3 billion apiece. Combined, that was more capital than for all the NYSE member firms at the start of the 1980s. In six years Drexel had boosted its capital base fifteen-fold,[4] and the increases among its competitors weren't much smaller. The arrival of so much capital took dealmaking to frenzied heights and left the Wall Street houses owning securities and businesses of dubious value.

The rush of capital, of course, didn't all come from the pockets of the sugar daddies. Investors—public and private—pitched in by buying stakes in Wall Street houses. Also, retained earnings soared throughout the late 1970s and early 1980s. So much so that no one could call Wall Street a tiny or inconsequential business. Thanks to the magic of leverage, the industry's balance sheet—its capital plus its liabilities—had soared from a mere $25 billion in 1975 and was approaching half a trillion dollars going into the crash.

A great deal of capital should have left the investment business after the market crashes in the late 1980s but didn't. In the panic that began in the summer of 1987 (and which Milken claims he forecast), most of the Street's newer big-time backers found they couldn't get out. The exit doors were blocked. Almost without exception, the sugar daddies gritted their teeth and dug deeper into their pockets to keep their investments solvent.

A slew of big-name firms were technically bankrupt, but they didn't fold. Only Drexel Burnham went under, victim of its own short, but ill-advised, fight against the charges of insider trading, stock manipulation, and various and sundry other wrongdoings, plus the federal government's equally misguided war on junk bonds.

Instead, those deep-pocketed parents rushed to the rescue, bailing out First Boston, Shearson Lehman, and Kidder, Peabody and pumping in enough capital to cause a glut. No wonder Gantcher laments, "The returns on capital are terrible, particularly for a risk business."

This is no exaggeration. During the 1980s, a period when investment bankers made vast personal fortunes, the return on equity for the industry skidded from above 40 percent to zero. True, the returns have improved somewhat in the 1990s, but to less than half the level achieved a decade earlier. Permanent prosperity can return only if Wall Street shrinks its capital base or reduces its operating costs. Or both.

Capital is the fuel that drives and lubricates Wall Street. The investment community's need for capital appears insatiable, no different from that of the airlines, the phone companies, or any other business coping with a changing technological and regulatory environment. Except in one particular. In financial services, geographic boundaries are even less secure, safe havens far harder to find. Wall Street's historic businesses—the raising of capital for others and the distribution and trading of securities—are so intertwined that a problem in one area soon spills over and causes troubles in the other. Here the glut of funds fosters the inefficient, lets weak competitors survive, while creating overcapacity and devastating profit margins. Even in good times, mediocre firms with funds to spare can replicate the products and services created by smarter competitors, crimping everyone's returns. This is as true in the bidding wars for new issues as it is for the creation of indexes and all the other new derivative products flooding into the financial arena.

For an example of what this superabundance of capital and capacity does, look at what's happened to two basic Wall Street functions—its creation of research materials and its hunt for commissions.

Research reports don't come cheap. To keep a hundred researchers tracking some eleven hundred companies, Merrill spends around $100 million annually.[5] The better analysts earn high six-figure salaries and more. It isn't money well spent. Research reports litter the desks of most money managers. Much of this material gets tossed into the trash, unread and unwanted. It's the investment community's version of junk mail. There's no charge to the big customers, the institutions, for this research, but then, arguably it isn't worth much. Most of the ideas proffered are knockoffs of the common wisdom. Few are sufficiently original to make the investment recommendation worthwhile.

So why bother? The brokerages send the research out by the carload. The payoff, they hope, will come when institutional clients buy a few extra shares of tough-to-sell issue and steer commission business their way. Mostly that's wishful thinking.

Take a look at Wall Street's approach to billing institutional traders for handling their transactions. It's crazier than the way Crazy Eddie sold TV sets before he went over the brink. These prices aren't just insane, they're ludicrous. Most houses *pay* the institutions to trade with them.

Welcome to soft-dollar deals—a practice that's more pernicious than any loss leader tried in the retail electronics business. Since May Day 1975 the commissions charged institutions have fallen inexorably, dropping from twenty-six cents a share to a couple of cents or so. Yet so desperate are the brokers for business that they also supply for free many of the computers, monitors, information services, and other paraphernalia that the institutions use to track movements in prices and markets.

Each year Wall Street gives away possibly as much as $3 billion in soft-dollar services in the hope of recouping its costs through execution and transaction charges. Mostly the firms are hoping in vain. It's doubtful if this is a viable approach for any of the major houses.

In fact, Morgan Stanley and Goldman, Sachs became sufficiently disillusioned that they threatened to walk away from the business of trading shares for commissions. In a sense, they can afford to do so. Thanks to Michael Milken, their primary business today is acting as principals rather than agents. Their absence from the commissions business might reduce but it won't eliminate the industry's excess capacity. And commissions are only one of the many troubles on Wall Street.

* * *

Management guru Peter Drucker once admitted, "We know nothing about motivation. All we can do is write books about it." Drucker is probably right, but within the jumble of motivating thoughts that lay behind the sugar daddies' movement into Wall Street, one stands out. Simply put, the grass looked greener. Prompted by regulatory changes, many firms decided they could make money easier and faster if they moved their capital into financial services. And why not? If an upstart like Drexel Burnham Lambert could become a multibillion-dollar operation in the space of a few years, why couldn't others?

No group bought its way into this business with as much determination as the insurers did. Travelers took over Dillon, Read. St. Paul's grabbed John Nuveen to get into fixed-income investing, while Equitable Life bagged Donaldson, Lufkin and Jenrette, which a generation earlier had broken ground by being the first house on Wall Street to issue public shares. Metropolitan Life put up money for a 10 percent stake in the holding company that owns First Boston, a move it now must regret. John Hancock owns brokerages on both coasts, and Kemper bought no fewer than five regional firms.

Money had an affinity for Wall Street. It just kept coming. For a while, Wall Street became a hot investment. After watching Merrill Lynch's stock quintuple in the early 1980s, insiders at Morgan Stanley and Bear, Stearns tapped investors' pockets, turning their partnerships into public companies but still retaining virtual control. From the viewpoint of the houses, but not their investors, their timing was exquisite. Merrill's stock had already peaked. Wall Street as an investment wasn't so hot after all. Caught in the downdraft of the 1987 crash, shares of both Morgan Stanley and Bear, Stearns would struggle for several years, frequently trading at sizable discounts to their issue prices. Merrill's stock would take eight years to regain its peak.

Firms didn't even have to sell out entirely to get funds. Goldman had no difficulties in raising more than $700 million from Sumitomo Bank and a slew of Japanese and U.S. insurance companies. The backers received shares in Goldman, but these didn't give them any say about the way in which Goldman would conduct its affairs. Their shares were the nonvoting type but—as it turned out— among the smarter investments made.

When added together, these cash infusions became significant. What concerns thoughtful folk on Wall Street today is that the ranks of corporations who want in—either as passive investors or to run their own securities operations—is hardly diminishing. True, some Japanese bankers aren't as well heeled as they were and have had second thoughts. This still leaves plenty of potential competitors among the big European and U.S. commercial banks. Whether they still believe that this is an easier business than their own is beside the point. They yearn for a piece of Wall Street because they believe its prospects are at least better than their own.

Besides envy and fear, the motivating forces here include the expectation of regulatory change. The neat divisions that for six decades separated the money suppliers into two groups and the insurers into a third are fast breaking down. Minimonopolies are being overrun by ferocious competition. Many commercial bankers, notably those running the money center banks, are in deep trouble. They have committed one breathtaking blunder after another, from recycling petrodollars into Latin America to funding the glut in real estate. Now these banks must worry about the growing competitive threat to their home turf.

The banks' traditional role as intermediaries, of taking deposits from customers and making loans, is up for grabs. Finance companies, department stores, and even Ma Bell are direct competitors, offering mortgages, credit cards, and even the money for leveraged buyouts plus commercial and industrial loans. AT&T could have as many credit card customers as Citicorp by 1995.

The attacks don't stop there. IBM and American Airlines don't seem likely threats to the neighborhood bank or to Wall Street, but they are. Besides selling computers when it can, IBM also is in the business of taking deposits and acting as a money manager.[6] Through its credit arm, IBM runs a sizable money market fund. On a smaller scale, American has experimented with a money fund that awards one free flight mile for each ten dollars deposited.[7]

Initially, IBM created the fund with its employees in mind, but there's nothing to stop outsiders giving IBM their money to manage. Many do, attracted by IBM's guarantee that their returns will exceed the average of all money funds.

There's a double whammy at work here. IBM invests those funds in its own commercial paper. Bang goes a hunk of fee business for its traditional bankers. First IBM, then American, then who? Where the computer giant goes, others are sure to follow.

Robert Dugger is chief economist for the American Bankers Association and recognizes the threat. His words are verbose, but their message is important. Says Dugger, "We are in an era of aggressively intensified competition, rapidly shifting definitions of what financial products are, a general slowdown in world economic growth, and much much tougher risk management demands."[8] In plain English, everybody wants into somebody else's backyard.

Officially, Glass-Steagall, the legislation enacted in the aftermath of the great crash of 1929, is still in place. Fire walls still separate investment and commercial banking. A decade ago bankers would have laughed if someone had suggested that the Berlin Wall would collapse before Glass-Steagall. Back then Glass-Steagall's fall was a foregone conclusion.

The nub of the argument for throwing away Glass-Steagall, then and now, is that it puts U.S. banks at a competitive disadvantage. If restraints are lifted, these banks will no longer need to fear the huge globe-girdling European and Japanese banks, many of which also run sizable investment-banking and stock brokerage operations.

The argument might carry more weight if those same money center banks hadn't frittered away fortunes. Besides their ill-conceived lending to third-world countries and domestic property developers, several gambled and lost large sums on trying to become investment bankers, both here and overseas. Commercial bankers lost a ton of money in the follies of the 1980s acquisition binge. In the apt words of one critic, "the trendiest takeovers were of failing companies expensively sold to their failed managers."

The money center banks also lost a bundle abroad, trying to learn the craft of investment banking ahead of Glass-Steagall's demise. Citicorp and Security Pacific, in particular, emptied their wallets in London and the Far East as a prelude to getting into the business in the United States. The results were horrendous. Both had to back away and take sizable write-offs. "It was just a disaster," says James Hanbury, who follows investment banking at Wertheim Schroder. All told, Hanbury reckons Citicorp blew half a billion dollars in trying to become a player in the securities industry. "They were just in time to get killed in 1987 when the business dried up," says Hanbury. "It was not very well planned."

Wrong execution, right motive? The breaching of Glass-Steagall will continue even while Congress remains in a dither over its repeal. The Federal Reserve Bank apparently worries less than the politicians about offending the thousands of small bankers, who rightly fear they would lose out in any banking free-for-all.

The irony of the Fed permitting J. P. Morgan to become the first U.S. commercial bank to underwrite and trade U.S. stocks in fifty-seven years didn't go unnoticed on Wall Street. Morgan was the bank whose monopolistic shenanigans triggered the original Glass-Steagall separation in the wake of the 1929 crash.

This could be like letting Godzilla loose in lower Manhattan. With $5 billion in capital and its rare triple-A rating, J. P. Morgan is often the biggest profit maker in banking. Leaving no one in doubt about its aspirations, the bank has erected a new headquarters at 60 Wall Street with thick carpets, walnut paneling, and delicate Oriental vases, plus an equally lavish pad in London, at a total cost of $1.5 billion. In its first year of regulatory freedom, J. P. Morgan underwrote about 6 percent of all equity issues in the United States, and its roster of blue-chip clients includes Procter and Gamble, PepsiCo, and American Brands.[9]

After Morgan, the deluge?

What worries securities firms is how commercial banks can unfairly twist the arms of their corporate clients. According to this argument, customers may get sent to the back of the line for loans if they don't give the commercial banks their underwriting business. The Securities Industry Association, a trade group, is lobbying Congress to prevent other banks' being allowed to lend and underwrite simultaneously.

The timing for a full-scale drive by the larger commercial bankers into Wall Street's terrain is right. Loyalty between borrowers and any kind of banker went out the window with the entry of shelf registrations. Treasurers of corporations seeking funds say the services of most bankers are overblown. They don't see a whole heck of a difference between one stripe of banker and another.

Twist that thought around and see what it means from a banker's perspective. If the chief financial officer at an Exxon or a Union Carbide isn't going to respect whatever his bankers—commercial or investment—do, then the smartest banker is the one managing to collect the highest fees. In this jungle, being nice to customers doesn't make sense if that customer is a price shopper. Shopping for money isn't quite as cutthroat as shopping for electronics, but it's headed that way.

You cannot but appreciate the irony of the situation here. The shadow of J. P. Morgan is spreading, even while the securities industry wrestles with the legacy of Michael Milken. Many contend that when the history of twentieth-century finance is written, Milken will be regarded as the preeminent figure of his era, as old J. Pierpont Morgan was of his. If that judgment is rendered on the basis of one man's ability to change the way Wall Street conducts its business, then Milken will be long remembered, perhaps even for as long as Morgan.

Milken was a spellbinder, a natural orator who could captivate seasoned corporate chieftains and hold them in the palm of his hand. He liked to argue that through debt came safety. In times of trouble, he would say, the highly leveraged company could exchange its debt for equity. The savings produced by no longer needing to service that debt would turn the cash flow positive. In Milken's reasoning an unleveraged company didn't have this advantage since it didn't have any debt service charges to eliminate. But as one critic rightly observed, "That's something like saying a drunk is better off than a teetotaler because a drunk can sober up and a teetotaler can't."[10]

A lot of baloney gets spoken about Milken by people you might expect to be less naive. Milken shouldn't get the credit—and he doesn't claim it for himself—for inventing and issuing junk bonds. They have been around at least since the late 1960s, only then they masqueraded as Chinese paper and carried the imprimatur of the conglomerators Larry Tisch, Charlie Bluhdorn, and Jimmy Ling, among others. Only later did Drexel and Bear, Stearns issue low-grade bonds for corporations, triggering the wave of leveraged deals.

Something close to the truth about Milken came out in a piece by *Forbes* magazine. "Milken wasn't just a step ahead of his Wall Street peers, but a quantum leap ahead, acting as a venture capitalist, investment banker, trader, investor," wrote the magazine's top investigative journalists with rare insight. "What counts with Milken is that he changed the way Wall Street houses played the game. He showed them that the more hats you wear the more money you make."

This was heady wine, and Wall Streeters were ready to sup from the same cup. With Milken as Bacchus, staid bankers threw aside thoughts of probity and reveled in leverage. Unbridled, they were no longer content to run their business only as agents, acting for others. To compete with Milken and the Drexel Burnham Lambert money machine, firms on Wall Street became principals, putting their own funds into one deal after another.

It didn't matter that the air would soon go out of the Drexel machine, or that its success depended upon sleight of hand rather than sound practices. Or that evidence was available about how dangerous such deals were. For example, long before Drexel's troubles became apparent, a Morgan Stanley high-yield financing for Oxoco, an obscure energy company, had bombed. A red-faced Morgan Stanley was left holding three-quarters of what luckily was a relatively small offering. But Wall Street was in heat, and to borrow a quotation sometimes attributed to St. Augustine, "a Stiff Prick hath no Conscience."[11] Apparently, few on Wall Street paused long enough to analyze the way the game worked. Milken was operating what would later become known as the "mutual convenience routine." As *Forbes*'s Howard Rudnitsky and Allan Sloan would reveal, Milken, in effect, was running a laundry operation where the clients took in each other's washing—the latest junk bond offering.

Through his close ties to some of the most controversial figures in big-league finance, Milken was able to ensure an ample number of subscribers for any new issue of junk bonds. In fact, Milken would raise more cash than participants needed for their own uses, ensuring they had surplus funds to invest in the junk bonds of the next issuer in the Milken queue. And so the gig kept going.

Instead of heeding the fragile base upon which Drexel had grown, Wall Streeters went after their own pot of gold. Fearful that Drexel would monopolize the takeover game with its infamous "highly confident" letters—bragging notes that said it could raise funds for deals of almost any size—the other houses set out to compete by using their own funds in bridge loans. These proved to be anything but temporary. "It was disastrous," says Oppenheimer's Gantcher. Flush with capital and overconfidence, the houses staked and not infrequently lost a bundle in buyouts.

Merrill Lynch gets credit for starting the bridging craze by supplying $400 million in July 1985 to Comcast for its unsuccessful bid for Storer Communications.[12] Merrill Lynch was in an unenviable position. Its attempts to become a big-league banker were going awry. Blue-chip companies snubbed Merrill, preferring to get their investment advice from the likes of Morgan Stanley and Goldman, Sachs or even First Boston. The raiders and other adventurers also turned their backs on Merrill, choosing to trek to the Beverly Hills printing press run by Milken. "We thought we could get clients from both ends of the spectrum," said Kenneth Miller, who did as much as anyone to put Merrill Lynch into the bridging business before he left to set up Lodestar as a takeover boutique.

As their name implies, bridge loans were designed as short-term loans, a bridging device available until more permanent financing could be arranged. The interest rates were always high and sometimes the borrower put up collateral. But it was the dealers who were taking the risks, supplying the money, much of it raised by leveraging their own balance sheets with commercial paper and other short-term borrowings. Most felt they didn't have much choice. Any banker who refused to fund a bridge loan risked seeing the takeover artists cross the street to the competition. The prospect of rich fees blinded bankers to the perils.

Wall Street had always risked modest amounts of its capital in deals, but here we are talking about big money. Investment bankers were plunking down as much as a third of their firms' total capital on a single deal. At one point in 1987, Merrill had committed to $2.5 billion in bridge loans when its equity capital totaled only $3.3 billion. Merrill even agreed to lend the Anglo-French raider Sir James Goldsmith almost $2 billion for his takeover attempt of Goodyear Tire without bothering to get any other bankers to share in the risks.[13] But then, Merrill was hardly alone.

For a brief while, bankers in their snazzy suspenders believed and acted as if they were omnipotent. A banker at First Boston kept a cowboy hat on his credenza inscribed with the words BET THE RANCH. He wasn't kidding. His firm had committed almost two-thirds of its $2 billion in assets to bridge loans.

If anything, Shearson Lehman plunged even deeper into the hole. Its funds went into no fewer than twenty deals at one time. Its bankers bragged that the firm's capital base could handle five different deals each worth $1 billion—not sequentially, but simultaneously.

Making such commitments was all too easy. Deal designers expected a payoff at the end of three months or, at the most, six months. Only their deals didn't meet their schedules. Three years beyond the due date, Shearson was still holding paper that Prime Computer, an ailing minicomputer maker, couldn't repay.

While it lasted, bridge building was quite a business. The braver you were, the more you extended your firm, the richer you became and the higher the firm rose in the banking league tables. In funding bridge loans, the firms, in effect, were writing checks against their ability to sell junk bonds at a later date. The fees were enormous, twice or even three times higher than those the firms could charge if they were only offering advice rather than putting up their own moneys. And remember: in addition, the bankers levied an interest rate for the bridge loans that smacked of usury. Charges of five points over the prime rate weren't uncommon, at a time when the prime spent more time above than below the double-digit mark.

There wasn't much that was nice about the way some merchant bankers operated. Any borrower foolish enough to fall behind in his repayment schedule faced the prospect of his interest rate escalating each month. "We want the chief executive to hear the clock ticking away as he lays his head on his pillow," said a dealmaker, sounding much like a loan shark. "We are not holding a gun to anyone's head. We are just providing the incentive to pay back quickly."

First Boston, with the deep pockets of Credit Suisse and Metropolitan Life behind it, was unrivaled among the bridge builders for its enthusiastic dealmaking. It even coined and copyrighted a cute term for its bridge loan business—*MBA*, for Merchant Banking Acquisition—and bought newspaper advertisements to herald MBA's debut. The firm's top merchant banker then was Bruce Wasserstein, who liked to proclaim, "This is the dawn of a new era of merchant banking." Wasserstein was right, but not in the way he meant.

First Boston achieved what became the era's high- or low-water mark, depending upon your viewpoint, through its dealings with Robert Campeau, a little-known Canadian real estate developer with a widely publicized history of mental and marital problems. It offered to lend the entire $1.8 billion needed for his bid to acquire Allied Stores. Two years later First Boston was again Campeau's lead investment banker, supplying much of the $2 billion bridge loan he needed to bag Federated Department Stores.[14]

The Campeau deals came to epitomize the foolishness of the times, and it's worth recalling the fees First Boston hoped to recoup on just one part of the Allied deal:

Commitment fee	$47.4 million
Aggregate on bridge loan	31.0 million
Solvency letter to comfort banks	1.0 million
Advisory fee	7.0 million
Success fee	7.6 million
TOTAL FEES	94.0 million
TOTAL BRIDGE	$865.0 million

Source: *Investment Dealers' Digest*, June 1, 1987, p. 18.

In this feast, these fees were only the first course. First Boston figured to collect a further flood of income for selling off bits of Allied when the time came for Campeau to repay his loans. Dessert would be the charges levied by First Boston for recycling as a new public company whatever was left of Allied. A veritable feast of fees.

In the midst of the Federated deal, Bruce Wasserstein quit First Boston to set up his own boutique. First Boston went ahead anyway. Whether its managers were indulging their egos by trying to prove they didn't need their former dealmaker hardly matters. The Campeau financings weren't markedly different from many others of the era, only bigger.

Should all the bankers have known there was a catch? Of course. The clients weren't crazy. Most were paying such high fees because they couldn't get the money elsewhere. Did these clients think they would repay the loans? Maybe. This wasn't a time to worry about the future.

It was a time to acquire and accept the bankers' terms. Conflicts of interest? Few cared if the bankers offering "impartial" advice on the merits of a deal were the same guys who would loan the money needed to complete it. Some deals were so complex even the lawyers were hard-pressed to understand them. The documentation needed to describe the fees alone often ran to several pages.

The mistake Wall Street made was in believing that the fine print meant what it said. By definition, these bridge loans were to be temporary loans to cover a gap between the initial takeover and its final refinancing. PaineWebber loaned Campeau the equivalent of half of its own net worth and two years later found itself lining up with the other unsecured creditors.

You might say Wall Street was using a strategy popular with home buyers, who use bank money to buy a swank seven-bedroom mansion until they sell their dilapidated three-bedroom house. Trouble was, merchant bankers were no smarter than the typical house buyer in a fading market. In fact, even as they were putting their jobs into jeopardy, many were mortgaging away their futures. They were using the bonuses they expected to collect for what they thought were "done deals" to buy pricey condos on Manhattan's Park Avenue. Five years after the Campeau crash, those condos were selling for a fraction of the prices the bankers had paid at the peak of the market.

* * *

In their rush to cut deals, too many bankers overlooked or chose to ignore the inevitable consequences. This was a game like the lottery. The odds got worse with every new player. In this case the jackpot also was shrinking. Dealmakers abused the rationales they had concocted for justifying takeovers. Their theory that the sum of the parts would always be greater than the whole came back to haunt the bankers.

At the start of the 1980s bull market, raiders could scoop up assets at ridiculous discounts. Typically, you could spend forty-four cents in the stock market and own a dollar of corporate assets. By 1989 that gap had narrowed, leaving only a modest difference between the worth of a company in the stock market and the value you could expect from breaking it up into salable parts. On top of this, owners were demanding—and getting—a 30 percent premium over the market price for transferring control of the company to the raiders.

In the words of one player, "Prices had gotten so high in the late 1980s that the winning bidder was often a loser. Especially since it should have been clear that a capital crunch was coming." The player's name? Michael Milken.[15]

For anyone sober enough to look there were signs aplenty that this binge would end in a bust. To take just one. At midyear 1987, a tally of the money available for leveraged buyouts showed a breathtaking $17.5 billion accumulated by twenty-seven organizations, most of them raiding parties. And that didn't count all the dough in banks or securities firms or insurance companies that stood ready to participate in yet one more deal.

That same year Wall Street took in well over $1 billion in fees for its merger advice and its bridge loans. Three years later the gusher of money was virtually extinct.

Outsiders are often puzzled why the bankers and raiders kept on with the takeover game when the mathematics of deals had long since ceased making sense. The only plausible answer seems to be that the participants were like St. Augustine, pleading, "Give me chastity, but not quite yet."[16] Not while they thought they could plunder and reap all those juicy fees.

In fact, dealmakers were encouraged to keep dealing because of the way Wall Street houses structured their compensation packages. Of this frenzied era, Miller once commented, "People in investment banks don't get rewarded for not doing jobs. So those in charge of making money by placing capital have a proclivity to do it."

Few firms held money in escrow until the deals were concluded and the loans repaid. That would have been like the pope questioning his faith in front of St. Peter's. In fact, by way of showing the strength of their convictions, most firms gave out generous bonuses based not upon the ultimate returns but on the original terms of the deal.

Worse, many firms—Merrill, Shearson, First Boston, and Goldman, Sachs, normally the epitome of rectitude, among them—allowed their senior officials to coinvest in the deals through special limited partnerships. Consider how these partnerships worked. Whatever the limited partners put in, their firm, in its role as general partner, typically leveraged fourfold. Put in $10,000 and you have $50,000 working for you in a deal that will yield a 50 percent compound annual return, if it pans out. Chastity, anyone? Not yet, Lord.

Around the time of the Campeau deal, members of the red-suspender set began to call themselves *merchant* rather than *investment* bankers. This was more than a change in semantics. It signaled an alteration in mind-set that has cost Wall Street dearly.

For outsiders, the distinction between investment and merchant banking is more subtle than obvious. The roles overlap. Both sets of bankers give advice, take positions, and earn huge fees. About the only discernible difference is this. If the investment bankers' fees are outrageously large, those of the merchant bankers are obscenely so. This, supposedly, is compensation for supplying last-resort financing.

Traditionally, investment bankers put up funds to ease the progress of an underwriting. They made sure the offering didn't collapse in the first days and weeks of trading. That obligation fulfilled, the bankers collected their fees and moved to the next deal. In contrast, the newer breed of merchant bankers locked up their firms' funds in what with depressing regularity turned out to be long-term illiquid investments. As one participant would ruefully acknowledge, "In a principal business life begins at the closing. You own it and cannot walk away."

In the 1980s merchant bankers used those investments to move far beyond the funding of deals. Their firms bought into real estate, went prospecting for oil and gas, and became venture capitalists. Morgan Stanley alone wound up owning over forty different industrial companies.

According to many of the participants, merchant banking was to be the new wave on Wall Street. "Merchant banking is not a fad," insisted William E. Mayer, whose twenty-three-year career at First Boston had brought him to the chief executive's office. Oh no? Not long after uttering that forecast, Mayer would be gone. So would dozens of colleagues, most of them unceremoniously fired at the insistence of the firm's largest stockholder, Credit Suisse. There was, apparently, a limit to the patience and indulgence of this deep-pocketed parent. Still, the cleanup act at First Boston came too late. Shortly before Mayer's departure Credit Suisse and Metropolitan Life needed to bail out their wayward offspring by buying up most of the unsalable paper in its $1.1 billion bridge loan portfolio.

More prescient than Mayer was Lazard's Felix Rohatyn, who around the same time observed, "There have always been fads in investment banking. We have had our short skirts and bouffant hairdos. Today we have merchant banking. Next week we will come up with something new."

Although he didn't know it at the time, Robert Pirie, a top officer at Rothschild group, which eschewed this business, would utter the era's epitaph. "Merchant banking is like those mushrooms that only grow where corpses are buried," he said. "It could only flourish in a mad, hectic bull market. It cannot flourish in a rational market."

Today its critics call merchant banking Wall Street's most costly and shortest-lived indulgence. Its obituary may be premature.

However abrupt its demise and however much red ink it generated, merchant banking may return in a different guise. In time, Wall Streeters will recall the fees that merchant banking generated, while forgetting the losses and pain that accompanied them.

Merchant banking faces a troubling question. Whom is Wall Street in business for, its customers or itself? "You cannot honestly advise a client and at the same time have your merchant bank be in the market competing with that client," says the head of one brokerage house. "I don't think you can do it with any degree of honest explanation. Your client wants the first crack at the company you might buy. It makes for a very awkward situation."

How the houses choose promises to be the debate of the decade. If this executive is right, they have no alternative but to decide whether they want to be advisors or investors. They cannot straddle both camps. Their clients already are too angry to tolerate that.

Assessing Michael Milken's role in the mergers and acquisitions binge is difficult even now. The claims of investigative journalists and the counterclaims of defense lawyers make for bestselling books but don't clarify the issue. So much of the evidence of what really went on probably never will surface. That's the price we pay for a justice system dominated by plea bargaining. The $1.3 billion settlement for civil claims plus Milken's ten-year sentence in return for some guilty pleas left the public still pondering exactly what had gone on during the eighties. Milken's return to society early in 1993 didn't lessen doubts among critics about the fairness of the system.

Was Milken an updated version of the century's most celebrated financier, J. Pierpont Morgan? There are parallels, but author Ron Chernow, who has labored long over the Morgan files, is probably right in dismissing such claims. Morgan could be arbitrary and intrusive with companies he financed, according to Chernow, who wrote the prize-winning *House of Morgan*. Yet Morgan also insisted on sound, professional management and—with some notable exceptions—conservative financial policy.

"Milken was an anti-establishment maverick who financed raiders lacking any experience in companies they bought," says

Chernow. "Far from trying to develop their targets for the long haul the Milken minions broke them up for quick gains."[17] By emphasizing debt to such extremes, Milken and the other investment bankers, plus, of course, the raiders, left the country with weaker rather than stronger companies. As Chernow says, Milken "typified a decade in which financial machinations stymied long-term corporate growth."

Milken had his own perception of what it had been all about. "Finance is an art," he told members of the American Academy of Achievement when he was guest of honor at their annual banquet. "Not yes or no, right or wrong. It is an art form, an understanding of who should be the companies of the future, and how to structure transactions. It's an art form greatly misunderstood."[18]

A better assessment of Milken's talents comes from comparing him with Samuel Insull, the legendary utility tycoon, according to James W. Michaels, the perspicacious editor of *Forbes* magazine.[19] At his zenith in the 1920s, Insull controlled an empire worth $60 billion in today's money and was lauded by the press. But Insull, too, was thrown into jail, and eventually died broke and in disgrace.

Both Milken and Insull were geniuses at raising money from the public and were instinctively in tune with the economic trends of their times. The way Michaels tells the tale, Insull was every bit Milken's match at the leverage game, at one point controlling as much as twenty dollars in assets for every dollar of his own wealth through multitiered holding companies.

Milken and Insull made the same point. There was little risk in leverage while the operating income from the underlying business was predictable. The problem was that neither man knew when to stop. Michaels twice interviewed Milken in the federal prison camp in Dublin, California, and believes Milken, having popularized junk bonds, hated giving up even a corner of the business. "Through stretching the rules and selling junk securities as sound investments," says Michaels, "both men ended with their empires destroyed and their accomplishments buried."

Few on Wall Street noticed the signs that were flashing the end of this party. They were too busy making money. Here Milken was as guilty as anyone. Swept along by the spirit of the times, Milken had stopped doing basic research and, by his actions if not his words, failed to acknowledge that the inefficient market had disappeared. The test no longer was whether today's junk issue had a superior risk ratio, but rather whether it would sell.

Robert Campeau's junk-burdened retail–real estate empire became a paradigm for the outrages of the 1980s. As one observer put it, "the definitive LBO [leveraged buyout] in reverse, the first great bankruptcy of the 1990s." But its lesson goes deeper than that.

The dealmakers did more than ruin other people's companies. By ignoring the pitfalls of leverage and by grasping for fees, they weakened their own franchise. Wall Street had left its flanks open. New competitors, particularly the banks, are storming the bastion.

A sensible approach at this point would have seen the investment bankers pacifying their angry customers. Or at least acknowledging the need for different strategies as the global economies swung from inflation to deflation. But no, Wall Street's preoccupation was in patching up its crumbling bridges. As Nate Gantcher at Oppenheimer recalls, "Everybody said if you could bail out of a bridge loan in 1987, then there was never going to be a problem with a bridge loan." Wrong.

The worst-hit firms simply dug deeper into pockets of their sugar daddies, leaving an excess of capacity if not competence in place. One result: the industry's pretax profit margins plunged from double to single digits and then entirely vanished.

In their feverish pursuit of fees, the merchant bankers also failed to scan the horizons for what others might be doing. If they had, they might have spotted that plenty of banks, domestic and foreign, now harbor aspirations to offer a fuller range of financial services. These bankers had their eyes on some of Wall Street's prime customers, particularly their larger corporate clients, who do business around the globe. By one count, there could be as many as four dozen banking operations that are preparing to throw down the gauntlet and enter the lists for Wall Street's business.

Of course, not all of these banks will have the moxie or savvy to pinch too much of what Wall Streeters consider *their* business, but some will. George Vojta heads strategic planning at Bankers

Trust and is well aware of this movement. "To be competitive you need to be a universal banking institution," says Vojta. "You need to be able to take principal risk and put it on your balance sheet." Vojta thinks maybe as many as ten out of the four dozen will soon be offering tough competition. Bad news for a business that's already struggling with a capacity surfeit.

The reason Vojta's list isn't longer is cost. The price tag for entry into the global stakes is enormous, particularly for communications gear to keep pace with the technological winds of change. Bankers Trust, for example, spends about $350 million annually on its computer operations. "The cumulative technology is reaching the point," says Vojta, "where we develop barriers to entry and others don't even want to try to compete."

Those costs are something Wall Streeters are slowly coming to grasp. Kidder, Peabody, for example, thought it had gained an edge when for a song it picked up all of Drexel Burnham's newly installed communications equipment after Drexel went into bankruptcy. Less than three years later Kidder was ripping out and replacing that system. Such is the speed of technological change.

The difficulties General Electric has had with Kidder, Peabody underscore the excess-capacity problems in this business. Even after the Siegel affair had taken away that made-in-heaven glow, plenty of pundits thought this partnership would succeed. In its own right, General Electric is a dynamo in finance. Its GE Capital runs a largely successful, multibillion-dollar business that takes the firm into leasing, insurance, and lending.

By rights, GE's knowledge of the financial business should have brought the right mix of disciplined aggression into Kidder, plus the capital clout for it to rise into the top tier. Clearly this hasn't happened. GE hasn't succeeded either in getting the returns it expected from Wall Street or in eliminating the turf wars that periodically flare between subsidiaries that should be allies rather than enemies.

For the sugar daddies, finding the way out of Wall Street is proving a lot tougher than getting in. Every few months another rumor swirls through the community that GE is selling out its Kidder stake. Nomura and Smith Barney both have sniffed, but didn't buy.

Sears also couldn't find a buyer and is spinning off its stake in Dean Witter to its own stockholders. Travelers, the insurance firm best known for its red umbrella advertising campaign, did slightly better. It managed to off-load Dillon, Read to the latter's employees and a British merchant bank. Travelers had used Dillon to get into risky buyouts and other projects needing venture capital funding. With its own problems in real estate mounting, Travelers wants less, not more, exposure to high-risk financing deals. Part of the money for the buyout came from Barings, an old-line British banking firm, whose claim to fame is that it helped arrange for the Louisiana Purchase.[20]

As for the rest of the sugar daddies, they are zipping up their wallets. And they are doing so at precisely the wrong moment, lessening the chances that their wards will remain competitive. We will examine the consequences of their reluctance to keep funding Wall Street in a later chapter. First we need to see how technology is tearing down the barriers that for years protected the New York Stock Exchange.

CHAPTER FIVE

At the Closing Bell

SHORTLY AFTER MIDNIGHT ON THE THIRD DAY of Christmas 1990, an explosion shattered the brief stillness that comes to lower Manhattan at that hour. An electrical transformer had blown up. The event might have gone unremarked except that the transformer was standing outside 55 Water Street, nerve center for the nation's stock markets.

The significance of the explosion wasn't in the physical damage—a few broken windows—but in the fatal flaw it exposed in the structure of the New York Stock Exchange.

Fifty-five Water Street is a hub. Into the building flow the details of every transaction consummated on the major exchanges. From it the ticker tape flashes electronically into brokerage houses across the country and around the world. In many minds, the tape is the quintessential symbol of capitalism. That morning, the tape faced a crucial test. As workers arrived for the start of the business day, city officials refused to allow them into the building, fearing chemical contamination. The stock exchange, a few blocks away at the corner of Wall and Broad streets, also remained closed, its trading floor, normally a scene of frenetic activity, stilled by congressional fiat. Years earlier, Congress had ruled that anyone trading stocks has a right to know the latest price. No ticker tape, no trading, decreed the regulators, whose job at the Securities and Exchange Commission is to translate law into regulation.

Yet that morning, while the exchange remained closed for ninety minutes, trading in Big Board stocks continued. Many investors reckoned that their own market information made the ticker tape less than essential and saw no reason to have their hands tied. Several dealers, including Donaldson, Lufkin, Shearson Lehman, and Montgomery Securities, ignored the regulators and made their own markets for institutional clients. Reuters, by far the largest supplier of electronic information in the securities industry, was also active. "If I wanted to trade I could trade. There was nothing stopping me," said an institutional trader.[1]

Why did so many market participants tweak the regulators' noses? If New York brokers hadn't offered to trade that December morning, their institutional clients could have executed their transactions abroad.

Modern technology is pushing the securities business beyond the reach of the regulators. Erecting artificial barriers in New York makes little sense if the trading still gets done electronically in Tokyo or Frankfurt. Why shouldn't pension funds, insurance companies, or banks trade if they determine they have adequate information? A few taps on the computer keyboard, a transocean phone call, that's all it takes to make the Securities and Exchange Commission and its rules redundant.

Petty restrictions on trading are becoming as irrelevant as blue laws once were to Sunday shoppers. Worse, instead of protecting small investors, as Congress intended, many of the rules preserve an aging cartel at the New York Stock Exchange.

The impact of technology on financial markets isn't often as clear-cut as it was that December morning. Certain trends, however, are discernible. At the very least, computers and electronic communications will:

- let anyone (who has the stamina) trade for twenty-four hours a day;
- shrink the profits of market makers and middlemen;
- cut thousands of jobs and push others away from New York;
- make stocks and bonds less important;
- promote indexing as the best way to beat the markets;
- drive investors offshore and out of the regulators' reach;
- limit how much regulators, central bankers, and legislators know about the markets;
- shift power from the Wall Street houses into the hands of the information suppliers;
- create a two-tier stock market with one section for amateur investors and another for professionals.

Before long, the ringing of the closing bell at the New York Stock Exchange, a favorite scene of television newscasts, may be a memory. "The days of the physical trading floor are numbered," says William Freund, the former chief economist at the NYSE, who now teaches finance at Pace University. "Time is running out for the NYSE," he says.

Also headed for extinction are the Chicago commodity pits with their bellowing, hand-waving traders. The Chicago pits, hardly the epitome of efficiency, are a prime target for the electronic information systems peddled by Reuters and the other wizards of technology. Reuters already is experimenting with a system called Globex that links traders in futures and options around the world and around the clock. At peak performance, a trading pit handles about twenty transactions a second. At the moment Globex isn't much faster, but it comes with an enticing guarantee. It promises eventually to execute a trade in three seconds from anywhere in the world. That's three times faster than a customer takes to dial his broker's phone number. Start saying goodbye to traders with sore throats and aching arms.

Once it gets up to speed, Globex also could challenge the NYSE. A few changes to the Globex software programming and it could handle equities as well as commodities. Another threat to jobs.

* * *

Trying to fathom where the New York Stock Exchange fits into an increasingly electronic world isn't easy. Big Board officials often sound like the proud mother watching her son's first parade at an army boot camp. "They're all out of step but our George."

With its heavy dependence on labor, the Big Board cannot compete in a technological era. Since NASDAQ launched the electronic era two decades ago, exchanges from London to Toronto have eliminated floor trading. Daily trading volume on the NASDAQ often approaches the Big Board's level. True, most of this trading involves the shares of smaller companies. Still, among these firms could be tomorrow's giants. Years ago firms switched their listings from NASDAQ to the Big Board once they became successful. Lately, few bother.

As if in a world of their own, New York's floor traders and specialists act like old-fashioned bankers, resisting attempts to extend their hours or modernize their operations. Yet customers, the bigger ones at least, feel a need to trade around the clock, driven by news events that don't occur on a rigid schedule. Cable News Network beams details of an assassination attempt in Baghdad or a currency crisis in Stockholm whether or not the New York markets are open.

As other markets and prices react, plenty of investors believe they cannot afford to wait for the NYSE to reopen. Increasingly, these money managers trade after hours in other markets where disclosure rules also happen to be less onerous.

In an unkind cut, *Fortune* magazine likened William Donaldson, the NYSE chairman, to the leader of the Flat Earth Society.[2] "All that electronics stuff, machines talking to machines with no human in the middle," insists Donaldson, "is about as realistic as airplanes taking off and landing without pilots. There are people who predict that will happen someday. I doubt it."

Donaldson only sounds like Neanderthal man. He arrived at the exchange with impressive credentials after pursuing an eclectic career. He was a cofounder of Donaldson, Lufkin and Jenrette, the first investment house to issue public stock. With his fortune secure, Donaldson left Wall Street initially for Washington, D.C. He made policy in Foggy Bottom as an under secretary of state for Henry Kissinger, then became the founding dean of Yale's business school before running his own venture capital firm.

For years, critics have compared the exchange to a dinosaur and forecast its imminent demise. And for as many years the exchange has brushed aside such attacks by seeking support among politicians and the business community to ensure its survival.

Since taking charge at the exchange, Donaldson has barnstormed across the country, trying to alert the public to his fears about electronic trading and what he calls the "fractionalization" of our marketplace. "I am worried," says Donaldson, "that in this pell-mell pace of new trading techniques we are going to lose a great national asset."[3]

Drawing upon his Washington connections, Donaldson trumpets the exchange's role in the financing of America as effectively as any of his predecessors. "No other country," says Donaldson, "has developed an equities market system so attuned to the broadest possible public participation and so encouraging to entrepreneurship."[4]

Ironically, it is this entrepreneurial spirit that now poses the most serious threat yet to the survival of the exchange.

Steven Wunsch looks improbably cast for the role of dragon slayer. Slightly built, Wunsch exudes little of the charm characteristic of a born salesman or entrepreneur. He is as unprepossessing as the bare-bones office he occupies steps away from the New York Stock Exchange. The walls are bare, the desk rented and filled only with business cards. Yet this is the man the governors and officials of the Big Board fear will put their institution out of business.

Wunsch lives to overcome challenges that would daunt lesser men. Before he confronted the Big Board, he won fame as a fearless mountaineer of world class. Now he has set up his own exchange. Wunsch's backers include the state of Arizona and his exchange officially operates from Phoenix. Through the wonders of electronics, Wunsch as easily could have located it in Minneapolis, where he keeps his main computer.

Wunsch runs a call auction. On his exchange you don't get to trade when the whim or the news suits you. It opens for business only thrice daily. At these preset times each day, Wunsch assembles all the bids and offers that come into his office via computer. He uses an algorithm, a mathematical procedure, to calculate the price at which the most buy and sell offers match for any particular stock. Say most people want to trade IBM at 50. In Wunsch's auction any bids above 50 and any offers below that will get filled, while any bids at, say, 49 or less or offers at, say, 51 or more won't. In trade parlance, they're "off the market." Ironically, Wunsch uses the same algorithm as do the NYSE specialists when they set opening prices each morning on the Big Board.

The advantages Wunsch's exchange supplies are rock-bottom commission charges—under a penny a share—and anonymity. The computer screens on Wunsch's system only reveal the numbers of shares available for trading, not their owners. Better still, Wunsch cuts out the traditional middleman. His customers only buy or sell at the price they specify. They don't hand over part of the transaction price to a trader who is making a market in those IBM shares, for instance.

What Wunsch offers flies in the face of conventional wisdom. The New York Stock Exchange boasts of its continuous flow of trades. Stock markets move up or down in reaction to the latest economic tidbit—the number of houses started by builders or the tally of those joining the unemployment line. All irrelevant for most people, contends Wunsch, who stands the argument on its head. "I have trouble finding many investors who *do* need to trade continuously all of the time," he says, arguing there's far less need for immediacy than the NYSE assumes.

Some of what Wunsch says makes sense. Most individuals and even a number of institutions have neither the inclination nor the mandate to trade based upon the latest news flash. The news moderates their thinking, but reaction comes with reflection. Investors might make fewer mistakes if Wunsch's argument were to take hold.

So far there's not been a flood of individuals or institutions transferring their business to Wunsch. Still, Wunsch says he isn't daunted. As a mountaineer, he knows what it takes to hang on by his fingernails.

As it is, Wunsch terrifies the NYSE. The Big Board pleaded with the SEC to ban his operation, raising the specter of one market developing for institutions and another for retail customers. In a letter, one stock exchange official warned the SEC that unless it prohibited competition, liquidity would fall and price volatility rise.[5]

For the regulators there looms a bigger concern. Once institutions get a taste for avoiding the exchanges, will they hunt for other trading arenas—particularly abroad—where the rules are lax? This is the concern that lies behind what the SEC is calling its Market 2000 probe, and it isn't misplaced. Market 2000 will examine what technology is doing to securities trading and promises to rank among the most important studies undertaken by the SEC since it probed the fixing of commission rates. When the study is completed sometime in 1993, the SEC could recommend more competition for the New York Stock Exchange.

Already within the United States, some twenty entrepreneurs in addition to Steve Wunsch have set up alternative trading systems. So far, these all comply with SEC mandates. As more trading gets done away from the traditional exchanges, who is to say some rules won't get bent? That's what's worrying the SEC and why it's investigating where electronic trading is headed. To see a prototype of what's in store, the SEC could begin by visiting a mid-Manhattan office block where one of the more successful among the alternative arenas is in full swing.

Bernie Madoff claims he doesn't run a stock exchange. "I'm a market maker," he likes to say, "no different from the specialists on the floor of the New York Stock Exchange."

In fact, from his computer-laden quarters in New York, Madoff makes a market in most leading industrial companies that trade on the Big Board plus another hundred or so from the over-the-counter market and a bunch of convertibles. About eight hundred securities in all.

His clients are other dealers, particularly the discount brokers, the Fidelitys and the Schwabs.

Why do they turn to Madoff? For one compelling reason. They don't pay him to execute trades; he pays them. Madoff gives the broker one cent for each share sent electronically to his office in midtown Manhattan. Until recently, the Big Board charged a broker about two cents a share to trade.

In the past, the NYSE claimed it needed the money to cover overheads, including specialists' fees and regulatory costs. In an about-face in January 1993, Donaldson said the exchange will cut its fees to stem competition from Madoff and others.

Madoff is no philanthropist. His money comes from astute trading. "Hopefully," Madoff explains, "we are buying those shares on the bid and selling them on the offering at a later time. We don't charge commissions." Again let's use IBM as an example. Madoff might offer to buy shares at 49⅞ and moments—or even days—later sell those same shares out at 50 or more. The price difference is his gross profit.

Donaldson and other officials like to say that people trading off the exchange don't get the best price. Sure, they might save a few pennies on commissions, goes the argument, but what about the eighths and quarters they lose on the execution prices?

Baloney, retorts Madoff. "We all execute at the same price by law." Everyone in the business, Madoff included, has studies showing they give their customers the best price.

Still, he must be doing something right. Madoff handles some twenty-five thousand transactions daily sent to him by three hundred brokerage firms. What's more, he claims he can execute a transaction marginally faster than any other exchange, including the Big Board. Unlike Reuters' Instinet, another off-exchange dealer, Madoff doesn't handle big blocks of shares. His customers are discount brokers trading for individual investors.

Madoff likens his role to the competition that discounters offer full-line brokers. "When people send us their orders automatically we save money," he says. "We eliminate clerks. We eliminate errors. We eliminate a lot of manual labor that used to be necessary."

By dealing only in a fraction of all the listed securities, Madoff is creaming the market. "Everybody puts out a product for which they feel there's a market," he says with a take-it-or-leave-it shrug.

What Madoff is to small trades, Reuters' Instinet aspires to be for the large blocks of shares. For its part, Instinet focuses on the big investors. Reuters acquired Instinet in the late 1980s and competes with the NYSE for heavy hitters. "If you want to talk about a trend," says a Reuters man, "it's in institutional portfolio managers doing their own trading." Anonymity and control are the major reasons. Information between traders passes across Instinet's screens rather than over the phone. Nobody need know who is buying or selling. Costs, too, are a factor. Wall Street is labor intensive and pension fund managers see no reason to pay for unnecessary overhead when there are excellent alternatives.

Instinet's terms aren't quite as generous as Madoff's, but some customers pay only half a cent a share to execute their trade.

Madoff started his business with five thousand dollars and claims his capital is now worth $80 million. His achievement is attracting imitators. A realist, Madoff acknowledges further growth will be difficult in his own business, since other brokers see what he and Instinet are doing and want in. A dozen years ago Madoff was one of several brokers offering this type of service. They were participating in an experiment quietly launched by the regulators to stimulate competition. Salomon, Goldman, Dean Witter, and Merrill Lynch all dropped out quickly, saying they couldn't make money. Politics was also a factor, with pressure on the brokers coming from the NYSE, to which, by tradition, they belong.

Now outfits such as Dean Witter, Merrill Lynch, and Shearson Lehman have had second thoughts and are offering their own off-exchange services. At present, restrictions limit the number of securities they can handle, but the SEC may lift them. That would really give the NYSE and Bill Donaldson something to worry about. Every day twenty million shares of companies listed on the NYSE already trade on other exchanges. That may not sound like much, but put it in perspective. On a typical day in the 1960s, the New York Stock Exchange was lucky if it traded ten million shares in total.

Supplying Information to the financial markets is big business. Already huge sums—$5 billion or more annually—go to the peddlers of electronic data and systems. Most of the vendors, whose half-million terminals carry the precious data, are newcomers to the financial arena. They pinched the business while Wall Street slept.

Only reluctantly did the Wall Street houses enter the computer era. Barely more than two decades ago, the firms still had a Dickensian quill-pen approach to their operations. In many offices, stock quotes arrived via telegraph, and the floor of the New York Stock Exchange looked much as it had at the turn of the century. It was only after the 1970s paper crunch swamped and wiped out some of the better-known names that the survivors accepted the need to spend for technology.

The biggest of the info vendors by far is Reuters. The British foreign news agency used its reporting skills to become *the* source for information about foreign exchange and commodities. No one trades currencies—and $750 billion worth changes hands daily—without consulting the latest prices flashing across Reuters' 190,000 terminals. Now Reuters is seeking a similar edge in stocks and bonds.

Behind Reuters and ferociously fighting for their share of the business are a slew of other newcomers. Among them are the likes of Telerate, Bloomberg, Automatic Data Processing, PC Quote, and Quotron.

The crux of the electronic wars is a battle for real estate. Space on traders' desks is tight. So is money to pay for services, even after the prosperity of recent times. Since the crash of 1987 there are fewer occupied desks on which to put the terminals. Since screens and keyboards cannot get much smaller, growth must come at the expense of someone else's machines and programs. Price wars rage, competition is brutal, and the failure rate keeps climbing.

In theory, vendors think there's a market for almost a million of their machines. One for every professional investor at work and another at home to keep pace with the market around the clock. Demand, in practice, is much less. Telerate and Quotron already have seen their installed bases almost halve to around 50,000 or so each. Bloomberg has 15,000 tops and has tried diversifying with modest success into supplying information about petroleum and real estate. While denying competitors' claims that it swaps newer hand-held devices for machines installed earlier, Reuters does admit growth has stalled.

Whether anyone makes much money is debatable. Not long ago, the cost of equipping a foreign exchange trader with electronic paraphernalia ran around $75,000. By mid-1992, the tab was down to $25,000 and still falling. If anything, the price wars among vendors of equity programs is even more cutthroat.

"You have a great deal of price competition," says Robert J. Casale, who heads up ADP's sales efforts to the financial services business. That's by way of understatement. His firm dominates the market for retail brokers with a tad under two-thirds of the machines installed. To fend off competition, ADP has halved the monthly rental to around $250 a terminal. "It's not a business for the faint of heart," says Casale.

Indeed, several firms are wondering if this is a business for them. The gossipmongers say Citicorp would pay somebody at this point to take money-losing Quotron off its hands. The alternative could be worse. If Citicorp shuts Quotron and lets it default on its existing contracts, the bank could face another sizable write-off on top of the $400 million it's already taken. That's something Citicorp doesn't need with all its other problems. Dow Jones put $1.6 billion in goodwill on its books when it bought Telerate, only to discover it had purchased a company of dubious merits. Merrill Lynch talks of bailing out of its investment position with Bloomberg but has yet to find anyone willing to pay its price.

Time was when one or two vendors dominated a single market. Thus Reuters controlled the foreign exchange desks, Telerate, the fixed income, while ADP and Quotron battled for the equities market. Each firm supplied the hardware and real-time prices for a discrete set of financial products. They dictated the terms to a marketplace enthralled at finding information so abundantly available.

The info vendors could charge almost what they liked and for years their revenues and profits climbed prodigiously. No more.

During a New York technology trade show, a Quotron saleswoman is asked about growth prospects. She gives a hollow laugh. "The play is beating your competitor, taking business away," she says. "Nothing more."

Reuters still owns the currencies markets, but competition is increasing and the other arenas are wide open for grabs. Name a security or commodity that trades anywhere from Mandalay to Milan and somebody will supply real-time information on its price. Lately Telerate has taken to running advertisements touting its ability to bring traders forty thousand computer screen pages filled with different prices and quotes. Sounds great for Wall Street until you remember what all this instant information creates—tighter spreads.

This is a serious threat to Wall Street's profitability. Once market participants base trading decisions upon the same information, the spreads between the bid and asked prices for any security shrink. Bang goes any chance for large or quick profits.

Does all this readily available information improve the performance of anyone trading or investing in securities? That's hard to say, and it may be beside the point. For better or worse, technology changes markets. Among those who trade regularly, few dare fall behind, no matter how steep the tab for installing the newest technological gizmo.

Nowadays the info vendors concentrate on supplying software, preferring to let others supply the hardware as smart personal computers replace dumb terminals. That's sensible. The peddlers of personal computers and workstations are price-cutting each other out of existence. The competition for software orders also is intense, but at least users will pay higher prices for programs they think might give them an edge.

In the 1992 currency crisis, traders in Europe were using software based upon chaos theory to predict where exchange rates were headed. The predictions weren't always accurate, but the word spread that any trader armed with the software could outwit a competitor operating alone.

In less time than it takes to read this sentence, a broker with a personal computer and the right software can execute and confirm a trade while instructing another computer on the network to process and print the order. Productivity increases? You bet.

Reuters reckons only 5 percent of the trades on its Instinet system involve any form of phone conversation. In the other 95 percent, traders at each end of the transaction press keys to execute their orders.

Coming soon, say the programmers, is software that automates most of the investment process. It will analyze an investor's needs and create a "perfect" portfolio out of a tailor-made set of financial products. All crafted and traded on the fly and with minimal human involvement.

Productivity is something few in the business like to talk about. Even the info vendors go coy at mention of the word. They don't want to remind the customers about redundancy.

Speak to Reuters about screen-based trading replacing people and you get a ten-minute lecture on why the idea is preposterous. "Oh, no, no," huffed one Reuters man in London. "The screen doesn't actually replace people at all. It's an efficient way of replacing the telephone." Perhaps.

An industry rule of thumb in the brokerage business is that one computer equals twelve people sitting around a room, and no holidays or vacations to fund. Far fewer registered reps will sit in those offices five years hence unless they can convince millions of people to start investing.

For the moment, the securities industry is still reveling in the power of computers. Brokers and investment bankers are playing the what-if game. By applying real-time market quotes to hypothetical portfolios, they hope they can push investors into new products and indexes.

The unanswered question is whether so much readily available information improves investment performance? If it doesn't, many in the business may find technology only speeds their redundancy. This is no idle threat when you consider how many customers—retail and institutional—already question the value of their broker's contribution.

* * *

In a wired world, Wall Street's role is changing, not least in the way markets are made. The creation of electronic information and automatic trading programs driven by computers could herald the biggest transfer of power yet to occur in financial services.

Without question Reuters and the info suppliers have used technology to lessen the traditional importance of investment bankers and brokers. Technology also pushes power into the hands of the buy side, the mammoth, asset-rich institutions, who for years swallowed whatever investments Wall Street sold them. Armed with their own computers and programmers, the pension funds and insurance companies can analyze and manipulate the outpourings of the information suppliers. As their confidence grows, the need for middlemen will shrink. So will Wall Street's profits. Another indication of this came when Morgan Stanley and Bear, Stearns, among others, added to their soft-dollar offerings all the information and technology needed for program trading. It's the Crazy Eddie routine all over again. Give away your proprietary knowledge in the hope that the fund managers will respond by executing their program trades through your office. Better that than seeing the funds execute even more trades via a private trading network far away from the stock exchanges.

Among the first to spot what was happening with information and technology was Walter Wriston, the former chairman of Citicorp and Reuters' director. "Reuters invented this wonderful system," Wriston explained. "You give away your inventory to them and they sell it back to you. That's tough to beat economically."

Incredible as it sounds, that's exactly what Wall Street has been doing. The houses pass their bids and offers to Reuters and the other collectors of information, who then beam back electronically what's happening in the market. For the privilege of reading on their computer screens information they once owned, everybody pays Reuters et al. a fee. Clever that.

Information is power. The information suppliers in effect become the market with their ability to collect and send information about what's actually taking place. At some point they—or their machines—could usurp yet another role: determining the value of securities in those markets. If they do, much of traditional Wall Street becomes redundant. Here we have the essence of the threat facing Wall Street and other financial institutions. Electronic markets diminish the influence and control of those who formerly dictated market behavior. This is as true for specialists responsible for maintaining orderliness at the stock exchange as it is for central bankers monitoring currencies and interest rates. "When the president goes out into the Rose Garden and says something," as Wriston once said, "over two hundred thousand screens light up in the trading rooms of the world." If the customer is as knowledgeable as the broker, who needs the broker? Equally, who needs exchanges of the type that began in the era of quill pens?

Until recently, only Merrill Lynch among the old guard had tried to compete with the information interlopers. For example, Merrill once teamed with IBM, the two aiming to knock Quotron off brokers' desks with their own razzle-dazzle technology. They found few takers and shut the venture after three years.

On its own, Merrill has another campaign aimed at preventing Reuters' Instinet from becoming the preferred outlet among institutions. Merrill is offering special deals on commissions. Again there are few takers.

In the early 1980s, seed money from Merrill went into Bloomberg Financial Markets, in which it now holds a 30 percent stake. Bloomberg is the creation of Michael Bloomberg, a former boss of equity trading at Salomon Brothers. Neither Solly nor any other house except Merrill would fund his venture.

From a plush office on Manhattan's Park Avenue, Bloomberg dominates the information market for fixed-income securities. Initially, Merrill was the source of Bloomberg's information. In turn, Bloomberg gave Merrill an edge. Since institutions were trading off Merrill's quotes, they were more likely to place their orders with Merrill than with any of its competitors. These days Bloomberg claims to be less dependent. He uses a network of bond dealers to supply the Street with the current prices for Treasuries and corporate bonds.

In a business of upstarts, Bloomberg has skillfully expanded by providing sophisticated analytical packages to his institutional clients. Nowadays he even emulates Reuters with his own news service that employs dozens of reporters and editors. Inevitably, Bloomberg is running into competition. The surprise is one source of the challenge. It comes from a consortium of high-powered Wall Street houses. In the spirit of the join-them-if-you-can't-beat-them school, five have joined forces to form EJV Partners as a vendor of information on a variety of fixed-income securities. Among them are Goldman, Morgan Stanley, and Salomon. Their avowed aim is to annihilate Bloomberg.

With such illustrious parents, EJV appeared destined to be an overnight star among info vendors. In fact, since its start in April 1990, EJV has had a spotty record. It refuses to disclose its client list—"fewer than expected," chortle competitors—and is guarded about describing the services it offers. In its first couple of years EJV did little more than assemble historical data bases. When quizzed, an EJV official resorts to gobbledygook and talks of developing a "generic technological infrastructure," whatever that is. Perhaps this vagueness reflects the consortium's ambivalence about venturing far into the information business.

Since Bloomberg's arrival, spreads on fixed-income securities have shrunk, making it tougher for traders to make profits. Selling data is a way to make a few extra bucks, but the same information could aid the competition. Detractors say consortium members keep the better material for themselves and only supply the consortium with basic data.

In private, Bloomberg tells his sales teams they have little to fear. Their system carries bond quotes from a wider and more pertinent array of sources than EJV's does, Bloomberg assures them. In fact, Bloomberg people spread the word that the partners formed the consortium, in part, as a delaying tactic while positioning themselves for more proprietary trading.

Another way to look at EJV is to regard its creation as an insurance policy. Consortium members worry that if they don't supply information, their large institutional clients will desert them and trade elsewhere. At first glance that may not appear such a big deal, considering how much spreads have narrowed. Now put yourself in the shoes of a trader at a Wall Street house whose main business is its own account. The big fear for that trader is losing track of what other big investors are doing. When the time comes to unload the house's holdings, he needs to know the number of buyers and how much each will take of whatever he's selling. Wall Street must keep its fingers on the market's pulse. The agency business serves a purpose, even if the commissions are vanishing. It helps the houses make better trades—and profits—for their own accounts.

For all Michael Bloomberg's brave talk, the consortium and its many powerful members aren't to be taken lightly. Not the least because of the other markets they may enter. Also among the members is Citicorp, owner of the floundering Quotron. Through the consortium, the bank may find a way to help Quotron regain its position as a supplier of information about equity markets. "It is entirely within reason we will go out to other instruments beyond fixed income," says an EJV spokeswoman enigmatically.

Only individuals and a few traditionalists among the mutual fund managers invest the old-fashioned way. Crossing their fingers, they neatly divide their portfolios into so many stocks, bonds, and so much cash, then pray their individual selections pan out.

The smart-money crowd today uses complex computer programs. These daring managers hedge their bets through intertwined investments that link a slew of different products, currencies, and markets, both domestic and international. This is the world of derivatives and indexing and swaps. We will look more closely at these arcane products and trading methods in chapter 6. But first there's a crucial problem to consider: how computers change markets and market participants.

Swapping people for computers is about the only way this labor-intensive industry can hope to raise its margins. To a degree, it's happening already. For example, consider the success of a prominent Wall Street house trading commercial paper. Not long ago each salesperson handled two clients and the firm handled about $33 billion in transactions. Okay, but not great. With computers, the volume of business has expanded to more than $100 billion, and seventy-five staffers are handling five hundred clients. New workstations allow them to filter data. No more wading through screen after screen of irrelevant information. By pressing a few keys, any salesperson knows what a client prefers or can buy.

Computers do all the paperwork but the actual trade is still done over the phone. Why? The sales teams insist they cannot negotiate a deal electronically. Maybe not. Still, this doesn't mean their jobs are safe. This firm already has put twenty computer terminals on the desks of its biggest clients. This ensures it gets the business even when the salesman is out. At once, this reduces the salesman's grip on the client and lessens his middleman role between client and trader.

Why not have the client push the button and send the trade directly to the trader and cut out the salesman? It's a matter of time, says an executive. So is the expansion of such programs into more complex product lines like corporate or government bonds.

"We must aggressively pursue technology or the Reuters, Telerates, and Dow Joneses will own this business," says this executive. "Data is the most valuable resource in this business. We give it to the info companies and then pay to get it back."

A specter hangs over the Street. Hardly a firm isn't experimenting to see how it can use computers to improve productivity. When Morgan Stanley pitted its computers against its staff, there was no contest. Computers executed trades for a third less cost than humans, and they did it faster. Tests such as this send shivers down the spines of the thousands of salesmen and traders employed on the Street.

Of course, human foibles can still flummox the best automated systems. Computers are no match yet for the idiosyncracies of some investors. Most programs can handle small shifts in price. The large moves send them into a tizzy. An old-time trader turned info vendor explains the problem. Suppose a stock selling at twenty dollars drops to ten. Logic says demand should rise as the price falls. Human nature says differently. Demand is often less at ten than at twenty and less still than it would be if the stock rose to thirty. Explains the trader, "There's no fund manager who wants to have that goddamn stock on his books at ten, and everybody wants to have it at thirty."

No amount of artificial intelligence yet available can overcome that level of human foible.

A mantra among information vendors is that people, not machines, make decisions. A screen gives the watcher a price, not a reason. This sounds more reassuring than it is.

According to this argument, people do their best trading as a result of conversations with other market participants. There's some truth in that, but less than there used to be. In the past the best market tidbits often came while rubbing shoulders at Harry's and other watering spots. Social contacts still count, but their importance is fading. Blame the pace of today's markets and the immediacy of news. By the time the noon-hour crowd gets back from Harry's, chances are CNN will have thrust another emergency into our midst. What seemed relevant at lunchtime often isn't by three o'clock.

The wealth of statistical information on computer screens is producing a resurgence of technical analysis. Fundamental analysis is out of fashion. Investing is becoming a by-the-numbers game. What does this mean for the habitués of Harry's? Only that the time is coming when the screens will supply more and better information than Harry's can. Then both bartender and arm bender will find themselves out of work.

Already plenty of firms are preparing for that day. They recognize the game of the future is custom-designing products for the asset-rich institutions that generate fat fees. The race is on to craft merchandise complex enough not to become a commodity. These firms deploy their best people accordingly. In the 1990s product manufacturing will outrank product trading.

As he watches this trend, Bryan Cavill, the former trader who now runs Instinet in Britain for Reuters, ponders an intriguing question. In five or ten years will there be enough people with the street skills left to do the buying and selling? Maybe to trade in a smallish group of companies that everyone feels comfortable owning. But beyond that Cavill and others see a desert littered with stocks no one wants. In this scenario, the Nifty Fifty of the mid-1970s becomes this decade's Global 100, the select band of popular securities every manager wants. Every other company becomes an orphan, for whom the capital markets are closed.

Suddenly there's a chain reaction. Without trading, there's no liquidity, only volatility. Without liquidity, there's no research and fewer commissions. And so it goes. And so too, eventually, goes the underwriting of issues for all except the pristine few. "In the future," says Cavill, "an entirely different way to trade smaller companies will evolve." Cavill pauses and adds, "But it may not. They may have been dealt some dastardly blow."

The Luddites are as prevalent in the financial services industry as they were in textiles almost two centuries earlier. David Jeffrey has met them and lost. His plan to use technology to boost efficiency and lower underwriting costs fell foul of those who don't want fees to fall any lower than they have.

Jeffrey learned about underwriting in the Treasury departments at Joseph E. Seagram and Atlantic Richfield and figured there had to be a better way. He called it CapitaLink. His idea was to let big corporations bypass the underwriters and auction their bonds via the wonders of electronics directly to institutional investors. The big institutions—the T. Rowe Prices, the Fidelitys—would use their own PCs to hook into CapitaLink's host system and actually watch an auction take place on the screen. No names would appear and participants could adjust their bids based upon what they were seeing. The potential savings on a $100 million issue: roughly half a million dollars.

With the backing of J. P. Morgan and the sanction of the Securities and Exchange Commission, Jeffrey's firm soon began collecting clients. A dozen or so issuers, including John Deere and Exxon, named CapitaLink in their prospectuses.

"We were not only eliminating the middleman," says Jeffrey, "we were making the process a lot more efficient by providing more information to the market."

There was the rub. The bidders were becoming as knowledgeable as the underwriters. They would have that "feel" of the market, what middlemen everywhere get paid for possessing.

"Somehow," says Jeffrey with a deep sigh, "the market just wasn't ready for it. So we dissolved."

Squeezed out, more like. Jeffrey believes he got his comeuppance from underwriters, who warned issuers their future offerings might become more costly and difficult to handle. Jeffrey cannot prove that and is too wise to voice a grudge.

Perhaps it was coincidence, but around the time of Capita-Link's debut, underwriting fees began to dip. "What the houses did, I think," says Jeffrey, "was offer very good pricing." The issuers had gotten what they really wanted, a better price. The old guard had stood its ground. Strike one against the electronic market.

It's hard to believe this idea will not catch on one day for certain transactions. The advantages of narrowing spreads are too strong for issuers and buyers to ignore. Already a growing band of issuers place their commercial paper and medium-term notes directly in private deals with insurance companies.

Jeffrey chafes at the thought of being right in principle but wrong in timing. "Five years from now," he says, "the large corporations will issue their plain vanilla bonds through a system that will look like mine."

If he is right, Wall Street can get ready to wave goodbye to a wad of easy underwriting fees.

Legend has it that the specialist system began on the Big Board in the early 1870s when William Boyd injured his leg. A floor trader, Boyd couldn't scurry around for business. Positioning himself by the post where Western Union traded, he agreed to look after other brokers' orders in that stock. Soon Boyd realized he also could make a bit of money trading for himself. Presto. A specialist had arrived.

Boyd's successors occupy favored and prosperous positions by dint of knowing what other brokers are doing. Today specialists may not be popular, nor add much to market efficiency, but they are pillars of the exchange's establishment. John Phelan was a specialist when he became chairman at the exchange. His successor, Bill

Donaldson, owes his position to the votes of specialists. The specialists are a powerful constituency and don't brook the idea of change readily.

Each specialist makes a market in a handful of stocks and acts much as a contrarian might. When everyone dumps IBM, the IBM specialist buys. And vice versa. The specialists' role is to reduce volatility. Does the system work?

Thirty years ago, the SEC lambasted the exchange's specialists in a vitriolic report. "They aim more at increasing their profits than at lessening radical swings in stock prices," the SEC charged. Staffers at the SEC demanded a sharp reduction in the number of specialists, the abolition of floor traders, and higher standards of self-regulation by the exchange. Joining the fray, the *New York Times* raised a moral question. "How can a man deal for himself and serve the public at the same time?" it asked.[6]

Today the question remains unanswered and the specialists and floor traders are as numerous and powerful as ever. A recent study by a couple of professors at Memphis State University charges that specialists rig prices. They don't let other traders know the best bids and offers available. Result: more profits go into the specialists' pockets.[7]

No surprise, the SEC has ordered yet another study to update its old study. At least one congressional committee also plans a probe to see if investors are being shortchanged by the system. A donnybrook of a power struggle lies ahead with the gloves coming off, as they did almost two decades earlier when the SEC forced the brokerage houses to stop price fixing on commissions.

The vested interests are girding for battle, preying on the fears of politicians by emphasizing the dangers of change. As their standard-bearer, Donaldson bravely promotes the exchange as an icon for individual investors. He comes across as the defender of the indefensible, much as another nice-mannered man with Yale connections did in the 1992 presidential campaign while trying to defend the state of the U.S. economy.

Does it matter if individuals tire of being whipsawed by the markets and put less money into equities, whether directly or through professional managers? Not as much as Donaldson and others would have you believe.

In the raising of capital, the exchange's role gets overblown. For every dollar of new common stock, companies issue nine dollars' worth of debt, and that's not even counting high-yield bonds.[8] Even new issues of junk bonds are in demand again, with $30 billion expected in 1992, up from barely $5 billion only a couple of years earlier.

So while Washington probes and debates, the Big Board resists. And technology moves yet more trading away from floor-based exchanges. At the center of the battle of electronics versus specialists is the question of liquidity. In the 1987 market collapse, the electronic system pioneered by NASDAQ and copied around the world failed. Brokers refused to answer customers' calls and orders went unfilled.

The regulatory changes designed to fix that problem will get tested in the next crash. Whether they work or not is almost irrelevant. What counts more in most investors' minds are the trading patterns on a normal day in the markets. Lucky the investor who hasn't had a stock pummeled by unexpected news and wondered what, if anything, the specialist did to prevent the damage. In truth, there's not much specialists can do. We are now in an era of investment by knee-jerk reaction. With institutional investors peering at the same data on their monitors, the reaction to any event is instantaneous. Hit the sell key and bail out immediately if the news is the least bit disconcerting. That's the style of the day. And that's why the specialists' role is so questionable.

Specialists spend much of their day trying to avoid trouble. At most only one trade in eight goes through a specialist on a typical day. When volatility rises, specialists often will only participate when the exchange's floor supervisors pressure them to do so.

Dean LeBaron of Batterymarch, the Boston-based money manager, is as shrewd a judge of how technology shapes markets as anyone in the business. "Information that used to be received at different speeds by different investors," he says, "is now received essentially at the same speed." Specialists can no more resist the avalanche of orders to buy or sell than King Canute could control the waves.

So why do they resist change?

"If you or I were specialists we'd make the same stupid arguments that their jobs cannot be automated," says an information vendor, who insists on anonymity. "They have spouses, and children and significant others. They are all addicted to three meals a day, and that's a hard addiction to get over."

Time was when specialists minted money. A *Fortune* reporter in the aftermath of the 1987 crash managed a rare peek at the books of one specialist.[9] Between 1980 and 1987, this specialist had achieved an average annual return on his capital of 55.4 percent, which is probably why he insisted on speaking with the reporter anonymously. A specialist would stake a minimal amount of capital back then, an amount equal to 1,250 shares of each stock in which he made a market. With that level raised after 1987, many specialists now complain that they can make money only on the most actively traded stocks, the top two hundred out of the eighteen hundred or so listed.

The system might have collapsed long ago if the exchange hadn't tinkered with the rules, insisting each specialist handle a mix of stocks, including some that trade infrequently. The less often a stock trades, the wider the spread and the greater the risk to the market maker. This is the rub. If Madoff, Reuters, or the European exchanges cream off more of the trading in those treasured two hundred stocks, as is likely, the privileged specialists will be in deep trouble. What next?

Call for Steven Wunsch or a system remarkably like his. Ahead, we will probably have two markets, one for active stocks, the other for inactive ones. Trading in the more active stocks will continue much as it does now, only with longer operating hours. The smaller, less active issues will go into an electronic market. These will be available for trading in auctions at set times. In effect, the exchange will acknowledge that Wunsch is right with his call auction and that many investors don't need to trade throughout the business day or around the clock.

None of this, of course, will stop the skimming. Money managers at the Fidelitys and Batterymarches are discovering they can bypass not only the exchanges and Wall Street, but the Madoffs and Instinets as well.

"It's not hard to see the day when major pension funds do a big part of their buying and selling directly from each other's port-folios," says consultant Joellin Comerford. "How long can they keep forcing themselves in as intermediaries, without adding a lot of value?" she asks rhetorically.

Institutions don't trade among themselves only to save the odd penny. They want privacy. Here we enter the gray area of what in the parlance of the trade is known as *front running,* or *scalping.*

At the New York Stock Exchange traders spend much of their time watching the antics of Fido. That's their nickname for Fidelity. In the public arena, Fidelity, the world's biggest mutual fund organi-zation, trades through National Financial Services, whose orders account for roughly every tenth share traded on the Big Board. Knowing whether Fidelity wants to buy or sell a stock is prime intelligence to others, who adjust their own holdings accordingly by front running.

So Fidelity encourages its mutual funds to trade among them-selves away from the public spotlight whenever it can.

Front running in its broadest sense is nothing more than trad-ing on the basis of information about impending market transactions that the public doesn't know about. It's all a big no-no and against the rules. It's also widely practiced.

"Front running is probably even more widespread than it was a few years back, but less talked about," says John Morton, a former trader turned consultant. Morton believes many traders have come to the conclusion that they must front-run to survive. "Institutions pay so little for execution—one or two cents a share," he explains. "Brokers don't feel their customers should have a right to ask for perfect agency execution at those levels."

At the exchanges, the floor brokers trade in gossip as much as in securities. They live on their wits, always trying to figure out the next turn in the marketplace or in an individual issue. From the floor of the exchange the investment horizon is five minutes or less. Information comes to these swarms of gesticulating, yelling traders for reasons an unsuspicious mind might regard as a legitimate and necessary part of their business. If an institution calls a broker with an order to purchase a large block of General Motors stock, for example, the broker's instinctive reaction is to find the other side of the transaction, someone eager to sell General Motors. This cuts transaction costs and doubles the commissions.

All aboveboard so far. But where does the broker get to know who is selling GM? On the floor, dozens of middlemen make it their job to know, swapping intelligence among themselves. A tip here, a wink there. But rarely anything the regulators can point to and call trading on inside information. No question, plenty of middlemen earn an adequate living by going with the flow. They trade ahead of the large transactions the broker is attempting to put together. Illegal? Try and prove it. Often this trading also spills over into the futures markets, where the leverage is greater and the execution costs are lower. It's this fear of everyone knowing your business, of course, that promotes off-exchange trading through Instinet and other systems that guarantee anonymity.

Sometime in the 1990s, institutions could supplant specialists and brokers as the liquidity providers in whatever forum becomes the marketplace. If sheer size counts, then the balance of power will move. Institutions and the sponsors of pension plans control over $5 trillion in assets, far more capital than the Wall Street firms that serve them.

Multiple markets, multiple prices. Does that matter any more than it does in groceries, with A&P undercutting Safeway? Most of the time the price differential won't matter because few will bother to check. But watch out for the day the market really hits the skids. Furor and congressional inquiries will follow when individual investors discover that prices in the markets used by their neighbors differed markedly from those in the markets they used.

The New York Stock Exchange trumpets its efficiency and its use of electronics, claiming it needs fewer people to handle a billion-share day than it took to trade ten million shares in the 1960s. That's true, but the story needs to go further than that. Over time the volume of trading on the Big Board has risen, but at nothing like the rate once expected. Nor at anything like the rate of growth in other investment markets such as options, futures, currencies, and asset-backed securities. In fact, since the 1987 crash, the exchange has become thankful for days when volume reaches two hundred million shares, a far cry from the billion-share days once expected.

During the year roughly $1.5 trillion worth of equities change hands at the NYSE, about a third more than on all the exchanges in Europe combined. That too is impressive, but not as significant as it might appear. There's a hollow ring to the New York Stock Exchange's claim that it is *the* market. One day soon, more than half the trades in the stocks listed at the Big Board will change hands on some other exchange.

As a reformer, Bill Donaldson wisely has set modest goals. Even so, he keeps setting off fire storms. His members threw a tantrum when Donaldson suggested they open for business at breakfast time and staunch the flow of trading into London. The SEC publicly ridiculed Donaldson by suggesting he emulate the American Stock Exchange's new business program and forget his own plans to get more foreign firms listed on the Big Board.

Of late, the Amex has run rings around Donaldson's exchange, gaining a sizable lead in the newer securities, particularly futures and options. "Donaldson is scared his will become another regional exchange," says a somewhat biased official at the London Stock Exchange. "He's worried it's going to go the way of the Pacific exchange or the Boston exchange and have a very small niche."

In this sense, the New York Stock Exchange is parochial. Fewer foreign companies list their shares on it than on any other major exchange.[10]

A smart move would be for Donaldson to seek a grand alliance. He should negotiate with his counterparts in London and Tokyo so that a selection of stocks from each of the world's biggest exchanges would be available for trading around the clock, and around the world. An index of this Global 100 or 500 would carry great marketing appeal. If Donaldson doesn't launch such an index, somebody will, perhaps even the American Stock Exchange. Others also might find ways for institutions to trade derivatives based upon such an index and do it among themselves, far away from the official exchanges.

Complacency is always dangerous and particularly so in a competitive business such as this. The Swiss learned the hard way what happens if you fall behind in technology. Switzerland automated its futures and options exchange, but was slow to do the same for equities. Result: every fifth trade in Swiss equities changes hands in London in its screen-based market.[11]

The brokerage community has found reasons aplenty why it shouldn't heed Donaldson and operate beyond what used to be regarded as bankers' hours. That's understandable. Banking didn't change much until someone invented the automatic teller machine.

The day may never come when people stand on a street corner and buy a hundred shares of AT&T while taking a cash advance from a machine. Yet, questioning who needs a twenty-four-hour stock market is like wondering who needs a twenty-four-hour corner deli. Somebody, somewhere will pander to the insomniacs among investors, as they did when others had an urge to buy a jug of milk at 3:00 A.M.

Already a brisk trade in NYSE-listed shares occurs in London during the night hours in New York, and that's only a beginning. Alarmed at how much off-hours trading in U.S. stocks was slipping across the Atlantic Ocean, the SEC has loosened its rules. Starting in 1991, the regulators let the automated NASDAQ open its computers before dawn for trading in its own and certain Big Board stocks. They also ruled that NASDAQ could copy the London practice of not immediately reporting trades.[12]

Officials at the Big Board could only stand by and fume. Less trading is now done overseas, but its specialists and floor traders still don't get the business.

James R. Jones, the former congressman from Oklahoma, is now head of the American Stock Exchange. He predicts a changed arena ahead for the trading of stocks. "I can see a time," says Jones, "when a person sitting before a single computer screen anywhere in the world can pick a company, say Amdahl, trade it in dollars when our market is open, and when Frankfurt is open trade it in Deutsche marks. When both are open they can pick the best price in either market or in any number of markets."[13]

When will this happen, and more to the point, when will we see a twenty-four-hour global market? Sometime around 1996 for both events, predicts Jones.

As the price of electronics drops and computers get easier to use, the debate about continuous worldwide trading becomes less a question of when than how.

In Yokohama at the Nomura Research Institute, Japan's largest broker has joined forces with Nintendo in an experiment to let investors trade stocks through their television sets in their living rooms. If they're successful, that will be a game of a whole other sort.

Don't expect more than token changes, however, at the corner of Broad and Wall. Matching members' and customers' needs has never had the highest priority there. Long ago, New York Stock Exchange members set a tone for its dealings with the public. At the turn of the century, when the members decided on a new home, their architect created an edifice of white Georgian marble in the Roman Renaissance style, with fluted Corinthian columns. The cost in 1903 dollars: $4 million, hardly a trifle. The exchange came complete with trading floor and elegant baths where the members could soak away their fatigue.[14]

More recently, plans surfaced to build a new exchange nearby. Developers want to bring together under one roof the NYSE plus five commodity exchanges and the American Stock Exchange on property formerly occupied and still owned by J. P. Morgan. Local politicians were pushing the grandiose project. Olympia and York reportedly spent a million dollars drawing up architectural plans, which included—no kidding—a trading floor.[15] Perhaps it's fortunate the blueprints went back on the shelf when the development company headed off to the bankruptcy courts.

Still, don't be too surprised if one day the specialists insist Bill Donaldson dust off that plan. Their ability to survive is legendary.

CHAPTER SIX

Weird Products for a Wired World

FOR INVESTORS, THAT LATE WINTER'S DAY IN March 1992 had begun like so many others. The market was in a rut. For weeks the daily gyrations of the Dow Jones Industrials had been modest, up six points one day, down a half dozen the next.

In this torpid atmosphere, a clerk on the equities trading desk at Salomon Brothers misread a routine sales order. At precisely 3:58 P.M., two minutes before the closing bell, the clerk received a request to sell $11 million worth of stocks and began tapping into his computer terminal. Within seconds, he placed orders to sell eleven million shares worth *hundreds* of millions of dollars.[1]

If other traders were puzzled when they saw those sell orders flash across their computer screens, they didn't hesitate. They hit the sell buttons. Immediately the Dow, which had been inching upward all day, skidded into a stomach-wrenching tailspin. In the space of forty seconds what began as a simple clerical mistake had wiped $340 million off the value of the stock market. So dramatic was the plunge that onlookers feared a market meltdown had begun.

At Salomon, traders rushed massive buying orders into the market in an attempt to limit the damage. Even so it would take hours of hard trading to reverse a slip that had battered the investments of innocent bystanders.

The risk of a rout in the stock market is never far away. To prevent meltdowns, regulators now ban computer-driven program trading whenever the market moves more than fifty points. But investors cannot relax their vigilance for a moment, not with computers creating a never-ending stream of new products, any of which could roil the markets without warning.

Welcome to the scary world of synthetic stocks and derivative products.

Synthetics and derivatives are the driving forces of today's markets, the power behind the lightning-fast movements of money around the globe. They are the stuff of program trading, indexing, swaps, portfolio insurance, arbitrage, and tactical asset allocations. We are talking here of multitrillion-dollar markets, many of which have doubled in size in a single year. The value of swap contracts alone had climbed to the point in mid-1992 where it equaled the combined worth of the New York and Tokyo stock markets.[2] This is where competition is at its keenest in finance. Bankers create synthetics and derivatives as part of their hedging strategies while turning mortgages and other debts into newfangled securities. Insurance companies such as American International Group and foreigners like France's Banque Indosuez use them to widen their reach in financial services.

There are literally thousands of these newfangled products. Broadly, a synthetic is any financial instrument artificially crafted out of another, while a derivative, as its name implies, is one that's derived from another. Futures, warrants, and swaps are all derivatives and typically get used to hedge other investments. Yet the financial instrument that's created in the process of swapping is usually called a synthetic.

For investors, what's important is knowing that at a moment's notice any of these creations can roil the financial markets. The actual creative process, the terminology, or even an individual product is less important. Fashions change in finance as much as in clothing, and the life span of any product, while often dramatic, can be short. Then along comes a new terror.

At work here is a classic example of cause and effect. It took the widespread availability of cheap computing power to produce this bewildering array of new products. Without personal computers neither synthetics nor derivatives would have become so important.

The stated purpose of all this creativity is to reduce risk while lowering costs. As one player puts it, "A derivatives market is where you can get your wish list answered." Also, he might have added, where nightmares can come true.

Synthetics and derivatives were ingredients for portfolio insurance, which did nothing to prevent the October 1987 crash, and they probably exacerbated the market panics of 1989 and 1991.

After the 1987 crash, the Brady report—officially *The Report of the Presidential Task Force on Market Mechanisms,* a task force chaired by Nicholas F. Brady, then head of Dillon, Read—issued a prescient but unheeded warning about the dangers of derivatives growing at the expense of stocks. Five years later we are approaching the point where futures could supplant in importance the traditional markets they replicate. Today derivatives, notably futures, are the tails that wag the conventional stock and bond market dogs. Trading in futures has risen fivefold in fifteen years. This is another global business, with exchanges from Paris to Sydney competing with those in Chicago and New York.

Computer jocks—they're known in the trade as *quants,* for "quantitative analysts"—download these custom-designed products into the financial markets with only passing thought for the disruptive powers of their creations.

There's more than a touch of the sorcerer's apprentice about all this. Controlling the performance of these artificial securities is oftentimes more difficult than inventing them. "Where will the next credit crunch be?" Henry Kaufman, the economist, once asked rhetorically. "We're not even out of the current one, but the next one will be in derivatives."

This isn't a penny-ante market that can be swept aside and ignored anymore. According to the Bank for International Settlements, the global market in derivatives by mid-1991 had topped $7.5

trillion,[3] with the majority created for the private market rather than for trading on the public exchanges.

Sooner or later this stuff will manifest itself as the next big financial crisis. In the coming years, Michael A. Carpenter, chairman at Kidder, Peabody, expects "huge write-offs from derivatives." Within his industry, Carpenter has become something of a pariah for his belief that disasters loom. The problem with derivatives, he says, still lies ahead, "because the tail of the risk you are dealing with is not next week, but three years from now." Says Donald Marron, chairman at PaineWebber, "I worry about the lack of regulation."[4]

So do thoughtful regulators. "Getting your hands around these things," as E. Gerald Corrigan, president of the Federal Reserve Bank of New York, once said, "can be extremely difficult."[5]

The big fear is a domino effect. The fortunes of many firms are linked through intricate webs and hedging strategies built upon derivatives. If one fails, others could follow. There have already been several early warnings. The collapse of the Bank of New England and the demise of Drexel Burnham produced chaos when traders learned contracts worth billions of dollars were less well hedged than they thought. Drexel alone had $30 billion in swaps on its books. Bankers Trust got stuck with millions in worthless interest-rate swaps and collected an annuity business as partial settlement when Mutual Benefit Life collapsed.[6]

As derivatives increase in size and complexity, the fears grow. Corrigan was right when he said about derivatives, "High-tech banking and finance has its place, but it's not all that it's cracked up to be. . . ."[7]

Such warnings were underscored by J. P. Morgan taking a $50 million hit when a misguided bet in the market for securitized mortgages turned into a $300 million loss on paper. One of many banks playing this game, Morgan had misjudged the speed at which homeowners would repay their loans when interest rates declined.[8]

"It's a worry," says securities lawyer Sam Scott Miller, who has studied the risk of hedges going astray. "Anytime you've got unidentified exposure in the magnitude that I expect we have, you cannot be comfortable." Derivatives can become a nightmare for Wall Street's top executives who cannot match the Ph.D.'s or computer training of their younger employees. To the old guard what mattered most in investing was whether a stock or bond was headed up or down. To the players in derivatives what counts is the volatility, how fast prices are changing. The lesson for the unwary: the more complicated a derivative becomes, the harder it will be to unload in troubled times.

Much of the push into derivatives reflects the lousy state of profits in traditional financial services. This is another example where the Wall Street houses take on the role of principal rather than agents, hoping that trading for their own accounts will boost their margins. It's hard to see that everyone can be a winner. Derivatives are a zero-sum game. Winners and losers balance.

Nonetheless, the rush of those wanting to take risks accelerates. When Chase Manhattan wanted to expand in the trading of currency options, it turned for help to Susquehanna Partnerships, a fast-rising boutique. Susquehanna had entered the money game after its founders had honed their computer skills while betting on horse races.[9] When Goldman, Sachs and Merrill Lynch moved into derivatives, their lawyers advised them to create separate and independent units. This way, if things went wrong, said the lawyers, the whole firm wouldn't collapse.

This boom in derivatives ties into the movement toward indexing, the buying of whole markets or groups of stocks. Until the late 1970s, most institutions surrounded a passive core of assets with an actively traded shell. When their selections of individual stocks failed to beat the markets, fund managers began building portfolios around indexes. The trading of options and futures based upon those indexes became investing's new wave.

For the Wall Street houses, the cult proved equally irresistible. As commissions and fees from their traditional businesses shrank, they too increasingly used derivatives to hedge their own accounts plus the contracts they were undertaking for institutional and corporate clients as part of the underwriting process. These contracts are rarely simple and often involve many counterparties plus a multiplicity of financial instruments linked together in a chain. In turn, each of the counterparties has its own chain of hedged contracts. This is complex and risky stuff. Investing in synthetics and derivatives could be to the 1990s what funding bridge loans was in the 1980s.

Much of this trading in derivatives is shrouded in secrecy and takes place far from public scrutiny. The Treasury scandal did lift the curtain long enough to reveal how dependent Salomon Brothers had become on trading and arbitraging for its own account. At least four-fifths of its $3 billion-plus annual revenues was coming from conducting its own rather than its clients' business.[10] Much of this involved the intricate swapping of interest-rate and currency contracts.

Solly's Treasury desk was critical to those contracts. By dominating the markets in Treasury issues, Solly could outwit competitors in judging interest-rate and currency movements.

As soon as the Treasury auction scandal broke, Salomon was in deep trouble, its information edge blunted. Rumors swirled that Salomon could become another Drexel. Few bankers would risk taking the other side of swaps with a firm that might go out of business. Solly, yesterday's powerhouse, now had to pay a steep price in the form of the better terms its competitors joyfully extracted for letting it continue as a global player in the swaps market.

That Salomon ranks among the biggest plungers in derivatives should only surprise those who, during the Treasury scandal, believed every word of the firm's public relations campaign about a return to prudent investing under Warren Buffett.

When news of the auction rigging broke and its credit rating came under attack, Salomon did ease back. Much was made of the $50 billion or so it carved out of its portfolio of stocks and bonds.

What the public heard less about were the ways Salomon continued to use derivatives and leverage after the scandal. In fact, by mid-1992, according to estimates reported later in the *Wall Street Journal,* Salomon had swept past Goldman, Sachs and Morgan Stanley, both of whom rank high among the heavy hitters in derivatives. Measured against their equity bases, Salomon was betting one-third more in derivatives than Goldman and twice as much as Morgan Stanley.[11]

Hubris? You bet. Solly had taken a $185 million charge against earnings for its hanky-panky at the auctions and was the only major house that didn't report record earnings in 1991. Regard that as a temporary setback. Thanks to its prowess in heavily leveraged principal trading based upon derivatives, Solly is playing catch-up at a phenomenal pace.

Imagine walking into a Chevy dealer and asking the salesman to custom-design a car or pickup truck for you from a thousand different options and colors. The result might differ from what you expected, but at least you wouldn't leave driving a vehicle that looks like your neighbor's. That's how it is with modern investing.

Simplicity in investing ceased with the arrival of cheap personal computers and workstations. A couple of decades or so ago, the choice of vehicles traded on Wall Street was meager, considerably smaller than the array offered each year by Detroit. There were only about a half dozen alternatives available for investors—common and preferred stocks, plus corporate and government bonds. Henry Ford's dictum was any color so long as it's black. Wall Street gave two choices. How many do you want? And at what price?

Nowadays the choice of investments is overwhelming. This is how one bewildered investor described the opportunities that confronted him after emerging from the financial pages of his daily paper. There were, he said, "options on stocks, options on stock indexes, futures based on stock indexes, options based on the futures based on stock indexes and a railcar full of other futures and options thereon, covering every financial, agricultural or import-export arena in which an investor or speculator can test his expertise."[12]

To that list he might have added *swaptions*—options on swaps—or *circus swaps,* which combine interest-rate and currency swaps, or *spiders,* which involve the tracking of the Standard and Poor's 500 index and depositary receipts. If they're not exotic enough, how about acid rain futures or property right derivatives?

The epitome of financial engineering, and something at which U.S. investment bankers excel, is the creation of customized derivatives. Reputations are made—and lost—by how far a financial engineer can push the edge of the envelope. A team from Kidder,

Peabody recently was trying to create futures in the emissions allow-ances, or rights to pollute, that came with the 1990 Clean Air Act.

While the most creative derivatives spring from the fertile minds and computers of Americans, the trading is often a foreign affair. This is an offshore business that thrives in such places as London, Stockholm, Paris, or the Cayman Islands. Regulations and capital requirements there are less stringent than in the United States.

What the quants and their computers are doing goes by many names. In Tokyo, it's called *zaitech.* In London, *bespoke investing.* In New York, *financial engineering.* A better term might be financial *alchemy,* if only gold were not being turned to base metal for inves-tors innocent to the inner workings of modern financial markets.

Today the biggest buyers of the exotic are the professional money managers, particularly those running pension funds, univer-sity endowments, and mutual funds. Even some money market funds are into this game, spurred by falling interest rates. Competi-tion plays a big role here. If investors see a Fidelity Spartan Fund offering a return that's a fraction higher than Dreyfus, with no dis-cernible extra risk, you know which fund gets the money.

In today's financial world, a neat division of synthetics and derivatives is tricky. They overlap, intersect, and mingle with each other. Definitions at times are hardly meaningful. Even among the more articulate of the alchemists, jargon abounds. The uninitiated feel perplexed and wonder if that's what the high priests and crea-tors intend. So first a little learning.

At its simplest, a derivative is nothing more than what its name implies. It is a financial instrument extracted from another, for ex-ample an index of stocks such as the S&P 500 or the Wilshire 5000. Buying an index is a cheap and easy way of mimicking the actions of the overall market.

Synthetics are more complex. Investors are buying an illusion, financial alchemy at its most mysterious. As one trader tries to explain it, "Synthesizing means creating things that look like securi-ties, but are something else."

A synthetic is an artificial product. Typically, it combines and replicates various characteristics you might find in a group of traditional securities—yield, term, or currency, for example. The aim is to capture cash flow in a manner that's impossible with a single security. In theory, this sounds fine.

The tricky part comes in deciding who owns what and who gets paid when. Unlike a stock, a synthetic doesn't signify ownership in an asset. Many times all the investor has is a private agreement with a broker-dealer. If certain events occur in a string of markets, the broker promises to pay out vast sums, typically millions of dollars. If they don't, the investor doesn't collect.

With their computers, the quants can create a single instrument or contract to imitate the performance that might come from many. A synthetic might mimic the investment returns you would expect from owning a collection of blue-chip and over-the-counter stocks plus a thirty-year government bond and some global currencies such as the yen or the dollar.

Why bother with something so complex? To boost yield is one reason, to end run the regulators is another. A clever alchemist can sidestep the time-consuming regulatory and filing requirements needed for ordinary securities. When billions of dollars are at stake, time saved can mean a heck of a lot of money earned.

All this is akin to gene splitting or hybridization. The quants subtly change the composition of a portfolio or an index by emphasizing certain features while playing down others. Let's say you're managing a university endowment fund and cannot invest in politically incorrect companies that do business in South Africa or mess up the environment. Or that you worry about heavy exposure to the vagaries of European currencies. Yet you don't want to be totally unexposed to companies that only get a fraction of their earnings from such sensitive areas. No problem. For a fee, the quants will create a synthetic security tailor-made to include only the pieces you want.

Or imagine you are an antsy fund manager with hundreds of millions of dollars at play. The stock market is rising, but you think it will fall in a while. If you sell into the rise and take some profits, are you smart enough to buy again when prices are lower? Not many do that well. Worse, switching the contents of a sizable portfolio takes weeks, upsets prices, and alerts the competition. By then, the markets may well have changed, forcing you to repeat the performance. With derivatives there's an easier way. You purchase stock index options to replicate the stocks or bonds you want. Later you buy the actual investments at a more leisurely pace. Worldwide, the volume of equity index derivatives is now running at an annual rate far in excess of $10 trillion and approaching the volume of the cash markets they replicate.[13]

Indexing and futures have a couple of neat advantages for the fund managers, but not their brokers. Probably one-tenth of the cost is involved when a fund buys an S&P 500 contract rather than the stocks in the index. Then there's the leverage. A fund manager buying stock worth, say, $172,000 on margin would need to put up half the amount. To buy a like amount of futures on margin, he might spend only $9,000. Translate this into the figures dealt in by the big players and the leverage becomes enormous.

The head of one of the largest brokerages once explained the advantage this way to a congressional panel. By using a futures index, a customer could buy nearly $1 billion worth of stock market action for something less than $40 million. At the time such a purchase was equal to about a fifth of the daily volume on the New York Stock Exchange. Conversely, it represented only 4 percent of the total amount of futures contracts outstanding. That's a formidable amount of power and leverage. Since then the leading commodity exchanges have notched down their margin requirements, to the benefit of both speculators and hedgers.

Fund managers bridle at suggestions they speculate with derivatives. They claim to use futures as insurance, much as farmers have done for aeons with commodity contracts. Futures do tend to move in the opposite direction to stocks and bonds. This, say their proponents, makes them safe vehicles for hedging strategies. Nonetheless, speculation abounds.

The big game on the Chicago Mercantile Exchange is no longer agricultural products, which account for but a tiny fraction of today's trading. For action and speculation at the Merc look to financial futures. Pension moneys going into futures climbed in four years from less than $100 million to a couple of billion dollars.[14]

Hope and pray the pension plans do better than most individuals. A safe guess is that seven out of ten individuals lose money trading in futures.

Futures are "the most significant innovation of the last twenty years," says economist Merton Miller, whose work made him a Nobel laureate and helped change the financial markets. He could be right, if the measuring tool is power to control markets. The futures market is in the driver's seat. Frequently, the stock markets react, the futures lead. To put it bluntly, stocks are dangerously close to becoming derivatives of futures in this Alice in Wonderland world. Larry Zicklin, in his role as managing partner at Neuberger and Berman, one of the shrewdest money managers in the business, has warned of the dangers. If we're not careful, Zicklin said, stock exchanges could become "manic-depressive through speculation, leverage, and disturbing conflicts of interest."[15]

Here's a paradox. If investors worry more about risk, they can blame the work of three ivory-tower economists whose intent was to make markets less unpredictable.

The three—Harry Markowitz, William Sharpe, and Merton Miller—gained recognition as Nobel laureates for their insights into how markets work. Wall Streeters may not have understood the academics, but they adopted their theories with gusto, believing they contained prescriptions for safer and less volatile markets. Result: a radical change in how markets function and more, not fewer, dangers.

Vastly oversimplifying, from Harry Markowitz, a professor at New York's Baruch College and a consultant to Daiwa Securities, came an asset-allocation theory. Markowitz showed how companies and householders alike can achieve the greatest wealth and reduce risk by distributing their assets among investments offering different risks and returns. From William Sharpe, his protégé, came the foundation of the price theory for modern financial markets. Sharpe, who teaches at Stanford and advises pension funds, also supplied a financial asset–pricing model to value securities in relation to other possible investments.

Meanwhile, the University of Chicago's Merton Miller contributed a theory relating market value to a company's policy on paying out dividends and taking on debt.

Described so starkly, their theories have an innocuous ring. Yet it didn't take long before Miller's views were extended to mean that the best mix of debt to equity was simply the cheapest mix available. In the late 1980s, that meant more debt, less equity thanks to the federal government's bizarre approach to taxes and interest charges. Leverage? Wall Street and corporate America couldn't have enough. You might say Miller inadvertently ratified Michael Milken and all the overleveraging follies of the 1980s.

To simpler minds, Sharpe's and Markowitz's views on risk might sound remarkably akin to what grandma told us about not keeping all our eggs in one basket. Yet among those who handle money for a living the insights of the academics came as a revelation. Fund managers adopted these teachings as a panacea for overcoming their own failure as investors.

"Tactical asset allocation" became the buzz phrase of the late 1980s, indexing and program trading the means to lessen risk.

All that was needed to complete the revolution in finance was one more piece of academic thinking—the introduction of *options theory*. Simply put, this theory asks, Do you want to be holding more or less of a product—or a market—if it goes up? And, if the price goes down, do you want less or more? Options theory got its start with a paper by a pair of University of Chicago theorists, Fischer Black and Myron Scholes. Their work arrived just in time to endorse the then newly opened options exchange in Chicago and transform the art of hedging.

For Wall Street there are many ways of making money in derivatives. The houses collect fees for hedging as well as custom designing new products for their clients. When they issue and sell derivative contracts, the houses frequently take the other side of whatever is being sold. This gives the clients and customers some peace of mind since part of the risk is reduced or eliminated. This is the hedge.

Joseph R. Schmuckler, head of derivative trading for Nomura in New York, explains. "In this business there's no commission paid, nothing for research," he says. "There's a deal based upon a price. If my price is no good, I get hurt. If my price is good, I win. It's that simple."

The horse trading begins when the dealer decides he doesn't want a particular position and exposure just because the fund manager does. "I'm not looking around and saying, 'You want to be long and I want to be short, so gee, we have a trade,'" Schmuckler explains. Mostly his firm wants to get rid of the risk. That means Schmuckler must go out into the capital markets and sell his position or hedge it with yet another contract. And so it goes.

Sometimes this works, but not always. Rapid changes in interest rates can clobber the best-laid hedges. In what may be a record, Merrill Lynch once suffered a one-day trading loss of $377 million in mortgage-backed securities that the house had neglected to lay off on someone else.

Part of the hedging strategy behind derivatives involves selling the underlying securities short. That in turn creates another specialist business, the lending of shares to the short sellers. Lenders are a secretive lot, but, by some estimates, if you count all the loaning around the world you quickly get into the hundreds of billions of dollars. A good business for brokerages that have ample inventories of stocks? Not anymore. A few years back, lenders were asking and getting as much as 8 percent for the service. Fierce competition has lowered that to 1 percent or less.[16] The loaning isn't to be confused with the baffling business of swaps.

Why do companies issue bonds or paper with fixed rates of interest and immediately swap them for others carrying variable rates of interest? Or raise funds through dollar-denominated bonds and swap those for others pegged to the yen or the deutsche mark? This is another part—and a big one—of the mystery of financial engineering. Swaps is another trillion-dollar market.

Here, too, competition is ferocious. In almost no time, the number of bidders for this business has increased tenfold, and yields have dropped to a tenth their former levels. A dealer nowadays is lucky to pick up $20,000 for arranging swaps valued at $100 million.

The big banks play the leading role in the swapping game by dint of their huge capital bases. Wall Streeters, for their part, supply both brains and capital. How risky is a swap? "Its originality has made its riskiness practically unfathomable," says a market watcher. Drexel was running a huge book in swaps when it went under. The holders had to settle for a stiff 30 percent discount on their money in the settlements.

In one farcical case, a London municipality defaulted on swap contracts involving several billion pounds. The royal borough of Hammersmith and Fulham wasn't trying to change the characteristics of its debt, but was gambling on the direction of interest rates. Its losses at one point amounted to twice the borough's annual revenue, a scary thought for voters and taxpayers. After the borough's bet unraveled, Britain's highest court—the House of Lords—ruled that local governments had no business in interest-rate swapping. Few would disagree, but the verdict immediately put in jeopardy a further half billion pounds or so in debts related to swaps that other municipalities owed scores of banks.

Twenty years ago, when a company wanted to raise $100 million the choice was simple. Should it sell equities or debt—senior or subordinated—or, if it wanted to be a little bit exotic, convertible bonds? That was about as far as the equation went.

Today, a McDonald's or an AT&T asks an underwriter for the cheapest possible financing for, say, seven years, and in dollars. If demand for dollar issues is slight, that's no longer a problem. The underwriter's derivatives specialist might concoct a yen-denominated note, whose return depends upon the rise or fall of the Tokyo stock market. The underwriter takes the yen and starts a hedging process.

The aim is threefold: to protect McDonald's or AT&T against a collapse in the Tokyo market; to turn the yen into dollars; to get the cheapest cost of money available.

Where this process gets tricky is: Who goes into the hole if things go wrong? In this particular case, the swapping would last for the life of the seven-year notes, and maybe longer if other hedges are involved.

For part of the time, Wall Street firms end up holding sizable chunks of the paper in these complex transactions. This means three types of risk are now involved—trading, hedging, and credit, with the latter growing in importance.

As the swapping and hedging of deals get more involved and the time span of contracts lengthens, the business flows to the underwriters with asset-rich balance sheets and the better credit ratings. The brains on the Street, who devise the derivatives, follow the assets.

For a while, its quants turned PaineWebber into a hothouse for creativity in derivatives. But PaineWebber lacked funds, boasted only a modest credit rating, and awoke one morning to find its derivative team had decamped to Deutsche Bank. With its prized triple-A rating, Deutsche can underwrite, if it wants, far more derivatives than PaineWebber, or just about anyone else.

Risk is a big part of what the modern Wall Street is all about. Go back to that hypothetical seven-year note for McDonald's and the hedging that might be needed. The investment house has now created an option that's obscure, unique, and that cannot trade on the Chicago Board Options Exchange. To lower its exposure, the house must attempt to replicate the option through trading strategies in the cash market. More contracts. More risk. There's no end to this process or its perils.

Listen to what a big-league arbitrage player says: "You have a lot of twenty-six-year-old hotshots, two years out of business school, who think they know everything." Their predecessors, he says, had similar thoughts and faith in portfolio insurance before the 1987 crash. "You see a lot of guys pricing things on theory, but there are certain practical things, like liquidity, that they tend to forget."

What it boils down to is judgment. Wall Street's judgment was sadly wanting both with portfolio insurance and with bridge loans. The one hope with derivatives, says this arb, is that everything balances. Given the number of players on the field and the complexity of the instruments involved, that's quite a hope.

If the dangers are so obvious, why have so many Wall Street houses plunged so deeply into derivatives?

Hubris is only part of the answer. A worried investment banker supplies the rest by rephrasing the question. "How many company treasurers," he asks, "will give you their straight debt and equity business if they think that's all you can do? They worry that, one day, they may want to be a little more innovative themselves."

Simple stocks and bonds? Forget 'em. In the quants' financially engineered world, simplicity is no match for complexity. No matter what the risks.

CHAPTER SEVEN

Into the Private World of the Program Traders

"The Dow Jones Industrial Average plunged sixty-five points this afternoon. Market analysts say program traders . . ."

FINANCIAL COMMENTATORS ARE QUICK TO finger program trading whenever trading is volatile. So does the Securities and Exchange Commission. The SEC believes program trading disrupts markets, drives away investors, raises the cost of capital, and makes a virtue of restless trading and a vice of long-term investing. Blame the academics again. Gregg A. Jarrell, a former chief economist at the SEC, says program trading "is a direct descendant of the theoretical innovations of Messrs. Markowitz and Sharpe."[1]

Program traders buy or sell securities in bulk rather than individually. By its simplest definition, a *program* is the simultaneous trade of fifteen or more stocks worth $1 million or more apiece.

You can divide program traders into two categories. There are the *net traders,* who buy or sell to change their exposure to particular markets. That's a brokerage business with the broker sometimes acting as agent and sometimes putting up his own money as principal. Then there are the *index arbitragers.* They comb the different markets for relative value differences. You can see some of this action as they make plays between the exchanges in New York and Chicago. Those are public markets, easy to measure. Houses such as Salomon, Merrill, and Dean Witter used to dominate, but became less active publicly when margins shrank.

Typically, a basic program involves an arbitrage play between the stock market and the index futures market. For example, a fund manager might arbitrage between the cash market—the stock in his portfolio—and the forward market of index futures. The idea is somewhat akin to a farmer hedging his crop through a commodities contract.

A flood in downtown Chicago in April 1992 illustrated how linking markets increases volatility. Among the buildings closed was the one housing the city's commodities exchanges. Eight hundred and forty-three miles to the east in Manhattan, activity on the New York Stock Exchange went into a trance. The result, as one observer aptly described it, was Wall Street's version of a flat brain wave. Traders couldn't arbitrage or hedge between futures, stocks, and Treasury issues. In despair, they retreated to the sidelines until the waters in Chicago subsided.[2]

On a more typical day, program traders figure they account for between a fifth and a quarter of the NYSE's volume. "It's easy to look at the market and say it went up or down because somebody did a program trade," says Nomura's Joseph Schmuckler, "but the real question is, why did he do it?" His firm pays Schmuckler handsomely to find out why.

Program traders are a secretive bunch, not eager to explain their moves or motives. Yet what they do has tremendous bearing on other investors. Each Friday the New York Stock Exchange issues and the *Wall Street Journal* dutifully publishes a list of the week's largest traders on the Big Board. Market participants say the list is meaningless. Rarely, if ever, does Credit Suisse's name appear on the NYSE list. Yet the Swiss firm probably does as much as anyone in derivatives and packaged trades. What's published is no more than the tip of another threatening iceberg.

The real action has moved into what's known as the over-the-counter market. This is largely a private arena where traders exchange information by phone and computer networks, far from prying eyes and public markets. This is the unseen part of the iceberg.

How much money is involved here? Nobody knows for sure because nobody knows all that's happening. As private transactions, these trades go unreported. A rule of thumb: the riskier they are, the more private they become.

Think of it this way. The public exchanges handle trading in what investors deem simple financial instruments by today's standards. You want a hundred shares of IBM? To these traders, no matter what Bill Donaldson says, that's a commodity. Since everyone knows IBM's present value, it makes sense to centralize all the buying and selling in one place.

But what about the present value of a six-month option in Germany on the Frankfurt Stock Exchange's DAX index backed by Salomon Brothers' credit? That's still a relatively simple transaction involving derivatives, but hardly a commodity. It has its own distinctive features. In recent times not everybody was prepared to take Salomon's credit for six months. If Solly were to go belly-up, the option would be worthless.

Now tie in some currency and interest-rate features plus the various credit ratings of the players involved and pretty soon you're dealing in some tricky instruments.

The key to whether trading occurs in the fishbowl or out of sight, say knowledgeable insiders, is how much value the dealers are adding. The less value added, the more likely the deal gets done at an exchange. For example, when trading in derivatives based upon the Nikkei market became commonplace, exchanges vied to list options.

The market for commonplace derivatives is brutally competitive. Dealers no longer make money on derivatives of the S&P indexes. The key to making real money is in packaging and pricing increasingly complex concoctions. Inevitably, the bigger the reward, the greater the risk. And more problems for investors.

Officials at the New York Stock Exchange like to say that the market cannot go into a meltdown, as it came close to doing during that terrifying week in October 1987. They have put curbs in place that reduce or completely halt program trading if the Dow falls more than a preset number of points. They point with pride to the placid behavior of the Dow these days.

This misses the point. The risk has moved from the public into the private market. Much of that risk has also landed upon Wall Street's shoulders. Nomura's Schmuckler explains why. "Before the crash the client was trading in the market to hedge his exposure," he says. "After the crash an investment dealer was selling him a contract to hedge his exposure. All this does is transfer the risk of hedging to the investment dealer."

One result: a giant game of pass the parcel. When the music stops, no one wants to be left holding the contract. So the firms undertake these sophisticated maneuvers to offset the equally complex hedges they have sold to major institutional clients.

In this game, somebody's credit is always on the line. Whose credit and how much are the questions traders like Joe Schmuckler are always trying to get answered. So are the regulators. Too often they don't know either, as we will see in the next chapter. In the meantime remember this. When it comes to synthetics and derivatives, pretty well the whole panoply of institutional investors—banks, insurance companies, pension plans, and, of course, the Wall Street houses—are playing the game. The assumption within financial circles is that since these are sophisticated participants, everyone knows what's happening. Perhaps everyone does. But the market crashes of the late 1980s tend to belie that thought.

What newspaperman Charles Dow started over a hundred years ago, Wall Street has turned into a cottage industry. Everybody knows of the Dow Jones Industrial Average. Few realize there are 950 or so other equity indexes in the United States and a further 1,000 or more outside.

Indexing is another of the voguish trends in finance. Investors increasingly buy indexes or contracts based upon indexes rather than assembling portfolios of individual stocks. Their aim: to match market performance while reducing risk and trading costs.

"This is a straightforward and boring quantitative exercise," says Larry Rafsky by way of describing the process of index creation.

Besides tracking the number of indexes, he supplies their inventors with a key ingredient, the historical data for the securities contained in them.

Rafsky earned his doctorate in statistics at Yale, and is one of the new breed in financial services. His career has included stints with Bell Labs, Chase Manhattan Bank, and Automatic Data Processing. Twice Rafsky has run his own business, only to sell out, latterly to IDD Information Services, which boasts what may be the biggest data base in the industry.

If you like, Rafsky will custom-tailor an index for you on the fly, statistics, graphs, and all. A simple one, involving the twenty-year performance of some seventy-one hundred companies, takes less than fifteen minutes to create on his computer.

At the other end of the scale, Goldman, Sachs spent millions and kept two dozen staff analysts, economists, and portfolio managers plus assorted academics occupied for months producing a commodities index. Through its J. Aron division, Goldman ranks among the world's largest commodities traders. In a challenge to perceived wisdom, Goldman was pushing commodities as a safe and profitable way to make money for all investors.[3] The firm's timing, however, was off. With inflation no longer a threat, investors saw little need to trade futures and options based on the Goldman index.

Computer power is only one reason why indexes are numerous and widely followed. "The notion that one can beat the market consistently," says Richard Booth, who teaches law at the University of Maryland, "is rather like the idea that all the children in Lake Wobegon are above average."

From his ivory perch, Booth has put his finger on the market's prevailing philosophy. Professional money managers know how hard it is to beat the market and they have learned how to get paid for not doing so.

The investment vehicle of choice among pension managers is an index typically, but not necessarily, crafted on a computer. Some $200 billion is linked to the S&P 500, which probably makes it the most important of all indexes. Nationwide, every sixth dollar managed in a pension fund is pegged to an index rather than invested in an individual stock.[4] In California, at least half of the equity portion of state employee retirement funds is tied to indexes, double the 1988 level. Fund managers expect that figure to keep rising.

These managers don't have much choice. Remember the ERISA regulations for the proper handling of pension moneys? These days the concept of prudent management is also spreading into the handling of health-care benefits, another sizable chunk of funds. You don't get sued by irate workers for plunking their money into an index or a futures contract based upon an index. You might if you try cherry-picking the market. A study of the benefits of indexing by scholars at the Brookings Institution judged it "a very good strategy from the point of view of the beneficiaries and the corporations."

For some fund managers, indexing means survival. They've learned to hide their blemishes by convincing sponsors that failing to beat the S&P 500 isn't a disaster. These managers now insist they do well if they outperform a custom-designed index geared toward their personal investment style. A growth-based, small-cap index, for example, heavily weighted toward technology, say, or emerging countries. For these underperformers, there's an index to suit every excuse.

The Brady report in the wake of the 1987 crash summed up the essence of what's happening here. "All this trading in futures and indexes," it said, allows institutions to "trade the entire stock market as if it were a single commodity."

No wonder Bill Donaldson has sleepless nights when he thinks what that means for the New York Stock Exchange. The indexers, says Donaldson, "are accepting the limiting goal—one might even call it mediocrity—of just matching the market."[5]

Of course, Donaldson has a vested interest to protect. Still, his concern isn't without merit. Figure it this way: if the assets in pension funds keep growing at twice the rate of the gross national product, they will top $4 trillion by the year 2000. At that level, warns Donaldson, the funds "could own half of all corporate equity in this country."

Adds Donaldson, "All of us have to be concerned about passive investing, the commoditization of equities by trading them like pork bellies."

Wall Street may not share Donaldson's concerns, but it does fear its own version of trickle-down economics. Indexing translates into yet another squeeze on profit margins and wide-scale redundancy. When institutions trade whole portfolios rather than specific stocks, entire departments become marginal or redundant. Much of the infrastructure that Wall Street has carefully crafted over the decades begins to look fragile. Who needs expensive block trading or research when all you are buying are indexes?

The savings in transaction costs from indexing rather than trading in stocks add up. Those alone enabled index funds to outperform three-quarters of all dollars invested in the U.S. equity market over the last fifteen years.

This change represents more than a victory for technical analysis over fundamental analysis. It's a triumph of knee-jerk reaction over thoughtful appraisal. What's the use of checking a thousand analysts' reports if the market jumps or falls with the latest economic statistic? This month's housing starts, or the jobless figures or the trend in interest rates for the next forty-eight hours—that's what counts. This is a stock market for instant reaction and the simplest way to play it is via an index.

"Trading in individual stocks the old-fashioned way on the basis of fundamental analysis," as Booth likes to say, "involves unnecessary risks for which the market pays no returns."[6]

One reason indexing isn't more pervasive, according to the Brookings study, is, ironically, job preservation. While the indexers revel in the lower commissions they send Wall Street, they must wonder about their own fees. As the Brookings report concluded, "indexation has the disadvantage that it puts many of the people allocating the sponsors' money out of their jobs. Perhaps for that reason, it has not spread more widely." In plainer words, why should trustees of pension funds pay advisors millions of dollars if their advice boils down to one sentence: "Buy the market."

Plain old-fashioned politics may be another reason why fund managers don't push indexing. Think of all the power that comes with controlling massive amounts of money. Breathes there a manager of a state pension plan who doesn't believe in his right to tell

IBM or General Motors how to run its affairs? That's less easy to do if your fund only buys and sells indexes.

The managers of the larger funds are increasingly torn two ways. They want to exert power over corporate America, but they also need the lower cost and safety of indexing. ERISA is a hard mistress. Some funds think they have found a solution. Instead of holding, say, half of the five thousand stocks included in the broadest index, they trim their holdings to six hundred or so. That way they can focus their attention on fewer firms. It's a trend that neither chief executives nor securities salesmen much appreciate; the former get too much attention, the latter too little.

For the moment, the financial community is doing its best to delay the inevitable. Wall Street's creative geniuses have adopted a Baskin-Robbins approach. They have invented a thousand and one varieties of indexes. You want big-cap stocks? Here's a big-cap index. You think Asia will boom, but you worry about Japan? Then here's an index that weights by gross domestic product rather than by stock market capitalization.

The fees are sweet. Index suppliers get royalties—as much as $150,000 a year per contract—when their indexes are melded into financial products.

For an idea of how intertwined and complicated this global investment business has become, consider this. In Europe there's an index made up of one hundred blue-chip companies that are based in nine European countries. The choices for anyone wanting to trade derivatives of that index are legion on both sides of the Atlantic. In New York, warrants and options based upon the index trade in dollars. In Paris, futures based upon it trade in ECUs, the European currency. In Amsterdam, you can buy options also in ECUs. Go to Zurich and you can get either options or futures in Swiss francs. Take your pick and good luck in trying to figure out what everybody else is doing.

The better indexes have a life of their own, often a lengthy one, and firms get known by their indexes. For example, Salomon has the high-yield index, Shearson the T-bill index, and Merrill the muni-bond index. For a while, Morgan Stanley had a monopoly in industrial indexes in markets abroad. If you wanted an index featuring European telecommunications stocks there was only one place to go. Now international indexes are two-a-penny.

What's ahead? The volume of fund money heading into indexes isn't likely to slacken anytime soon. However, according to Rafsky, the pace of generating new indexes is slowing. Saturation is one reason, technology another.

The initial costs for the computer programming of indexes and derivatives are high, yet once a new product begins to trade, competitors set about replicating it. Before long what were lucrative proprietary products become commodities, and profits vanish. Already the profit margins for a typical new financial product start to shrink in the seventh week of its life cycle. Bad news for Wall Street houses looking to index creation as an easy source of rich profits.

Now Steve Jobs, the man behind Apple and Macintosh, wants to speed that process even more. With his new NextStep computer system he claims programmers can increase their pace of creation tenfold. "No longer do you have to be a rocket scientist to fully use a workstation," says Jobs. "They're now for mere mortals."

If Jobs indeed speeds the process of writing programs and applications, chances are the copyists will accelerate the pace of knockoffs, too. When they do, the margins of the originals will begin to shrink within days rather than weeks.

It's amazing what a friendly assist from the Federal Reserve can do for a market. Take the success bankers had in turning mortgages, credit card receivables, and boat loans into marketable securities.

Mortgage-backed securities came out in the early 1970s and by 1979 had become a $100 billion market. Then in 1981 the Fed propelled the business into the mainstream by insisting banks boost their capital. The banks didn't have much choice but to move loans off their balance sheets.[7]

Roughly every other mortgage now gets turned into a marketable security.[8] Consultant Lowell Bryan is right when he calls securitization "one of the most powerful forces at work in the financial services industry."[9]

On a bank's balance sheet, a $100 million loan is a deadweight. It could be worth its face value, or, more likely, a heck of a lot less. Repackage that loan as a security, and there's a happy banker. What was immobile becomes liquid, with its value set each day in the marketplace. "The force of securitization is unstoppable," says Bryan, "because it is driven by fundamental economics. Bluntly put, the securities business system is more efficient than the banking business system."

Turning loans into securities is duck soup for investment bankers. For the Wall Street houses, the amount of intellectual effort to package $100 million or $800 million is the same. That's the magic of any fee-based business. Unlike a manufacturer, whose profits are linked to output, the bankers' rewards come from the spread. Their profits are proportional to the size of the deal, not to the amount of effort or cost entailed.

The financial engineering involved here was relatively simple at first. Bankers did little more than create pools of mortgages backed by federal government guarantees. Soon the alchemists had more exotic wares to offer. They began chopping up the monthly mortgage payments coming from householders. Artfully, they tailored these cash flows to suit the needs of clients seeking differing rates of risk and yield. Presto, the bankers had a raft of new securities to offer. These are known as collateralized mortgage obligations, or CMOs for short.

In trading value, CMOs are a multitrillion-dollar market. This makes CMOs the largest single category of security derivatives.

Here there are real securities. You can see and trade them. But that physical presence doesn't make CMOs simple or easy to understand.

"CMOs are a misnomer," a practitioner tries to explain. "They're really a series of bonds created out of the cash flow from a pool of pools of pass-throughs." Huh?

You don't need to worry overly about another hard-to-comprehend definition, or that CMOs come with swaps, caps, belts, and goodness knows what else. The life of these engineered financial products is often short. Products go stale quickly. The geniuses with computers keep inventing newer versions.

What counts more is the arbitrage business they generate. This comes as investors weigh the merits of CMOs against other interest-bearing instruments. Call it the unfixing of the fixed income market if you will.

The CMO market can have a direct bearing on how a blue-chip firm like IBM raises money. Pension funds are cautious about holding embattled IBM's paper. Yet they still believe IBM's securities deserve some place in their portfolios. No sweat, say the alchemists. Using complex mathematics, they can clone an IBM bond. They create a CMO that simulates the characteristics of an IBM bond while eliminating the risk that the computer price wars might get worse.

This doesn't mean IBM cannot issue bonds, only that it might have to pay a higher rate of interest to compete with the clone. Another tail wagging the dog?

Credit cards, auto loans, and other receivables that once sat immobile on corporate balance sheets now follow mortgages into the securities markets. Of course, payments on a car in California aren't as secure as a house, but some investors don't worry. Spreading their net wider, bankers are creating CMOs out of small business loans, mortgages on commercial properties, and debts on recreational vehicles. The complexity of aircraft financing is fertile ground for creating securities and swap agreements. One deal involved no fewer than 240 swaps,[10] and aircraft leases today quickly turn into securities along with all the other receivables.

Even the Resolution Trust Corporation is into the game, putting loans for small office buildings into a pool for Wall Street to repackage.

It's hard to believe every CMO will prove to be the pristine package its sponsors tout. Over the years other Wall Street–repackaged offerings of real estate have proven dubious investments. CMOs may be no different.

Could securitization be a Trojan horse for the commercial banks to use to get deeper into Wall Street's bailiwick? Robert Litan, a senior fellow at the Brookings Institution, thinks so. The banks benefit by getting loans off their balance sheets, he says, but the price is high. His point is that banks are making themselves redundant.

Historically, a bank's job was to analyze the trickier credit risks, lend appropriately, and keep the loans in its own portfolios until maturity. If its credit officers knew their stuff, the bank prospered. Securitization makes that service redundant.

The pattern of the 1980s was for corporate customers to shun their banks and instead finance with securities. This shows no sign of ending. Says Litan, "It is not an overstatement that securitization threatens to make the large banks dinosaurs, since the customers of the large banks in particular ran most heavily to the securities markets in the 1980s for their credit needs."[11]

If Litan is right, the securities firms shouldn't feel complacent. Even dinosaurs could be dangerous before they became extinct. Chances are the banks will follow their clients and move deeper into the securities business. They will do so at both the wholesale and retail ends of the business.

Citicorp, which securitizes some $25 billion of its own loans annually, says it wants to concentrate on retail rather than wholesale banking. Why? If Citicorp gets permission to build a nationwide branch system, it could become a major threat to the big wire houses like Merrill Lynch and Shearson Lehman. Before long, Citicorp could offer its customers a complete range of services from checking to mutual funds to asset management and much more. Before this decade ends, plenty of other banks, particularly the superregionals, could also be lumbering their way into Wall Street's backyard.

CHAPTER EIGHT

The Nelson Gambit Goes Awry

EDWARD MARKEY IS THE WATCHDOG'S WATCH-
dog, and he's both worried and frustrated.

A sixteen-year veteran in Washington, D.C., Markey, a Democrat from Malden, Massachusetts, heads the House Telecommunications and Finance Subcommittee that monitors the regulatory
agencies with power over Wall Street. Time and again Markey has
hoisted warning flags, only to see the system over which he presides
lurch from one crisis to the next.

"We persist in regulating our diverse financial markets," Markey once said, "as if they were some barely connected quaint and
sleepy outposts of our furthest financial horizons."

If no one is listening, blame in large measure political expediency at home and abroad. Lawmakers and regulators alike have
concluded there's little personal reward to be gained from imposing
tough controls on the financial markets. Minor changes, perhaps, but
nothing draconian.

The public is right to worry. Their regulators appear determined to act like Keystone Kops. Hardly a day goes by without a regulator somewhere in the world being blindsided by agile market manipulators. Witness the scandals at the Bank of New England over derivatives and the rigging of the once pristine market for U.S. Treasuries. Or the ease with which organized crime in Japan gets its hooks into that country's financial markets. Or the Blue Arrow affair in Britain that showed executives connected with National Westminster Bank, that country's second largest, covering up their manipulation of a stock offering that went awry. (Blue Arrow, a British employment agency, had planned to fund its takeover of Manpower, its counterpart in the United States, by issuing new shares to its stockholders. When they balked, the lead underwriters fabricated a tale of how popular the issue had been. That's fraudulent, said a judge, handing out stiff sentences to some of Britain's best-known financiers.) Just how far the regulators are lagging behind became obvious with the collapse of the Bank of Credit and Commerce International and the uncovering of what may be the largest fraud in world financial history.

This was a paradigm of the complex nature of modern finance and regulators who are too compliant. BCCI kept its corporate headquarters in Luxembourg and ran its main operations from London and the Cayman Islands. That way the men controlling BCCI could sneak by the regulators and launder money in Peru or illegally control the largest bank in Washington, D.C., to name but two of their alleged sins. The losses from this caper, say the prosecutors, ran into the billions of dollars.

You might call what's happening here a misuse of the Horatio Nelson gambit. Every schoolchild in Britain is taught how the famous British admiral deliberately put his telescope to his blind eye so he could not see signals telling him not to attack Napoleon's fleet. Nelson routed the French, and the British are eternally grateful.

Almost three centuries later there's a surfeit of would-be Nelsons among the bureaucrats and legislators charged with overseeing the financial markets. Unfortunately, when they ignore signals and look the wrong way, we court global mayhem.

A close examination of the state of financial regulation in the United States reveals several disturbing trends:

- Competition within the various financial markets is escalating the risks firms take despite the establishment of new requirements for capital, liquidity, and business procedures.
- Financial markets are less regulated than the public imagines and more open to abuse than it suspects.
- Regulators concentrate their efforts on the least dangerous markets—old-fashioned stocks and fixed-income instruments— while shying away from the complexities of Treasuries, currencies, and derivatives.
- Wily traders are exploiting the numerous turf wars that abound between bureaucracies—domestic and international—to their own advantage.
- Paradoxically, when the regulators do make changes, opportunities for abuse and risk escalate.

Such is the ingenuity of artful market players that, as Markey says, regulators are left contemplating yesterday's problem. Fancy technology, instantaneous communications, and global money raise the stakes, frighten away individual investors, and should give perplexed regulators pause for thought. At any moment, some exotic financial product could explode and send shock waves throughout the financial system.

Among the least regulated markets, for example, is one of the largest and most volatile, foreign exchange. Currency speculation isn't new, it's just become more prolific and dramatic. Before governments began lifting exchange controls in 1971, traders were staging bear raids on sterling and striking fear into the hearts of British cabinet ministers. Beating up on a single currency was one thing; disrupting European unity in the summer of 1992 is something else.

Simultaneous attacks on lire, francs, punts, pesetas, escudos, and kronor indicate how big the currency binge has become. In the late 1980s and before the mauling of the Maastricht Treaty, the Bank for International Settlements in Geneva reckoned foreign currency trading had doubled in three years to around $650 billion. That's a daily figure for the spot market and was roughly forty times the value of a single day's trading of stocks on the New York Stock Exchange.

Among the financial markets, currencies have the least relevance to how the world conducts its business. Less than 10 percent, and maybe as little as 5 percent, of all the changing of dollars into deutsche marks or dinars or drachmas and back again has anything to do with trade or tourism. The rest is speculation. Swapping currencies is simply a game played by banks and securities houses among themselves to boost profits.

Hundreds of small firms and individuals make fortunes off currency speculation, but they are minnows. The big players in this pursuit are the money center banks, American, Japanese, and European, with a host of investment bankers in hot pursuit behind them. Maybe as much as half the profits registered by the big New York commercial banks comes from forex. By one estimate, Citicorp's earnings from foreign exchange averaged half a billion dollars each year in the late 1980s and early 1990s, a useful fillip when most everything else was going sour.

At its simplest, currency exchanges involve nothing more than, say, swapping pounds for marks because the Bundesbank is taking a harder line on interest rates than the Bank of England. Most trades are complex hedging strategies designed to offset a commercial bank's exposure in interest-rate swaps or in its portfolio of government securities. On a volatile day, trading in these interlinked but loosely regulated markets can tie up a trillion dollars or more.

The currency game begins each day in Australia, moves with the sun around the world via Japan into Europe, and then reaches the United States, only to start all over again as the Aussies go back to work. Most of the trading takes place abroad, with roughly 40 percent happening in London. The New York market accounts for less than a seventh of the currency exchanges.

Critics are right to brand the staking of so much money on interest-rate and currency movements a casino-style game. To be sure, participants say their hedging strategies are tied directly to economic factors, but, no matter how they rationalize and label this process, it's still gambling. And dangerous at that. While the jackals attack, propping up pounds or dollars becomes, for a few days, beyond the wealth of any individual nation. Anytime the central bankers step in prematurely and try to arrest a run on a particularly weak currency they risk losing a fortune of their taxpayers' money.

Which is why, if there's a lesson from the currency battles of the summer of 1992, it's that nations need closer, not looser agreements on currency alignments. This isn't the popular view, but it will take hold if for no other reason than this. The battering of currencies now cascades into the living rooms of the Western world via prime-time television much as news from Vietnam did a couple of decades ago. An informed public will only briefly tolerate news of currency speculators becoming wealthy if they believe their financial and economic worlds are spinning out of control.

In Washington, D.C., turf wars between the various agencies that control banking or between the Securities and Exchange Commission and the Commodity Futures Trading Commission do nothing to lessen the prospects for another financial crisis nor to assuage public fears.

An example illustrates the point: the collapse and subsequent probe of the Bank of New England. Early in 1990, federal regulators claimed to discover $36 billion worth of dubious investments in derivatives they say they didn't know the bank had made. That's a lot of money to tuck under the carpet.

The derivatives, being new creations, didn't fit neatly into the conventional accounting pigeonholes to which regulators assign traditional loans and deposits. So the bank, following the principle of what's not recognized is ignored, kept the derivatives off its balance sheet and enthusiastically traded them.

The derivatives went into deals made with other financial institutions in Tokyo, Frankfurt, and London and became part of contracts pegged to the future course of interest rates and currencies.

Everything was fine until the bank floundered. Quick to react, foreign bankers refused credit, and chaos swept through the Chicago Mercantile Exchange. "We moved risk out of the interbank system into the exchanges," the bank's former treasurer blithely commented.

A solitary case? Not according to a senior bank examiner in the Office of the Comptroller of the Currency. "For certain bankers there is a lot of exposure in the market for derivative securities," he said.

"If we had a real problem with one of the larger banks, a meltdown scenario would be a possibility."[1]

It doesn't take a great deal of imagination to see that happening. Just recall the mess Congress made of the junk bond market through its misguided interfering in the investment practices of the thrifts.

"Bank and thrift regulation in the 1980s in this country was an utter failure," contends Brookings Institution scholar Robert Litan. It's hard to know which caused the greater damage, the tinkering with deposit insurance at the start of the decade or the misguided legislation enacted in 1989 to get thrifts out of the junk market. The former permitted the thrifts to run amok with their speculative investments, particularly in real estate; the latter significantly increased the cost to taxpayers of bailing out those follies.

The thrifts started to get into trouble when short-term interest rates skyrocketed in the mid-1970s. Lacking sophisticated managers, they had about as much chance of mastering an inverted yield curve as a one-legged man going the wrong way on an escalator. Their traditional depositors departed to find happiness in the higher returns from money market funds, leaving the thrifts with an absence of customers and inventories stuffed with low-yielding mortgages.

Help was at hand. Unfortunately. Congress unshackled the thrifts with its Garn–St Germain legislation, permitting them to pursue more exotic investments. Back then many of the thrifts had unsullied credit ratings and could raise money relatively cheaply. By raising deposit insurance, the politicians also encouraged Wall Street to supply brokered deposits and show the thrifts how to invest them. Mayhem in the making.

Soon investment bankers were selling the thrifts a bundle of newly devised derivatives and hedging techniques, with the blessing and even the encouragement of the regulators. Few heeded the critics, who raised doubts about real estate and arbitrage deals for the thrifts or questioned the level of returns promised by the sponsors of those deals. The 1980s, with its can-do approach to all things financial, wasn't a time for heeding the Cassandras. The more exotic the deal, the greater its attraction to the thrifts.

"These were impossibly complex strategies that had never

been tested in the market," recalls Herbert Sandler, who runs one of the more conservative thrifts, Golden West Financial Corporation. In his view some thrift managers and the investment bankers involved were "simply charlatans." Others were "blinded by a consuming belief in their own supposed brilliance."[2]

Unfortunately, yet more congressional help was at hand.

In 1989, Congress, with its Financial Institutions Reform, Recovery, and Enforcement Act, in effect indicated how little its members understood the daily workings of the financial markets. FIRREA didn't order the thrifts to immediately vacate the junk bond market, but it might as well have done so. The legislation stipulated a halt in junk purchases and instructed the thrifts to unload their holdings over the next five years. Here's where political wisdom collided with prevailing accounting practices. The thrifts' new timetable meant they could no longer price their inventories as if they would receive the full redemption value when the bonds expired. Instead they had to value the inventories at current market prices. Even before Congress acted, the price of junk bonds was heading down and now would accelerate.

The spiral effect was traumatic. A sinking market lessened the inventory values, raised the thrifts' capital needs, and magnified the cost of taxpayer-funded bailouts. In the words of Brookings's Litan, "The thrift crisis drained what appears will be two hundred billion dollars in the nation's savings from the economy and put it literally down a sinkhole."[3]

Ah, if only the politicians in their rush to save the thrifts had paused long enough to read a report from the General Accounting Office. According to the GAO, the thrifts weren't up to their eyeballs in junk bonds but owned only a tiny fraction. And most of that was in a few hands. In fact, ten thrifts owned three-quarters of all the junk bonds purchased by the industry.[4]

Most of the junk bonds were sitting in the portfolios of insurance companies and mutual funds. By practice and inclination, these companies are long-term investors and could ride out most financial storms, probably even the collapse of Drexel Burnham. But now even their portfolios were threatened. Congress had decreed that junk was taboo. The markets overreacted, dumping junk and making a bad situation intolerable. Brave investors, who didn't panic or weren't forced into bailing out, were rewarded. The values of many high-yield bonds in 1992 were no different than they had been in 1989, and their 14-to-15 percent yields looked better than ever.

Political expediency and greed make a lethal combination. Salomon Brothers and the rigging of the U.S. Treasury auctions bear witness to that.

Outsiders to the financial process still find this event mind-boggling. How can a single firm corner the world's biggest and most liquid financial market? Equally puzzling, how could an outwardly serene thirty-six-year-old workaholic—the epitome of a yuppie—outmaneuver the combined powers of the United States Department of Treasury, the Federal Reserve Bank of New York, and the Securities and Exchange Commission?

The mystery vanishes if you place the event and its resolution in the context of the deregulatory mood of the times.

First, a brief recap. In September 1981 the Treasury department had set bidding limits at its auctions to ensure that no Wall Street house could dominate. In July 1990 the Treasury tightened the limits again. That apparently didn't sit well at Salomon. According to the SEC, the youthful head trader for Treasury issues at Salomon, Paul Mozer, and his assistant, Thomas Murphy, submitted numerous false bids bucking the limits. Their false bids totaled $13.5 billion in seven auctions over a two-year span. To cover their tracks, the pair altered the record books kept at Salomon and may have tried to get friends at another house to help them.

From its investigations, the SEC figured the three top officers at Salomon—John Gutfreund, then chairman, Thomas Strauss, his president, and John Meriwether, a vice chairman—neither knew what was going on nor participated in the phony bidding. Trouble was, when they did learn in April 1991 about the rigging of the preceding February's auction, they didn't take any action. Salomon's in-house lawyer even said Mozer's action appeared to be criminal. The brass, apparently, shrugged and let Mozer and Murphy keep working. Result: more rigged bids that enabled Salomon to corner a market that's critically important to the well-being of the United States. How could this happen?

Equally to the point, has much changed in how Wall Street and its regulators deal with ethical problems?

Start with the market rigging. Clearly within the Beltway and in New York there was scant support for a rigorous examination of the inner workings of financial markets until the bidding levels became preposterous. And there was great reluctance to do anything afterwards.

Move on to the resolution of the Salomon affair and a similar pattern unfolds. What emerged from the corridors of power was a plan designed mostly to placate public outrage. Little was done to upset the participants unnecessarily. The basic ingredients of this plan are worth recalling.

First find a Mr. Clean who could offer up the heads of Salomon's three top officers on a platter. Then, in front of the television cameras, hold several days of hearings on Capitol Hill with much hand wringing and promises of reform. Follow up with some legal charges, and, after accepting a monetary settlement that's not excessively onerous, everyone goes back to business as usual.

Hey, did anyone really expect anything more than that? Did it matter that the Mr. Clean in question was Warren Buffett, major shareholder and board director at Salomon throughout all the admitted wrongdoing? Apparently not. The order of the day was do whatever was necessary to keep the federal deficit funded.

The market for U.S. Treasury bonds and notes is a multitrillion-dollar affair. Paul Volcker once said the Treasury's auction system ensured the government it was dealing with institutions "of unquestioned probity and financial strength." Perhaps Volcker, who was then head of the Federal Reserve, was recalling an earlier era when deficits were small, regulators clear-sighted, and traders hadn't succumbed to a stop-at-nothing culture. In finance, the jackals move fast. It was probably more than mere coincidence that Salomon stepped up its bidding for government issues shortly after Drexel Burnham had left the market.

Why didn't the regulators ask a few awkward questions? The

General Accounting Office, which does investigative work for Congress, began suggesting around 1987 that all was not right in the Treasury market. Primary dealers were operating what amounted to a cozy cartel on price information while churning accounts and applying excessive markups. That message, too, fell on deaf ears.

At the start of the 1980s, the market for new Treasury issues was half a trillion dollars annually. By 1991, new issues had grown fivefold in value and daily trading in Treasury issues had passed the hundred-billion-dollar mark.

Here we have billions of dollars at stake, yet the Treasury auction ranked among the most antiquated of securities markets anywhere. On bidding days, dealers sent their clerks to join the throng on the ground floor of the New York Federal Reserve Bank on Liberty Street in lower Manhattan. There the clerks scribbled bids phoned to them by their houses and stuffed them into ballot boxes in the final minutes before the auction began.

Certainly the conduct of the market was odd considering how vitally important the issuing of Treasuries is, both to the economy and to high-tech finance. Some background.

In theory, virtually any dealer could bid at the government auctions. In practice, only a few houses bothered to join the fray, preferring instead to place bids through a select band known as the primary dealers. These dealers pledged to bid in most auctions and in return received special favors from the Treasury.

Participating at the auctions was more prestigious than profitable for all but a handful of dealers. Yet certain foreign banks and securities houses, notably the Japanese and the British, did apply to become primary dealers in the mid-1980s. They figured they might get an edge by learning which way U.S. interest rates—and, in turn, currencies—were headed. Vital information for anyone participating in swaps.

The newcomers soon became disillusioned. At the peak in 1988, there were forty-six primary dealers, ten more than there had been in early 1985 and seven more than there would be in 1991. An alert regulator might have pondered this sudden about-face by the foreigners.

The rookies had received a lesson in the realities of the New

York market. They discovered that an inner group was grabbing most of the bounty and getting access to the best information. Between them a handful of firms—Merrill, Goldman, Morgan Stanley, Shearson, First Boston, and of course Salomon—took the bulk of the profits. In a good year these ran around $800 million.

The newcomers might have tolerated the lack of profits if only they could have broken into the inner group of dealers, upon whom the Treasury relied for advice. This group, known as the Treasury Borrowing Advisory Committee, recommended the size and pricing of each issue. Each quarter, the Treasury invited committee members to Washington for a private powwow. No one missed these meetings. During the talks, officials would discreetly reveal the figure that everyone needed to know—the size of the Treasury's funding requirements for the months ahead.

The Treasury market is no different than a stuffy country club. A clique rules and new members aren't welcome, no matter that they pay their dues. At times the relationship between official Washington and the elite of Wall Street's dealers is more Japanese than American in its closeness. The official at the Treasury most responsible for overseeing the dealers often comes into government service after working for a bank or brokerage house. And this official later returns to the Street for employment.

Rules prohibit collusion and market manipulation in the Treasury market, of course. Prior to the Salomon affair, the interpretation of those rules had become liberal, to say the least. As issue time approached, dealers routinely checked each other's positions and the likely level of bids. All the evidence indicates officials knew this, but it also shows the key players knew more about what was going on than did the regulators. That, too, was almost inevitable, given the odd manner in which the supervisory powers were divvied up.

The chore of policing the market was split three ways. Treasury set the overall rules of play, but could not investigate. The New York Federal Reserve Bank had the task of keeping the scorecard of dealers' holdings, but lacked the staff for efficient information gathering and enforcement. As for the SEC, it's like the pathologist in a murder case. Its staffers only start work after someone else discovers the violations.

With the agencies acting like the three monkeys in their approach to evil, the rigging of the market became quite simple. In three of the five auctions where Salomon admits wrongdoing, the regulators never spotted anything wrong. Auditors from the New York Stock Exchange did take a routine look at Salomon's books while the firm was cornering the market. A NYSE official later confessed to a congressional panel that its green-eyeshade guys had spotted "non-material documentation problems" but "didn't think they were serious."[5]

Indeed, the regulators seemed determined not to act. The New York Fed investigated when some dealers complained of being squeezed out of the market. Details of its investigation went to Washington. The report raised some warning flags, but not enough to be taken seriously. After glancing at it, the Treasury's point man put the report on a back burner, judging he would be better employed shepherding the Bush administration's bank reform legislation through Congress.

In fairness, the Treasury had set a limit on transactions, restricting any firm to 35 percent of an issue. The shock came when Salomon admitted grabbing no less than 94 percent of the two-year Treasury notes sold to competitive bidders at the May auction in 1991.

End-running the rule wasn't difficult, according to the SEC. Mozer, the head of the government trading desk at Salomon, easily covered his tracks by bidding in the names of customers and then had a clerk destroy the confirmation notes that would have alerted customers to the unauthorized bids. Mozer even formed a bidding pool with some of the better-known operators of hedge funds to further muddy his tracks.

At the time, reporters highlighted a battle of wills that pitted Salomon's Mozer against the Treasury official who had imposed the bidding limit. Ego, if it counted at all, was only part of the event. The real motivators were money and information. As we keep seeing, the Treasury market is a crucial link to other markets. Control what's happening in Treasuries and you won't lose your shirt in currencies and other areas where interest rates are important. Treasuries directly influence many of the complicated transactions such as swaps, futures, and options. They set the prices for synthetics, derivatives, and a lot more besides.

Another factor influenced Mozer's and Salomon's determination to dominate the Treasury market. Profits. It's tough to make money solely by dealing in a limited number of Treasuries. The typical dealer's profit on a $1 million trade of Treasury notes had fallen in a decade from around $1,250 to below $313 by mid-1990. Yet the returns from holding Treasury paper can be enormous for those prepared to gamble in a big way on interest rates.

Look how $10 million becomes $1 billion thanks to the miracles of leverage. Dealers need to put up only 1 percent of the face value of a Treasury bond or note, and by using the paper as collateral can then borrow $990 million at preferred rates. With the proceeds, Salomon and other big players made other investments geared to the slope of the yield curve. In some cases with short rates declining faster than those on longer-maturing notes, their annualized returns were running at 50 percent. And that was only one example of how Salomon was prospering.

Salomon was putting the squeeze on smaller players. In so huge a market, Treasuries should be plentiful and easy to borrow. Salomon's voracious appetite left other firms in a bind. The short sellers—those who sold bonds they didn't own but expected to borrow from another dealer—found themselves lining up outside Salomon's door. As the only available source, Salomon could extract some pretty fancy terms.

Remember reverse repos from chapter 3 and how they are a vital source of industry profits? Salomon played this game full tilt. It would "sell" bonds to dealers in return for a cash loan, promising to repurchase the bonds and refund the cash. The lenders didn't set the terms of the loans, Salomon did. Often the rate was a mere 1 percent. That cash, shrewdly reinvested, became another source of earning power for Salomon.

The Salomon saga was taking on a life of its own as this book went to press. Early on the firm had paid $250 million to settle charges of rigging nine Treasury auctions. Salomon's three top executives—Gutfreund, Strauss, and Meriwether—had settled civil charges and received light smacks on their wrists. True, Gutfreund had to agree never to run another investment house, but between them the trio paid only $225,000 in penalties. That's hardly more than a good week's wage in this business.

Mozer was less fortunate. His attempts to plea bargain had run afoul of both a federal judge and the prosecutor, with the latter threatening tougher charges.

In another sign that the question of responsibility is a debatable matter, staffers at Salomon soon were attempting to get Meriwether, Mozer's immediate boss, reinstated. Meriwether's expertise at high-tech trading apparently was needed to keep Salomon on the come-back trail to greater profits.

Did taxpayers or other investors suffer from the Treasury scandal as they did in the thrift crisis? At the end of the day, no one could say for certain the government had paid more for its money. Will it happen again? Not a great deal has changed and what has altered is due as much to technology as political pressure. The information vendors are becoming a great factor in Treasuries with prices now funneling into the market from a number of sources. Disclosure limits the opportunities for rigging markets while reducing spreads and profits for market makers. At the auction itself, the Federal Reserve Bank of New York is installing automated screens to replace the hand-scrawled bids, and the primary dealers no longer occupy positions of privilege as they once did.

Whether all of this is sufficient to eliminate the worries the General Accounting Office had about accounting churning and excessive markups is debatable. Congress is still wrangling over who should set and monitor the rules. One safe bet: the Treasury won't let others decide what happens in the raising of money to fund the government's deficit—not without a fight.

The moral of this tale? That depends upon whom you ask. William Simon, the former Salomon bond salesman who became U.S. Treasury secretary, said the Salomon affair was more like a "Greek tragedy than an exposé of evil."[6] Others are less sanguine. According to Mark C. Hansen, a former prosecutor in the Milken affair, it was further evidence of "brazen indifference to the market police."[7]

At the height of the Salomon affair, SEC Chairman Richard

Breeden addressed a meeting of big-time purchasers of Treasuries. If his speech was meant to be an admonishment, it didn't come across that way. When he came to the crucial passages on regulation, a forlorn note crept into his voice. "It is not an adequate ethical standard," said Breeden wearily, "to aspire to get through the day without being indicted."[8]

If there's a lesson in the tale, it came when almost all the major Wall Street firms and nearly forty banks confessed they had falsified orders and filed false records in selling the debt of government-sponsored agencies. Their lawyers negotiated a blanket settlement with the SEC for abusing this trillion-dollar market. The sum paid? Slightly over $5 million in fines.

On Capitol Hill, the bill writers who would reregulate the financial services industry are opportunists, and proud of it. If an issue is hot, they pounce, figuring there's nothing like big headlines to get new restrictions through Congress.

Few pursue this strategy with greater zeal than Edward Markey as he chairs his subcommittee in the House. "We used the momentum of the Salomon scandal as a lever," explains a Markey aide, "to reform what would have been unheard of in the past."

High on the list of priorities in Markey's office as the 103rd Congress got under way was a significant rewrite of the Securities Exchange Act of 1934, which has governed the industry for six decades. If Markey has his way, the rules should go through Congress at least in time for the sixtieth anniversary of the original legislation.

Meanwhile, over at the SEC the staff is undertaking one of the agency's most far-reaching studies in years. The SEC is working on its first comprehensive examination of the equities markets since unfixing commissions two decades ago. Its Market 2000 study will, among other things, probe what technology is doing to competition, the flow of orders, and proprietary trading systems. While the Republicans still had the White House, the SEC promised not to dictate what the structure of the equity markets should be in the year 2000. That's likely to change, and the SEC could be opening a

Pandora's box of complaints by those who believe the New York Stock Exchange still runs like a club.

The bigger question is, will the markets have changed yet again by the time either the SEC study is complete or any new regulations get through Congress? Regulators follow behind market development almost by definition. Sam Scott Miller is a securities lawyer who understands the dilemma. "I get the impression," he says, "people at the SEC are aware there is this seismic event going on in the market. They are at least trying to understand and conceptualize it."

Paradoxically, the financial markets may need less not more rules. Among scholars and critics, it's fashionable now to say it's time to consider shuttering the Securities and Exchange Commission. The public spends $800 million a year on compliance regulation, an amount equal to $10,000 annually for every registered broker. That's overkill when so many individual investors have thrown in the towel and handed their money over to professionals for management. "The regulators," says Saul Cohen, "will need to ask themselves why they are taking all of this money to regulate when there is nothing there." Cohen is a securities lawyer who briefly served as general counsel during the winding up of Drexel Burnham and knows the seamy side of this business.

Specifically, Cohen contends the regulators should eliminate the thousands of prospectuses that never get read except by lawyers and a few analysts, while encouraging more and better earnings projections. Cohen boldly suggests the SEC should close down in 1999, when the agency turns sixty-five, and go into retirement.

Jonathan Macey, who teaches law at Cornell, also contends that the SEC is redundant. A champion of modern portfolio theory, Macey believes efficient markets make obsolete the SEC's historical mandate for regulation through disclosure. He is on even firmer ground when he calls the SEC "an ineffective, highly politicized agency that wastes a tremendous amount of resources in turf-grabbing."[9]

How futile are these turf wars that preoccupy the bureaucrats and politicians? Consider the knockdown fight going on between the SEC and the New York Stock Exchange. Each time the NYSE chairman, Bill Donaldson, proposes listing more companies from abroad on the New York Stock Exchange, Richard Breeden, chairman at the SEC, has a fit. If foreigners float and list issues here, the SEC insists, they should abide by U.S. rules. Fine, but shouldn't, by the same logic, U.S. firms abide by foreign rules if they float issues abroad? Breeden thinks otherwise.

Germany's accounting rules encourage firms to keep hidden reserves, which they can use at their discretion to produce a steady rather than an erratic flow of earnings. British rules permit corporations to forecast what will happen to earnings, particularly when they are offering new stock. The SEC allows neither practice.

Do the differences matter? Probably not nearly as much as Breeden and his SEC would have investors believe.

If anything, the SEC oversells itself as the protector of unwary investors. Chief executives of American firms have raised to an art form the publishing of meaningless annual reports. Firms routinely fudge their figures from one quarter to the next. In fact, the earnings reports of even blue-chip U.S. banks aren't always what they appear to be, let alone those of penny-stock firms. In an embarrassing exposé, *Fortune* revealed how Bankers Trust rigged its 1987 earnings report to avoid showing its first loss since the 1930s.[10]

Bankers Trust, it seems, was shy some $80 million in profits it thought it had gained from foreign exchange trading. To compensate, the bank did what any German firm might have done. With the blessing of its auditors, it adjusted the figures in the compensation expense account where, in effect, it had been accumulating a secret reserve. This only came to light, and then only partially, when the bank faced the dilemma of reporting different figures to its two regulatory agencies, the SEC and the Federal Reserve. *Fortune's* disclosure came four years after the event and long after the time when shareholders might have reacted if they had known the reality of Bankers Trust's earnings.

On another front, the SEC is fighting a decade-long battle over who should regulate the new derivatives. Here the SEC is in a standoff against the Commodity Futures Trading Commission. This struggle flared into prominence with the October 1987 crash and the publication of the Brady report on the causes of the crash. "From an economic viewpoint," said the report, "what had been traditionally seen as separate markets—the markets for stocks, stock index futures, and stock options—are, in fact, one market."[11] And, said the report with indisputable logic, one integrated market needed one regulatory agency to keep control.

Fat chance. That proposal died aborning, strangled by the bickering and turf wars among the regulators themselves.

When his name went on the report, Nick Brady was chairman of Dillon, Read, as blue-blooded a firm as ever existed on Wall Street. Brady was born wealthy. His forebears helped create the utilities that went into forming Consolidated Edison. For his advice and longtime friendship that began at Yale, George Bush rewarded Brady by naming him to succeed his other close friend, James A. Baker, as Treasury secretary.

Few positions in Washington offered a better chance for Brady to fight for his beliefs and bring about some meaningful changes in financial regulations. Brady even knew his way around the Beltway. For seven months in 1982 he had been New Jersey's senator, appointed to replace Harrison Williams of Abscam infamy.

Alas, Brady is too patrician a man for the infighting needed to ensure the financial markets don't go through another crash like 1987's. Fence sitting is a Brady characteristic. This became clear when, as Treasury secretary, he failed to push Congress on reforming the Glass-Steagall banking laws.

At the heart of the row between the CFTC and the SEC is the question of who will have the final say over futures and options and stocks and bonds. Pick apart many of the popular derivatives and you will uncover elements of both futures and securities. Deciding to call one a security, another a future, and a third a commodity alters the way each is regulated.

More than a decade ago, the heads of the two agencies met for a quiet lunch in a rear booth at the Monocle on Capitol Hill. There they hatched a plan to separate the regulatory powers for a common product. This was in the summer of 1981. In what became known among the bureaucrats as the Accord, options went to the SEC, futures to the CFTC. Two years later trading in stock index futures began at the Kansas City commodities exchange.[12] The regulators and the markets have been going their separate ways ever since.

This is no academic matter. Markets that become more entwined with every new product are ripe for disaster if no agency is responsible except in its own domain. What happens in the Chicago pits affects the stock exchanges in New York in ways we are only beginning to understand. And vice versa. Yet regulators allow them to operate as if the connection were tenuous and unimportant.

Option traders get a nineteen-to-one advantage over stock purchasers in terms of leverage under the different margin rules, for example, when both invest in the same company. Equally controversial are the margin rules for stock index futures that go into program trading. Congress late in 1992 set about redefining them but then backed away, leaving the self-regulating exchanges to set their own rules. Only in an emergency would the Federal Reserve be allowed to move in and make changes.

Why so much tiptoeing around and reluctance to deal with a potential problem? Fear of what investors might do is a big part of the answer. Markets are mobile. Geography and national boundaries count for little with modern communications.

When they testify in Washington, D.C., directors of the Chicago Mercantile Exchange rarely miss an opportunity to sound the alarm bells. They're quick to remind legislators that traders can operate as easily in London or Tokyo as in Chicago or New York. Or, for that matter, in Rio, Dublin, or Auckland, three of the dozen or more commodities exchanges to emerge in recent years. As traders say, all it takes to move $2 billion is a couple of phone calls.

The maxim at work here is: Probe too deeply and risk having little left to regulate. They may not admit it, but the regulators have learned this already with derivatives.

Increasingly, New York invents derivatives, London trades them. London's time zone, falling as it does between the markets in the Far East and the United States, offers traders greater convenience. But there's a more important reason—London's attitude about haircuts. We're not talking about the penchant of British males for long locks. *Haircut* is trade jargon for how much capital broker-dealers must keep on their books when trading in different securities.

The British regulators are far more liberal about capital levels than their counterparts in New York.

Typically, a U.S.-based broker-dealer must set aside as much as $30 million in capital when selling an option on $100 million worth of stock. This dealer needs to make at least $10 million on the transaction to justify tying up that much money for an option that could last three years, and he has to cover other expenses. Now go across the Atlantic.

In London, the haircut is zero for a perfectly hedged option. Dealers there can write that option for a hundred grand. No competition. London gets the business.

New York firms such as Goldman or Merrill still participate in the derivatives market, only they do so through units based offshore and beyond the reach of U.S. regulators.

Nowadays the execution of simpler transactions also goes overseas. Even stocks. This is the "fax market." In the United States, a broker-dealer and his customer agree to the terms of a trade involving American stocks and the broker faxes the order slip to one of his offices abroad for execution. The SEC calls this "a bookkeeping fiction, a foreign facade." All done, it says, to evade reporting requirements and exchange fees.[13]

The newfangled often equates with the nefarious. Synthetics and derivatives exist to help investors dodge taxes, margin requirements, and other nettlesome restrictions. For example, a manager of a fund that is prohibited from using options can buy a tailor-made derivative in the form of a bond laced with equity options. In Canada, pension funds regularly end-run rules designed to promote local investments and curb moneys flowing into the United States. These Canadian funds buy bonds linked to foreign equity indexes, keeping to the letter of the law, if not its spirit.

The regulators might get more support from the public if they didn't spend so much time in internecine warfare. The ongoing row between the CFTC and the SEC at the start of the 1990s was as much concerned with personal careers and family politics as with protecting markets.

The family was the Gramms. Senator Phil from Texas and wife Wendy, head of the CFTC under President Bush. Arguably this pair in the George Bush era became the most politically influential unit on Capitol Hill, at least where economics and market regulation mix. Neither Gramm wanted a single agency that would see the older SEC devour the CFTC.

The Gramms were not strong on market reform. Under Wendy Gramm, the CFTC earned a reputation for being lenient with brokers who misuse customers' funds or break commodities laws. Gramm was a champion both of deregulation and of turf rights and, said one former commissioner, was "drifting more toward a buyer-beware type of attitude."[14]

The CFTC historically hasn't concerned itself much with supervising what happens at the customer level, but under Wendy Gramm that lack of concern reached new heights that undoubtedly were applauded by her husband.

Phil Gramm was a Democrat while he was earning his doctorate in economics. He has since switched allegiances and has aspirations to be a Republican presidential candidate in 1996. His conservative views stir deep passions on Capitol Hill. A congressional aide once labeled Phil Gramm "a zealot, a one-man Inquisition who stops attempts to help individual investors." That's a reach, but on his own Gramm for several months did hold up reforms for limited partnerships, which rank high among Wall Street's bigger scams, as we will see in the next chapter.

On Capitol Hill, Wendy Gramm repeatedly beat back attempts by the SEC's Breeden to widen his agency's jurisdiction. But Breeden, a former corporate lawyer, was no less politically adroit, just intent on winning a different game. In Washington, Breeden was known for large ambitions and lengthy workdays, often keeping staff on duty until almost midnight. Breeden had made no secret of his desire for a Cabinet post, preferably Treasury. He could hardly be blamed if he thought it would be foolish to make enemies over what so many in Washington regard as nothing more than a petty jurisdictional tiff.

So Breeden, instead of fighting Gramm, became a frontline fighter for President Bush's deregulation drive to aid small business.

He lobbied for less public disclosure for firms issuing new bonds or stocks and urged the securitization of risky loans, while thwarting attempts by SEC staffers to rein in abuses in penny stocks.

With the arrival of the Clinton administration the Breeden-Gramm spat is history. A new thrust to greater regulation is likely. Shrewd as ever, Breeden pointed the way ahead before he returned to practicing law privately. In his farewell address to the heads of the securities houses, Breeden launched a tirade against low ethical standards.

Besides the highly publicized cases, he said, there's a "daunting volume" of less-well-known cases. Week after week, the SEC is faced with a "seemingly endless river" of cases, said Breeden, "involving little frauds and big frauds, cooked books, manipulated prices, overreaching, churning, unsuitable recommendations, imaginary earnings—sometimes imaginary companies."[15]

Faced with such a litany of malpractice, no wonder so many investors are turning their backs on the markets.

CHAPTER NINE

The Ripple Effect

Senator Daniel Patrick Moynihan wasn't about to mince his words that brisk morning early in November 1990. The scene was a private breakfast in the dining room at the *New York Times* in mid-Manhattan. For almost ninety minutes, a powerful gathering of political, religious, and civic leaders that included banker David Rockefeller, diplomat Cyrus Vance, and investor Preston Robert Tisch had made its pitch. Some cajoled, some warned, and now it was Moynihan's turn.

New York's senior senator peered over the tops of his spectacles and scanned his audience until his gaze came to rest upon the immaculately attired representatives from Morgan Stanley. "We live in a brutal capitalist system and if you leave New York you die," Moynihan said. Then Moynihan added with only a trace of that warm Irish lilt he uses to captivate his listeners, "We tend to help our constituents."

Dick Fisher, the newly elected chairman of Morgan Stanley, couldn't fail to understand the implicit message. That in a few years

Moynihan could be heading the Senate Budget Committee or that Congressman Charles Rangel, who also attended the meeting, might one day lead the House Ways and Means Committee. Dangerous men to cross, particularly for the head of a firm in a regulated industry.

The question on everyone's mind that morning was whether Moynihan's barely concealed warning and all the arm-twisting by the city's leaders would deter Morgan Stanley from delivering on its own threat. Morgan Stanley had quietly let people know it was considering closing its mid-Manhattan offices and selecting a new headquarters site, with Stamford, Connecticut, high on its list.

Morgan Stanley's leases wouldn't expire until 1998. Still, the mere thought of such a defection, however far in the future, was giving the local politicians apoplexy. If Morgan Stanley were to leave, who else might follow? Or, more to the point, who would stay?

Even while the city was cajoling Morgan Stanley, other government officials were offering a lush package of tax rebates and incentives to prevent the commodity exchanges from crossing the Hudson River to New Jersey. The package was worth $145 million.[1]

The politicians' fears only grew when Smith Barney casually confirmed it had hired none other than Morgan Stanley to study the costs of a move to Connecticut. Within days, Goldman, Sachs, in an internal memorandum, was telling employees that it, too, was pondering a move away from Manhattan.

In recent years, New York City has seen one industry after another decimated by defectors, from garment manufacturing to advertising to printing.

A scant quarter century ago, New York could claim to be headquarters for no fewer than 137 of the Fortune 500 companies. Today, with the likes of Exxon, Mobil, and American Home Products picking up sticks, it's home to fewer than 40.

Financial services is New York's most important business. For much of the 1980s, four jobs out of every ten created in New York were in finance. Wall Street still supplies thousands of jobs in New York, and even more if you count all the lawyers, accountants, printers, and journalists whose livelihoods depend upon the business of money. As Moynihan and the other politicians know only too well, investment houses aren't creating new jobs, as they once did. Their employment needs are shrinking, not expanding. But New York City's tax needs aren't.

For their part, the upper-crust bankers also were indulging in power politics. Threaten the politicians enough and who knows what tax breaks you won't get.

Still, that said, the job erosion within Manhattan won't stop anytime soon. The forces of change will see to that. Improved technology and the higher productivity that it brings, plus the greater competition from other world financial centers, along with the general disillusionment about the returns that come from investing are certain to take a toll. Bluntly put, investors, small and big, are fed up with Wall Street. Some are suing and winning for the losses inflicted upon them by their brokers. Far more are closing accounts or adopting strategies that reduce their dependence upon the Street. Technology lets investors, particularly the big institutions, conduct their business far from New York. A diaspora is occurring in financial services that can only mean less demand for people in Wall Street's traditional brokerages and investment houses.

Veiled threats and handouts can delay but not stop this migration, no matter how many deals the politicians try to cut. The exodus is under way.

In his widely acclaimed book, *The Competitive Advantage of Nations,* Michael E. Porter, the Harvard scholar, makes much of geographic concentration and the clustering of professional and industrial talents. Swiss pharmaceutical firms locate in Basel, their American competitors in northern New Jersey. Germany builds its printing presses around Heidelberg; the Italians create ceramics in Sassuolo.[2]

Significantly, Porter doesn't twin finance with Manhattan.

Modern electronics and telecommunications reduce Manhattan's allure as a place in which to conduct business. Already, of the twenty-five largest pools of investment funds, only seven keep their main office in New York.[3] Manhattan is a pleasant enough place to work if you are the kind of Wall Street superstar once wittily identified as "the honcho with the condo and the limo and the Miro and lots of dough."[4] For most of those employed in financial services, work means a day spent handling millions of other people's dollars, yelling into telephones, and staring at flickering screens in cramped, noisy offices. It also means miserable hours wasted at each end of the day, commuting on congested and unreliable trains. Glamorous it is not.

Why stay? Why indeed, firms and individuals alike wonder. Since the 1987 crash, real estate prices have stopped their skyward journey, but that's small solace. Even with a glut of office space, unsavory offices in Manhattan's financial districts continue to rank among the world's costliest spaces. In prosperous times, it was hard to justify paying more than forty dollars a square foot—the rate Olympia and York charged some tenants for space in its World Financial Center. In a recession no one wants to pay such a price. Moving offices to Connecticut, or to New Jersey, or to somewhere even further afield begins to look tempting. After all, that's where the big corporate clients are located.

In a business where communication is between electronically connected computers or between disembodied voices, location scarcely matters. Traders and bankers like to say they cannot do their job without seeing the whites of the other fellow's eyes. Or that the best tidbits of information come over a drink or a bite at Delmonico's or Sweet's. There's a modicum of merit in what they say. It is hard to get an edge when each of your competitors can buy the same computer program and run the same screens. Yet the argument has a hollow ring if you are counting costs or noticing what the customers are doing. The exodus that saw some back offices move to Queens or across the Hudson River to New Jersey is spreading. Florida is emerging as the industry's new back office. Salomon has moved its trade-processing unit to Tampa and Merrill is putting its mutual fund operation in Jacksonville. The attraction: lower wages and rents.

Budget directors talk of pushing the processing of accounts offshore to such places as Thailand and India.

*   *   *

Few businesses match Wall Street for its cavalier treatment of customers. Brokers rank in the public's mind alongside the builders of nuclear power stations and the makers of breast implants and cigarettes. Customers have learned to have little faith in this industry's ability to regulate or police itself.

The whistle-blowers hardly rushed into action when E. F. Hutton was making more money from kiting checks than selling stocks and bonds. Or when Marty Siegel openly bragged about commuting by helicopter to Kidder, Peabody. Okay, life-styles were different in the red-suspender set, but shouldn't some of Siegel's superiors have wondered whether insider trading might be covering some of his expenses?

Dennis Levine, sometime colleague of Siegel at Drexel, boasted how easy it was to trade on inside information. "If you do things right, it's pretty foolproof," bragged Levine when he emerged from a short stay in jail. "There is virtually no chance of getting caught."[5] Without a trace of genuine self-reproach, Levine asserts he would have eluded the watchdogs but for freeloaders.

As a dealmaker, Levine earned huge profits by investing in planned but unannounced takeovers. To cover his tracks, Levine traded shares through a Bahamian-based Swiss bank. Unfortunately for him, bank officers soon spotted what Levine was doing and hitched a ride on his system. Either because they weren't as smart or as devious as Levine, his bankers didn't conceal what they were doing. Their exposure led to Levine, who in turn fingered Ivan Boesky. From there it was only a jump to Beverly Hills and Michael Milken.

Ira Lee Sorkin had the unenviable task of being top cop on Wall Street during the takeover era. Said Sorkin of the participants on his turf while he was heading the SEC's office in New York, "Insider trading was just part of the scheme."[6]

A former New York Stock Exchange official, who was privy to top-level discussions on illegal trading, is equally blunt. He contends Ivan Boesky was only the icing on a large cake. "We didn't know what we were missing." In his view, the good guys didn't have a chance. "On the regulatory side we had a bunch of kids out of law school who didn't have a fucking clue about these deals. These are smart lawyers, don't get me wrong, but they're not sophisticated dealmakers and financiers."

Individual investors are right to worry about the game-keepers staying up with the poachers. A freshly minted business graduate or lawyer receives $82,000 and more in starting salary on Wall Street, and is soon earning well into six figures. All that the Securities and Exchange Commission can offer is $27,000 plus job satisfaction.

The SEC admits that compliance with its insider-trading rules is haphazard. A quarter of all the corporate executives who must make these filings fail to meet the deadline. What's more, the SEC acknowledges it has no idea how many executives don't bother to file at all.

The insider-trading cases generate the big headlines, but the burning of customers and the churning of their accounts hurts Wall Street more. Some cases might be funny if family savings weren't at stake. Critic Irving Kristol is a longtime industry watcher and adroitly puts the problem in perspective. "Brokerage houses may chatter about the advantages of long-term investing in the stock market," says Kristol, "but the truth is that the more long-term investors a brokerage house has on its books, the less money it (and the broker) makes."[7]

Say this for some brokers, they're creative in their skulduggery. For example, meet Dorothy Hutson, a fifty-one-year-old grand-mother who worked in Merrill Lynch's Houston office. In her thick glasses and dark suits, Hutson struck many as a timid broker, inter-ested only in conservative investments. What colleagues and cus-tomers didn't suspect was that she systematically cheated investors out of $1.4 million. The money went to finance her gambling trips to Las Vegas and Lake Tahoe. To cover her tracks, Granny Hutson mailed out bogus statements showing profits and even sent custom-ers interest payments on their accounts. Those funds didn't come out of her own purse, or even Merrill Lynch's. Hutson took them from the accounts of other customers, according to a civil suit.[8]

Or take the case of Leslie Roberts of Boca Raton, Florida. Rob-erts was in his early twenties when he accumulated $5 million in commissions in a couple of years mostly by trading the account of his multimillionaire great-uncle. Investigators took months to unravel the thousands of trades he executed and never did answer the critical question: Why had Roberts's activities gone undetected for so long while he progressed from working for a Denver-based penny-stock firm to becoming a star at the Miami branches of E. F. Hutton and then Merrill Lynch?[9]

Swindling is one thing; letting it go undetected is another. That worries customers, particularly if they lack the time, inclination, or ability to check their statements closely.

The Smiths, David and Virginia, a retired couple living in Coronado, California, weren't sure about the trading strategy their broker had suggested. Don't worry, they were told. The manager at the San Diego branch of Pru-Bache—later renamed as Prudential Securities—assured them their account was being handled in a responsible manner.

The strategy? Trade actively and catch the dips. In one twelve-month period, say the Smiths, Prudential turned over their account no fewer than seventy-two times. In three years their brokers generated more than $1.5 million in commissions by trading more than $230 million worth of securities. The capital in the Smiths' account? Less than $4 million.

The Smiths can consider themselves lucky. An arbitration panel awarded them almost $2 million. Fumed a Prudential Securities spokesman, "We think the award is unwarranted, incorrect, and unsubstantiated by the facts. We are considering appealing."[10]

Investigations of unscrupulous brokers can take an inordinate amount of time. Peter Anthony Ryan worked for seven brokerage firms during the four years the New York Stock Exchange studied his case. Ryan's last violation, which he didn't admit to or deny, was a beaut, according to Sam Scott Miller, the lawyer who handled the case. It involved lying to customers about their investments and millions of dollars in excessive or unauthorized trades. One customer claimed Ryan lost three-quarters of his initial $447,677 investment and collected more in commissions than the customer ended up keeping in capital. Eventually the Big Board did get around to barring Ryan.[11]

A few bad apples? That's what executives on Wall Street like to say. Crookedness isn't endemic to the business, they assert. Fingers in the cash register and pilferage, petty or otherwise, are hazards every business has to expect, right? Maybe.

The record, in fact, says otherwise. The number of brokers suspended or barred tripled in the late 1980s to more than nine hundred in 1991. Yet many brokers disciplined for client cheating soon get work in other houses. The *Los Angeles Times* traced forty brokers who went from one job to the next without difficulty even though customers had proven numerous cases against each of them. A Rolodex filled with the names of loyal and active customers is a wonderful asset to have when seeking fresh employment.

"Short of a smoking gun," says Miller, "it takes management and compliance departments a while to build their case. Usually the crooks have a pretty good antenna, so they shop around. Unfortunately, there is always another manager who looks at production and hires."

Boiler rooms—the scourge of the fifties and sixties—are again prevalent. The manipulation of penny stocks apparently is still considered an acceptable game in some quarters. "The rule of thumb is never, never hang up the phone until the person buys or dies," is the way one broker explained his craft. For years, J. T. Moran and Company, operating its largest retail branch out of Garden City, New York, ranked among the biggest penny-stock brokers. Moran built quite a reputation for its style of operation and in the process created plenty of unhappy clients among its 110,000 customers. One group claims it lost some $60 million, due to a combination of market manipulation, unauthorized trading, buying unregistered securities, and stock parking.[12]

Among the brokerage community's more pernicious practices is *cold calling.* Throughout the industry there exist numerous white-collar sweatshops populated by recent college graduates. For five dollars an hour plus lunch, these callers spend their days dialing for prospects. The pace is hectic. A *Fortune* reporter once visited a Shearson operation based in Manhattan and learned that in four days, forty-one callers had reached 18,004 prospects.[13]

Was the effort worthwhile? Probably not. Those calls yielded exactly forty new accounts, a figure that speaks volumes about the surfeit of brokers and disgruntled customers alike.

* * *

"Hustle!" is a standing order in many brokerages, denials notwithstanding. Tax shelters. Limited partnerships. Annuities. Penny stocks. Zero coupon bonds. "Sell the flavor of the day!" is the order of the day. A phone call from your broker can be hazardous to the health of your account.

One Dean Witter broker became so disillusioned that he actually sued his firm for harassment. He claimed he was hassled for not getting clients to buy his house's mutual funds. These, of course, bring in more fees than independent funds. No matter that many broker-managed mutual funds consistently trail the pack in performance.

A recommendation by regional broker Raymond James Financial in St. Petersburg ranks as a classic in the category of "do what I say, not what I do." The firm made Cascade International its number one recommendation while its analyst was selling the stock from his own account.[14] Months later, Cascade would be in bankruptcy, its chairman missing, and its stock decimated.

To the list of dubious investment advice add a new category—collateralized mortgage obligations. Brokers are peddling these as supposedly safe investments for investors who want something better than the miserly returns they now get from certificates of deposit.

The standard spiel is that these derivatives are carved out of mortgage-backed bonds issued by the Federal National Mortgage Association and the Federal Home Loan Mortgage Corporation. Safe as houses. Triple-A rated and backed by Uncle Sam. All true, but CMOs are so complicated and risky that they topple professional investors.

Lewis Ranieri, the man often credited with inventing the mortgage-backed market in his days at Salomon Brothers, fears these are lethal weapons. "The Federal Reserve, the Federal Deposit Insurance Corporation and the Comptroller of the Currency have decided that these are unsafe and unsound investments for banks because of their volatility and complexity," Ranieri once told a *Wall Street Journal* reporter. "If various classes of these have been made verboten for sophisticated financial institutions, how could it be okay for the average guy in the street?"[15]

Newsweek's savvy financial columnist Jane Bryant Quinn has repeatedly warned her readers about the perils of investing in CMOs, and each time received the wrath of brokers. Her biggest beef is the uncertainty about getting your money back. Investors buying a seven-year CMO, she warns, could find themselves stuck with it for a lifetime. If rates rise a modest 1 percent, they wouldn't get their money back for almost twenty-four years. And while they waited, they would collect a mediocre return.

The cries of anguish from upset purchasers of CMOs will one day resonate alongside those of investors who fell for another hot product—limited partnerships.

Billed as tax shelters, partnerships came into vogue in the 1970s and sold strongly until most of the benefits vanished with the 1986 tax reform and the plunge in real estate prices. Some eight million investors sank around $104 billion into partnerships, typically in $10,000 sums earmarked for college fees and retirements. Billions of dollars went to fund everything from shopping centers to oil wells to cable television and airplanes.

In the days when George Ball was running the firm, Pru-Bache could claim the dubious distinction of peddling more partnerships than any other house. Later a court ordered the firm to pay $1 million in compensatory damages to a trio of investors whose retirement funds went into a mixture of partnerships and junk bond mutual funds. Plenty of other aggrieved partners also wanted compensation. At one point, Pru-Bache faced no fewer than a hundred lawsuits, with total claims running over $2 billion.[16]

Still, Pru-Bache was hardly alone. Throughout the industry brokers promised wonderful yields but conveniently didn't tell gullible investors about the difficulties of selling these investments.

The resale market for limited partnerships in the early 1990s amounted to about $250 million a year at most. With few bidders, desperate sellers often found themselves paying dealers the equivalent of a 15 percent levy on an already depressed price.

There's probably no accurate tally of the amounts lost, nor of the ingenious ways Wall Street devised to skin its credulous clients through partnerships. When these investments floundered, Wall Street invented a new wrinkle for generating extra income. It proposed merging assets of illiquid partnerships into new entities whose shares could trade on an exchange. These are known as *roll-ups* in the trade.

For instance, a roll-up might ask limited partners to swap their holdings in some shopping centers for another investment that includes the centers plus some bonds in an ailing thrift. If the promoters' offers sound bleak, they generally are. For limited partners, this is a Hobson's choice. The alternative is sticking with the original investment, which by now, likely, is under water.

Plenty still balked, but to little avail. Any syndicator armed with 51 percent of the votes could ride roughshod over the protesters and force their deal through. These roll-ups often became bigger money losers than the partnerships they replaced.

You might say all of this was like putting a person with a cough in bed with someone with a cold and getting two cases of pneumonia. The roll-ups often were nothing more than a scheme to rebundle assets of dubious value and a way to bail out the general partners. Naturally, there were generous fees available to the arrangers of roll-ups and predictably the roll-ups performed as badly, if not worse, than the original investments.

At one point, the shares of the new partnerships on average had fallen 45 percent on the first day of trading. Over the following year, they dropped a further 23 percent.

In the midst of the outcry over roll-ups, SEC Chairman Richard Breeden confessed that federal rules didn't cover many of the problems. Worse, he conceded he didn't understand the language contained in the filing statements. Said Breeden with amazing nonchalance at a Senate hearing, "I'd like to meet the person who can understand all the provisions in the documents."[17] So much for the public watchdogs.

An investor group representing three thousand limited partners accused Dean Witter of using coercion and charging exorbitant fees in its roll-ups and called for a boycott of Sears, Roebuck, which at the time was the broker's parent company.[18]

Enter Phil Gramm, free marketeer. For a while, he derailed the move to reform this business. The Republican senator from Texas fought the idea that dissenting investors be allowed to claim compensation when they objected to a roll-up. In a filibuster, Gramm claimed this would ruin the business and encourage the abrogation of contracts. The majority in the Senate was more caring, and Congress late in 1992 did act to give investors in partnerships somewhat better protection.

Partnerships are only one of many failed ideas that have investors hopping. Shearson Lehman is a regular object of their rage. Every seventh case that went to arbitration in one recent reporting period involved this brokerage firm. In one case investors sued Shearson Lehman for hustling them into risky annuities issued by First Capital Holdings. Shearson had bought a 28 percent stake in the insurer, whose penchant for junk bonds would eventually take it into bankruptcy and leave Shearson with a $144 million charge against its earnings.

Still other investors took out after Dean Witter for luring them into the dangerous market for zero coupon bonds. Red-faced executives admitted the firm didn't tell investors about the volatility of zeros, or about the size of fees taken by the house.

Institutions also are hollering at Wall Street's chicanery. Weyerhaeuser, the pulp and paper giant, hired an outside manager to invest a portion of its billion-dollar pension fund. Weyerhaeuser thought it was getting what the professionals call a market neutral strategy. This means its long and short positions would always balance and so Weyerhaeuser would never be at risk no matter what the market did.

Imagine Weyerhaeuser's shock when, in the wake of the Iraqi invasion of Kuwait, this account suddenly showed a $30 million loss. Only after Weyerhaeuser brought a charge of "high-stakes gambling" did its outside money manager, without admitting liability, agree to pay $8 million to settle the lawsuit.[19]

In one of the worst economic scandals in West Virginia's history, the state investment fund lost $190 million from fixed-income investing strategies supplied by a passel of Wall Street advisors. Seven, including Salomon and Goldman, Sachs, settled out of court for $28 million. Morgan Stanley fought the suit, lost, and faced $48 million in damage payments. The judge said Morgan Stanley, which planned to appeal, had violated a state law prohibiting the fund from engaging in speculative trading. This, said the judge, meant any investment with identifiable market risk.[20]

The screw may be turning. Some governments are sensing that it makes good politics to support irate investors. For example, New York and Massachusetts tried to recoup $190 million lost in junk bond funds that they argued were unsuitable for many shareholders.[21] This was probably true. Still, where were those state officials when the fund managers were hooking in the unwary with misleading advice?

What are brokers doing to keep their individual customers loyal? Slotting them with higher fees whenever they can, that's what. With a surfeit of brokers, this isn't always easy to do.

Before commissions were deregulated, the average charge per share was thirty-two cents for an individual and twenty-six cents for an institution. Now, almost twenty years later, the national brokerages charge institutions a couple of cents a share but for individuals the average now is around eighty-eight cents. If they dared, the brokerages would slot their retail customers even more. Most brokers claim they lose money on the retail accounts except when volume is unusually heavy. Only fierce competition keeps them from raising their charges. Every day the discounters pound the airwaves with their ads telling individual investors that they, too, can trade for a few pennies a share.

To no one's surprise, the discounters in five years have nearly doubled their share of the commission business to 11 percent in value terms and a lot more in volume. The price of loyalty to a full-line brokerage is steep. A deep discounter, such as Waterhouse Securities, charges only $61 in commissions on a transaction valued at $10,000. This compares with $238 at Merrill and even more at

Prudential Securities. Few small investors realize it, but each time they trade a stock they are also, in effect, subsidizing the trades of the big institutions. Remember the soft-dollar routine described in chapter 4? Someone has to pay for all that craziness.

Most retail customers don't know about soft-dollar trading, but corporate executives responsible for their firms' pension accounts do. They're fuming. They pay handsome fees for outsiders to manage those pensions funds, and now here's Wall Street handing those managers soft dollars to cover expenses the corporations have already paid. "That's just like American Airlines charging $500 for you to fly from Florida to Texas and then using your credit card to pay for the fuel," says Bill Quinn, who supervises American Airlines' pension plan.[22] True enough, but, of course, the airlines have long had their own variant of the soft-dollar routine. They call it a frequent-flyer program. Whatever the label, what's happening merely indicates how lousy the travel and investing businesses are.

Small wonder the brokerages keep slotting their retail clients with extra charges. The bigger brokers slap on fees to cover postage and the nuisance of forwarding shareholder reports to their customers. Many also charge two to three dollars to mail confirmation of a trade and some levy a fifty-dollar toll on inactive accounts.

Still want to keep your share certificates? Merrill Lynch charges its customers fifteen dollars for that privilege and also lobs in a forty-dollar annual maintenance fee on any inactive accounts. Even research reports are becoming a source of income.

The real surprise is that more individuals haven't switched to the discounters.

How much higher the full-line brokers can raise their tolls is anyone's guess. They do have a couple of alternatives. More automation means big up-front costs but promises lower wage bills later. Discounter Charles Schwab cut out most paperwork years ago, a step few others have yet contemplated. Prompted by a computer, Schwab customers push buttons on their touch-tone phones, bypassing the brokers on every seventh trade. Fidelity is both a mutual fund manager and discount broker. Among Fidelity's many tools for generating business is a software program that prompts its sales staff about what to say when customers call. This speeds transactions and produces more orders. Better still, the program enables Fidelity to use newly minted college graduates and pay them a fraction of the rate commanded by fully qualified brokers.[23]

The second alternative is to manage more assets for a fee. This is one area where brokers believe they can hit pay dirt. Fees for managing assets grew tenfold in the early and mid-1980s and run around $2 billion annually. Most firms levy a 3 percent toll for this service, no matter how they perform.

Here again there's a snag. The crashes of the late 1980s jolted this business. Investors have become leery of handing their funds to professionals who prove no more adroit than they are at avoiding sudden losses. The value of assets placed with professional managers is now growing only a modest 5 percent or so each year, well below earlier rates. Competition is severe, with most brokerages touting a version of what they call wrap accounts. Worse, plenty of outsiders, including commercial banks and insurance firms, also want a piece of the business. The bandwagon of financial planners keeps growing too, with their numbers now exceeding twenty thousand. Their services aren't always cheap—fees sometimes exceed two hundred dollars an hour—but it's all competition for the main-line brokerage houses.

News that discounter Charles Schwab wants a bigger piece of the asset-management business sent shock waves through the brokerage community. Schwab hinted it could cover its cost for as little as 1.5 percent of assets under management, roughly half the rate most firms charge.[24] Competition is about to get brutal.

Promoting a fee-based business makes sense for the national, full-line brokerages for a couple of reasons beyond the immediate flow of income. The fees help smooth out the volatility of earnings coming from areas where they stake their own capital. Also, it's a way to ease frictions between customers and registered representatives. The reps are costly to train and, according to New York lawyer Saul S. Cohen, require constant monitoring. Their burn-and-churn tactics are an embarrassment to Wall Street's new corporate owners. Newspaper stories about the wrongdoings and court cases of their subsidiaries annoy and embarrass the Prudentials and the General Electrics, says Cohen.

With asset management, the frontline broker becomes less involved with investment decisions. The job for these brokers increasingly is to talk up the merits of their firm's asset managers rather than plugging the hot tip of the day.

Trouble is, with customers feeling much less affluent than they did before the recession began, there are fewer assets available to be managed.

The money flowing into mutual and pension funds will not do much for the employment rolls of brokers. Nor even for those seeking work in the funds themselves.

With some thirty-three hundred mutual funds trying to capture investors' attention, redundancy is rampant. If the number of funds hasn't yet peaked, it soon will. Probably half the funds manage less than $50 million, the minimal amount to be economically viable. Increasingly, the firms that manage families of funds are getting rid of their losers by merging them into stronger units.

Much of the money that goes into pension and mutual funds is conservative money. It needs little handling and will not generate much in the way of commissions for Wall Street.

Consider what's happening with corporate pension plans. Thousands of firms are shifting from defined benefit plans, where they guarantee the payouts, to defined contribution, where recipients determine how much they want to save. In part, this is the force of the 1986 tax reform at work, which made administering the plans a nightmare. As the responsibility shifts, so does the investment style. Safer investments, like guaranteed investment certificates, are replacing stocks and bonds.

So far only about a fifth of all pension moneys are in the defined contribution plans. That's because these plans are newer and don't come with any government insurance. But they will grow. In pensions as in health care, the trend is to put greater responsibility upon individuals.

Individuals also have about $300 billion invested through their 401[k] plans. This, too, is pretty dormant money. Over half of these funds are tucked away in guaranteed income certificates and money market funds.

For those in the investment industry the prospect is a chilling one. Picking GICs is a far simpler task than picking stocks or bonds, and the job gets paid accordingly. Bang goes another source of revenues.

Fidelity Investments, the biggest of the mutual fund families, runs a television commercial that's an updated version of the dizzy housewife needing help from the strong-voiced soap salesman. In Fidelity's commercial the actors pose as jurists, scientists, and other upper-echelon white-collar workers. All say they lack the time and know-how to handle their own financial affairs. Fidelity's less-than-subtle message is that even educated people are no more capable or self-sufficient in financial matters than the housewives of yesteryear were in getting the family's wash whiter than white. So, according to this message, the wise get on with their jobs and let the professionals manage the disposable income produced. Sounds reassuring. The record says otherwise.

Fidelity's flagship Magellan Fund has been a star performer, up 700 percent or more in ten years. But Magellan is in a class of its own. Among the forty largest funds, only a quarter managed to beat the S&P 500 over a recent ten-year span. A rather dismal performance. Even Peter Lynch, the man behind Magellan's success, is having second thoughts about the efficacy of mutual funds. Since his retirement he's advised investors to do their own thing and shun funds. All an investor needs for success, Lynch argues, is to find "two or three stocks a decade."[25]

In part, this reflects the steep fees many funds charge. But just plain bad judgment is also to blame. Most funds do perform quite modestly, trailing the market averages. Among the fifty largest, only nineteen beat the S&P 500 index over a five-year period, and sixteen over ten years.

These fund managers are no worse than any of the other groups earning their money as investment advisors. Three-quarters of all professionals fail to beat the market in any given period, according to studies.

Puzzled about this, the Brookings Institution, the Washington-based think tank, commissioned a study.[26] The findings are revealing. The professional managers trade too much and at the wrong times, so they incur large market impact or execution costs in addition to brokerage commissions.

Their second error lies in gravitating toward groups of stocks that are simultaneously overpriced yet easy to justify buying. In the 1970s it was the Nifty Fifty, in the 1980s the Wal-Marts and Mercks with their sky-high price-earnings ratios.

So why are so many fund managers earning fat six-figure salaries for giving such lousy advice? The Brookings scholars have figured that out.

At most companies the treasurer's office hires the money managers. Many of those treasurers, say the researchers, are often frustrated stock pickers, want an extra layer of people to blame, and like to pursue a sophisticated strategy to justify their continued existence.

Now comes the zinger. "Money managers who can provide a good story about their strategy have a comparative advantage," concluded the Brookings study. "In fact, the product sold by the professional money managers is not just good performance but *schmoozing,* frequent discussion of investment strategies and other forms of hand holding." Nothing like a bit of gossip to keep the client happy when all your stock picks are under water.

When it comes to investment ideas, the pros are as gullible as the amateurs, says Tony Russ at Dominick and Dominick, a New York investment advisor. In trying to spot the latest trend, "they allow themselves to be sold on concepts," says Russ. If you doubt he is right, just watch the professional rat pack rotating its way mindlessly through one sector or group of stocks after another. Pharmaceuticals today, cyclicals tomorrow, utilities the day after. And so it goes.

The point isn't going unnoticed.

Over breakfast one morning, British investment banker Nick Verey put his finger on Wall Street's people problem. There are too many of them. "How many analysts do you really need?" asked Verey, who was then heading up S. G. Warburg's New York operations. "The first ten in any industry might be all right, but what's the eleventh worth? Does it really serve any meaningful purpose to hear twenty different ways explaining how to get an extra one-tenth of 1 percent on a cash instrument?"

The professional managers of money apparently don't think so. This is why indexing is popular and why corporate pension funds resent paying stock pickers immodest amounts for modest results. Ditto small investors, who switch in droves to index funds.

Consider this: $10,000 put into the S&P 500 index in January 1980 was worth $49,973 in May 1990. The median return by investment managers was 15 percent below the index, according to a study by a monitoring service.

The more indexing catches on, the fewer drones you need peddling yesterday's stale stock tips or managing growth funds that don't grow. One day—and it's not far off—the computers will do it all, design the programs and execute the trades to fulfill them. Less and less will we need salesmen and traders.

Redundancy will plague the financial services industry throughout the 1990s. Sometime this decade, those who entered in the 1980s will become part of the fat generation, the unwanted midlevel managers. All Wall Street firms bulge at the middle. The pyramid of success is narrow. The word is starting to spread, says a New York headhunter. "We're telling people, 'Don't expect to be a vice president all your life. It's move up or out.' "

For the first eight decades of this century, people in the securities business could get by without a great deal of knowledge. Charm went a long way. So did a compelling sales pitch.

What will it take to succeed in the 1990s in financial services? For starters, a working knowledge of all the world's markets and economies and how they relate to each other. Add to that a real jock's knowledge of PCs and workstation technology. Only when those are mastered will the selling techniques of yore come into play.

Talk to the sellers and buyers of computers for the retail brokers and one thing becomes apparent. Most brokers aren't adapting well to the new technology. Mostly educated in the days before computers moved into classrooms and campuses, they're computer illiterate and scared. At PaineWebber, for example, a survey found three-quarters of its brokers couldn't remember how to run a program that required only a single keystroke. Even traders don't use their computers to their fullest. Most run their workstations at between 30 and 40 percent of capacity, says a Hewlett-Packard salesman.

The rub is that the need for a sophisticated mathematical and calculative kind of knowledge comes when many of the products are turning into commodities. It will be tough for the firms to pay top dollar to staffers who only know how to peddle products that carry low premiums.

Look how the ripple effect is at work here. As the management of money comes more under the control of professionals, so the instruments change. Derivatives replace stocks, quants replace brokers. With each change it takes more sophisticated but fewer people to handle the load.

Saul Cohen offers a view of what might lie ahead that's both intriguing and chilling. The stock market of the future, he predicts, will be devoid of trading floors, specialists, and to a large extent rules. "It may be," he says, "no more than a collection of linked desktop computers through which broker-dealers and institutions trade large blocks of securities." Not at all what the NYSE's Donaldson has in mind, perhaps, but quite likely, given the way technology is taking us.

In Cohen's blueprint, as public interest in investing wanes, so will the number of brokers needed to serve the public. Down, too, will go the revenues collected by the state securities commissions that grant the brokers their operating licenses. With lower revenues, says Cohen, the state regulators will cut back, confining their work to penny-stock manipulators and other scam artists. Bad news, he says, for those individual rich investors who stay in the market. "They can expect less regulatory help in dealing with the relatively few brokers who will handle their business."

As we saw in the last chapter, the regulators and law enforcers are playing catch-up in a game that's forever changing. For example, restrictions aimed at curbing market volatility probably will do little to stop the secular movement of money from individual to institutional management. Yet circuit breakers and other constraints could push institutions into less restrictive and more liquid markets, offshore ones if necessary. That's no idle threat. Foreign markets are ready to welcome all kinds of business. Ivan Boesky found receptive bases in Switzerland and England only months after he left jail. From there he could run an investment partnership specializing in takeover stocks. An extreme example, perhaps, but plenty of others also end-run the regulators, as we saw with derivatives registered and traded abroad.

The volatility factor is a real dilemma for Wall Street and its regulators. Let it rip and the public vanishes. We know about the benefits that come from individuals investing for the long haul, but there's another way they lessen volatility. Brokers "borrow" shares from individuals for short sales, which aids market liquidity. Cause and effect at work? It looks that way. The more individuals quit the markets, the fewer loanable securities are available and the more volatility rises. Caught up somewhere in the midst of this are the regulators seeking a balance between professional investors who want fewer restrictions and individuals who need the comfort of protection.

Does it matter that the independent investor—savvy, brave, or foolish enough to be a stock picker—is a dying breed, and probably knows it? Curiously, it does. When handling their own accounts, individuals invest in and hold securities for the long haul, unlike many institutions that simply trade. In the past, this helped smooth out the markets. Now with the dollars switching from one group to the other, volatility in stocks will rise, further disillusioning the small investors.

If you doubt this, consider this assessment of how a typical institutional investor approaches the selection of stocks:

> What the company itself does is largely irrelevant: its staff are of no consequence. It is a line on a chart, an object of risk assessment, a percentage point in an index matched fund, a name on a spreadsheet. Nothing matters about it except what may affect the immediate movement of its share price, such as

a change of fashion, a broker's lunch, a market rumor of disaster, the whisper of a bid. It is buy at 180 and sell at 230.

The writer? A top advisor to the Bank of England, Britain's central bank.[27] Fundamental analysis? Long-term investing? Forget all that. What concentrates the minds of modern-day fund managers is, will they perform sufficiently well over the next few weeks or months to keep their jobs?

The big question in every investor's mind is, Could all this impulsive investing ravage the markets again? Was 1987 simply a fluke or are our markets becoming more volatile with the freewheeling program traders and institutions pushing us closer to meltdown?

The Brady report is a chilling reminder of how little it takes to trigger catastrophe. Four sellers accounted for 14 percent of Black Monday's volume, and the concentration was even larger in the futures market. There the top ten sellers accounted for half the volume, if you exclude the market makers. One mutual fund hit the market with thirteen tidal waves of sell orders, each valued at over $100 million. Under such onslaughts, markets buckle, and they do so before most investors even know what's happening.

Mutual funds are now the most dominant buyers of equities, replacing pension funds. This increases market volatility and risk. Unlike pension money, mutual funds don't ride out storms. As money flows in or out from investors, they react immediately. A sudden switch in interest rates or the return of inflation could cause another panic along the lines of those in the late 1980s.

Yet there are some who contend that there's no reason for alarm. G. William Schwert, who teaches at the University of Rochester, looked at market swings going back seven decades. He counted the days on which the swings exceeded 2 percent and concluded that the fluctuations were greater in the 1920s and 1930s than in the 1980s.[28]

Trouble is, Schwert only measured what happened from one day to the next, not what happened during the day's trading. What scares the pants off many investors are the swings from one hour to the next. Or even when they think the daily trading is over.

Ignorance isn't bliss in the stock market, it's downright danger-ous. Investors in Employee Benefit Plans, a health-care supplier, might have had a celebratory drink after checking the Big Board's closing tape in early January 1992. Their stock that day had climbed to 64, a new high. Unfortunately, that wasn't the end of the invest-ment day.

Twenty-two minutes after the closing bell, the firm released an earnings report that didn't meet analysts' expectations. Institutions began dumping the stock, using one of the many private exchanges that don't stop working when the NYSE does. By six o'clock that evening, Employee Benefit's stock was changing hands at 32, its market value halved.[29] The fizz had gone from any celebratory drinks.

By some measures the 1980s was one of the best decades on record for equities. In round numbers, the Dow Jones Industrial Average tripled after barely showing any gain in the previous dec-ade. Yet in one six-year period private investors managed to lose half a trillion dollars.

Few investors operate according to decennial calendars. Most dart in and out according to need and whim. "As long as we have stock markets," the economist John Kenneth Galbraith once re-marked, "we will have people who operate on one of two assump-tions: that the market will go up forever, or that the market will go up for some time and they will be able to get out first when it turns."

Plenty of investors proved Galbraith right in 1987 and again in 1989, learning the hard way that the exit doors do get jammed. They have also discovered how difficult it is to judge the market's moods. According to one statistician, market timers have a four-in-one-thousand chance of consistently selling high and buying low.[30]

In lower Manhattan such pessimism is shrugged away. Sup-porters of the American approach to capitalism are quick to say the decline in yields for certificates of deposit makes the return of investors to the stock and bond markets inevitable. Indeed, money has poured into mutual funds at the fastest clip since the 1987 crash and trading on the New York Stock Exchange has climbed. The optimists point to one of their favorite barometers as an indication of the better times ahead—the price of an exchange seat is worth half again what it was in 1990.

That may become one of the least shrewd investments made in the 1990s.

The return of the individual investor is overblown, and, even if true, wouldn't guarantee a brighter prospect for those working in financial services. Even the tripling of the Dow hasn't stopped or even slowed what is now a three-decades-long exodus of individual investors from the markets. The equity investments directly held by individuals keep falling. In a couple of years, they will drop below 50 percent. Only one trade in four is now executed directly on behalf of an individual. The other trades are entered by the big institutional pools of money on behalf of individuals. As one sardonic observer sees it, if the trend continues, the last American to own shares directly would sell the final one in the year 2003.[31]

The folks at the New York Stock Exchange like to claim markets are less volatile than they were. If trading gets too explosive, the regulators step in, first curbing the program traders and then shutting off all trading, an hour for a hundred-point move, two hours for three hundred points. The hope is that sanity will return in these cool-off periods. With the markets closed, however, we will never know what might have happened. It could just be that we are setting ourselves up for long-drawn-out periods of pain rather than short bursts of discomfort.

The curbing of volatility, moreover, isn't likely to change the inexorable trend at work in the markets toward more indexing and fewer people. Nor in the long haul will it do anything to prevent the exodus from Manhattan. Nothing much has changed since that November morning when the New York politicians squared off against Morgan Stanley's Dick Fisher over breakfast. For the moment, the commodities exchanges have decided to stay in Manhattan after wringing even greater concessions from the politicians. And so has Fisher. Sort of.

Not long ago, Dick Fisher was chatting with some analysts and reporters about Morgan Stanley's future. "We are in the process of shifting," he said, "from an American firm that's strong internationally to a global firm that happens to be headquartered in New York."

Any sighs of relief from the politicians were premature. "I wouldn't be surprised," added Fisher, "if the chairman is based outside the U.S. in ten years."

Call that a reprieve for New York, not a final victory.

CHAPTER TEN

Strategies for Survivors

S WISS BANKERS ARE SOMBER-SUITED FELLOWS known for discretion and choosing their words with care. So you pay attention when they start talking about *natural selection* and how the Darwinian process is at work among firms offering global financial services.

Listen to Rainer Gut of Credit Suisse. "Financial institutions will undergo radical restructuring and only the fittest will survive," he likes to say.

Gut is the quintessential modern global banker, as much at home in New York, London, or Tokyo as in his native Switzerland. Handsome, multilingual, and married to an American, Gut learned investment banking at Lazard Frères and now is chairman of Credit Suisse, the Zurich-based banking empire, which controls New York's First Boston.

Competition, already fierce within the three major financial time zones, will become even more intense according to Gut. Switching his metaphor somewhat he forecasts, "The air will become appreciably rarefied and many financial institutions that have survived thus far by relying on oxygen masks will suffer a collapse." That is, warns Gut, "unless they withdraw to more gentle altitudes."

The irony is that his First Boston has been gasping for breath and would have fallen right off the mountain of high finance but for artificial resuscitation from Gut.

Still, that doesn't detract from the validity of his message. Rather, it shows how difficult it is to create and execute a survival strategy even when you know the dangers lurking ahead.

Boiled to its essence, Gut's message is a chillingly simple one. Dominate globally or find a defensive niche where you can ward off competitive attacks. Whatever you do, don't get caught in the middle, trying to run both strategies simultaneously with the wrong-sized organization. This is an either-or game. Either you are big and powerful or small and invincible. Stuck in the middle, you get pecked to death on both sides.

Trouble is, that's easier to say than to achieve. Shearson Lehman Hutton went for size and almost went under. Pru-Bache failed in its bid to go upmarket and become an investment banker. Now renamed Prudential Securities, the firm faces a modest future as an also-ran in retailing, its original business. For a while the hottest names on the Street were the investment bankers who opted for independence and set up their own shops. Much was made at the time of this new wave. After sprouting with much fanfare, many of the financial boutiques are proving to be nine-day wonders, as demand for dealmaking fades.

In this chapter we will follow the pursuit for the perfect financial services organization. This isn't a business where one style fits all. In fact, through a series of vignettes, we will see the difficulties many bankers have in making any style fit. For example, melding elements of commercial and investment banking may be inevitable for the bigger houses, but it's proving a hazardous and lengthy process. Credit Suisse has struggled for almost two decades to get the strategy right. Gut's only solace is knowing that plenty of other bankers also keep stumbling. Citicorp and Security Pacific threw their hats into the ring and got knocked out in the early rounds. Even

Morgan Stanley has run into troubles. Figuring there was money in ownership, Morgan got stuck running an industrial empire and became the focus of several bitter lawsuits. Several boutiques would be long gone but for funding from Japan.

We begin by examining Merrill Lynch's bout with bureaucracy.

One day Merrill Lynch may get it right. Lord knows, Merrill has charged bull-like in every direction in pursuit of the perfect organizational structure.

Just look at the businesses Merrill has tried and then quit, from real estate to insurance to commodities. It climbed aboard the foreign bandwagon, then dumped its Canadian and Australian operations and shuttered others in London. Merrill has centralized, then decentralized and recentralized its system of management. It has tried dividing the firm into fifteen segments, then two halves and, when that didn't work, redivided into six parts.

The crux of Merrill's problems: a bloated bureaucracy and an inability to allocate costs accurately among its lines of endeavor. The light flickered on briefly at Merrill in the mid-1980s. As a senior executive remarked then, "You reach a point where going for incremental revenues isn't a profitable decision."[1] This recognition that size might not be the solution still didn't end Merrill's problems.

In 1990, Merrill's internal controls still were in trouble, and the firm had to take a $470 million charge for layoffs and a major restructuring. This was yet another piece of bad news for Merrill's stockholders, who had missed out on much of the 1980s bull market, and it rekindled speculation of a management coup. Donald Regan, Merrill's former chief executive, the story went, would lead the rebellion with funding from Morgan Guaranty. Regan had left Wall Street to run Ronald Reagan's White House and then became secretary of the Treasury. He didn't curb his tongue. "They got too used to limousines and perks," Regan complained of his successors in the executive suite. The way he saw it, these managers had developed an edifice complex. "Look at the new headquarters," Regan griped. "Mahogany paneling everywhere. The swish dining rooms. The chauffeured cars."

His successors didn't stint themselves when it came to paying $122 million for not one but two new headquarters towers in lower Manhattan's luxurious World Financial Center. For years they would struggle to sublet half the space when demand for financial services evaporated. In a sign of the times, Japan's Nomura took over part of the space Merrill couldn't fill.

Nothing came of the coup talk. Perhaps because, paradoxically, the blame for much of Merrill's woes rests at Regan's feet. Under Regan, Merrill had set out to be a money-management supermarket, offering its customers, as one wag put it, womb-to-tomb financial services.

The Regan philosophy suited the period when managers believed they could run everything. It even fitted his firm's heritage. After all, founder Charlie Merrill had been the financial wizard who created what became Safeway Stores. The guiding dogma for Merrill's legion of brokers was to convince customers they needed a service or a product before they knew it themselves.

Cobbling together so many disparate businesses didn't work. Merrill was ill-equipped to cope with the winds of change howling through the financial industry. The retail business, Merrill's strength, was changing as much in finance as it was in the peddling of food and fashion. Discounting was on the rise. Worse, the customers were moving. Fed up with their own investment performance, many were passing their funds over to the professional managers of mutual funds.

To compensate, Merrill borrowed heavily, adding almost a billion dollars of new debt to its balance sheet each year, and set out to dominate institutional sales and underwriting. In a few breathless years, Merrill would surge from virtually nowhere to become the world's leading underwriter of debt and equity and a powerhouse in dealmaking.

The price Merrill paid for buying so much business was a crippling erosion in margins and profits. At one point Salomon Brothers, with one-seventh the head count, was comfortably leading Merrill in profits. Even Shearson employees were more productive, producing close to two dollars for each dollar netted by Merrill workers.

Schizophrenic is how critics described Merrill's approach to solving problems. That's harsh, but there were signs of desperation in Merrill's struggles to change its organizational structure. When an experiment in melding the investment-banking operations and the retail sales force failed, Merrill's management severed their firm into distinct halves. This only deepened the rift between the disparate businesses and increased the difficulty of allocating costs and overheads.

To its critics, Merrill was the Stumbling Herd or the Rodney Dangerfield of mergers and acquisitions. When the results weren't disastrous they bordered on the bizarre. For example, there was the $377 million hit Merrill took in a single day in mortgages when a trader was accused, wrongly it turned out, of hiding the mortgages in his desk drawer.

Merrill's current chief executive is Daniel Tully, a career stockbroker and a four-decade veteran of the Merrill system. For years, Tully had worked as the backup to his predecessor, William A. Schreyer, the affable, hardworking salesman who began his career in Merrill's Williamsport, Pennsylvania, branch under his father's tutelage. So close were Tully and Schreyer that employees often had a hard time distinguishing between their pep talks.

Tully shows no signs of changing the style set by Schreyer. He, too, is the salesman's salesman, a born optimist. Over the john in his executive bathroom Tully keeps a plaque known as the Optimist's Creed. In part, it reads, ". . . to look at the sunny side of everything and make your optimism come true. . . ."

Tully is on record as saying that the firm's aim to be the biggest broker and investment banker "was and will be the correct strategy." As the nation's top underwriter and with seven million retail customers and half a trillion dollars in assets under its care, Merrill does have clout. The test for Tully is whether such size allows for the adroitness needed in today's markets.

The verdict thus far: Merrill rates an A for effort, if not for success.

* * *

If Merrill Lynch does well these days, it is partly by default. Its major opponents in the retail end of the business—Shearson Lehman, Prudential Securities—are living down their pasts. Their strategic plans are in disarray.

Prudential Insurance's foray into the securities industry is a case study in mistake making.[2] In 1981, Prudential, the nation's largest insurer, had led the parade of companies seeking to get into the business. With a $385 million bid, it bought the Bache Group, a target that looked ideal for the Pru's diversification plan. Pru's customer base was eroding as individuals switched to insurance and savings plans sponsored by their employers. Bache was an old-line wire house that had fallen behind and on hard times—foolishly, it had backed the Hunt brothers in their abortive attempt to corner the silver market. Nonetheless, Bache had distribution and the synergy looked promising. Both firms had plenty of what you might term ambidextrous salesmen—licensed to sell both securities and insurance. The only noticeable hang-up: Bache lacked solid management, and Pru's officers lacked the time to supervise their acquisition. What looked to be the perfect solution came a year later with the hiring of George Ball, a twenty-year industry veteran who had helped build the retailing operation at E. F. Hutton, where he was president. At the time Hutton's profitability was the envy of the Street. Only later would evidence emerge that often Hutton's figures owed as much to chicanery and check kiting as to legitimate business methods.

Caught up in the hubris of the times, Ball convinced Prudential to expand far beyond retailing securities into investment banking and to pump hundreds of millions of dollars into his schemes. Briefly, Pru-Bache prospered, but excessive expenditures for sales and technology left the firm unable to withstand the collapses that came in all markets. In 1990 alone, Pru-Bache lost $243 million. The following year Ball was gone, along with most of the staff. Now renamed, under new management, and kept afloat with a further massive injection of capital, Prudential Securities talks bravely of getting back to basics and establishing a position in retail brokerage. Unfortunately, even that strategy could be hampered by its continuing legal claims from irate customers left holding limited partnerships.

At the time of its original purchase, the Pru in internal studies had figured it might take twenty years to get its plan to work. To date that's about the only forecast that looks accurate in this exercise.

On the day Pru went after Bache in 1980, James Robinson III, then the unchallenged chairman at American Express, uttered a six-word sentence that he would come to regret. "It's a new ball game now," Robinson told a friend, who quickly arranged for him to meet Sandy Weill, creator of what was then Shearson Loeb Rhodes. Within weeks, AmEx had scooped up Shearson for $900 million and Robinson was talking of supplying "the widest variety of consumer financial services from any single source."

Before the ink had dried on the takeover agreement, a perceptive reporter remarked, "This could prove to be anything from a beautiful piece of synergy to a $1 billion disaster."[3] Nine years later AmEx would spend a total of $1.4 billion in cash and shares to preserve Shearson's credit rating and keep the firm afloat after Shearson had reported a $915 million loss in one quarter.

Under Weill, Shearson entered the 1980s with a reputation of being such a tightwad it made brokers pay for their own computers. In pursuit of Robinson's aim to serve his customers' every need, the firm now chose growth by acquisition as its basic strategy and attempted to leave arch-rival Merrill Lynch eating its dust.

The acquisitions (first E. F. Hutton, then Lehman Brothers) plus poor management created a disaster. Weill has long since moved—or rather been moved from power—and now controls Primerica, where he is building another financial empire, as we will see in the next chapter. By decade's end, his successors at Shearson were wrestling with a bloated payroll and the aftermath of misguided deals. Shearson's involvement in the RJR Nabisco farce garnered the most headlines, but there were others almost as bad. Take the $500 million Shearson put up in 1989 to fund part of a leveraged buyout of Prime Computer. The deal called for a quick refinancing through a junk bond issue. What began as a loan soon became an "investment" in a company that couldn't even meet its interest payments let alone return the principal.

Move on to the summer of 1992. By then Prime's business had recovered sufficiently for the firm to issue stock and debt in the bubbling market for new issues. This only took Shearson partially off the hook. Shearson pocketed some of the cash Prime raised, but also had to take ownership of shares that it cannot sell for a year. Worse, Shearson had to acknowledge that the rest of the loan wasn't going to be repaid any time soon.

A chagrined Shearson and its parent American Express now have written off more than a quarter of the loan and taken a $84 million after-tax charge against earnings. Maybe one day they'll get lucky and Prime—now renamed Computervision—will sell enough products for the firm to repay the interest it owes Shearson.

These days Shearson's own survival depends upon the indulgence of its parent. Under new leadership and renamed Shearson Lehman Brothers, there's talk of consigning the Hutton name permanently to the trash can and of dividing the firm into two distinctive parts—retail and wholesale. In effect, this would copy what Merrill tried and failed to do a half-dozen years earlier with its own core businesses.

Fate is taking one of its wry turns already. The Shearson operation isn't doing much of anything, but Lehman is. Lehman's executives have recovered in spirit and prowess sufficiently to talk of buying themselves out and going public. While its client list isn't what it was, the Lehman name has historical cachet.

Of late, Lehman has polished its reputation for research and aggressively bid for bond underwriting business in the wake of the Salomon scandal. Lehman might not survive on its own, but a spin-off may happen if for no other reason than that American Express needs cash. On a good day a buyout might put $1 billion into its coffers. Such a sum would go a long way toward rejuvenating its ailing credit card and insurance businesses. There's also talk of a public offering of stock in Shearson as a means to lower AmEx's stake. If the folks now running AmEx are shrewd they will wait until

Sears goes ahead with its plans to offload Dean Witter to public investors. Should the public prove less than eager to buy into Wall Street at that point, AmEx can cancel its own bailout plan and say it was nothing but a rumor.

Pity the plight of Dean Witter, cast into the role of orphan by beleaguered Sears, Roebuck. As part of its get-back-to-basics strategy, Sears sometime in 1993 hopes to spin the brokerage off to its own shareholders and the public in a new offering of stock.

While the elephants were indulging in what some might call a dance of destruction, Dean Witter, like the wise mouse, had scurried to the sidelines to avoid being trampled underfoot.

Philip Purcell, a lanky six-foot-seven-inch former McKinsey consultant, runs the firm. He had advised Sears on its 1981 purchase and then got the job of making sense of his recommendation. His first attempts were anything but a success.

Purcell, too, wanted to be more than a purveyor of stocks and bonds to the middle-class masses who were Sears's customers. According to friends he yearned to rise above the hoi polloi and become an investment banker. His aspirations went unfulfilled and Purcell found himself forced into making an abrupt U-turn.

Sears's directors had watched in dismay as the investment firm failed in nine years to earn sufficient profits to cover its $607 million purchase price. Once Purcell changed tack and put his energies into finding a niche, Dean Witter began to prosper. In fact, the broker would start the 1990s reporting record earnings, while competitors such as Shearson and Pru-Bache were still drowning in red ink.[4]

Purcell has earned a reputation for paring expenses and being downright stingy in what he lets his brokers pocket. Much of Dean Witter's success comes from the lucrative management of its customers' funds. These have mushroomed from half a billion dollars to nearly $50 billion in less than a decade. The biggest blot on the firm's record comes from encouraging its brokers to hustle the firm's own mutual funds, several of which have performed abysmally.

Since Sears is letting Dean Witter keep its remarkably successful Discover card, the challenge ahead for Purcell will be to turn more of the forty-two million cardholders into investors. And that's no easy task.

"To survive today," says a competitor, "you must be a hit-and-run artist. You have to jump into something, make your money, and be ready to pull back if everybody else follows you in."

Witness the current rush into wrap accounts—the professionally managed accounts for individuals. This is a hot and much-touted new service. Already it's a $30 billion business, growing rapidly and supplying handsome fees for investment firms. Now banks, insurance firms, and mutual funds want in on what used to be Wall Street's exclusive domain. As they get in, you know the fat margins will shrink.

Purcell, however, has one thing in his favor. Technology. In the past, the bulge-bracket firms spent lavishly on technology and gained an edge over less affluent rivals. That's changing. Today when firms shop for technology, money matters less. In the mid-1980s the budget for a powerful minicomputer, a couple of programmers, and access to a data bank or software started at $150,000. Now that package costs under $10,000. Result: more experimenting, and more quants making something happen quickly and cheaply.

All of this gives second-tier outfits such as a PaineWebber or a Dean Witter a shot at challenging the Goldmans and Morgans in derivatives and mortgage-backed securities. Listen to Larry Rafsky, the programmer and index builder who has been selling to Wall Street for fifteen years. "It's clear," he says, "the computing power of firms in the second bracket now equals those at the top."

But that said, there's little else going for the smaller firms. Terrain that banks, thrifts, and securities firms once could call their own vanishes in a twinkling of an eye. Financial services is now as much the realm of a General Electric, or a Ford Motor Company, as it is of a Citicorp, a Merrill Lynch, or a Golden West Financial. General Motors now offers users of its credit card rebates that they can apply to their next car purchase.

Bankers Trust, an also-ran as a commercial banker, today handles more swaps for corporate customers than any other single institution and manages $90 billion for clients, much of it in index funds. It also competes fiercely for the physical management of stock and bond certificates. Sounds mundane? Only until you notice how often Bankers Trust taps that inventory of certificates. In four trades out of ten done for its index customers, the bank doesn't need to go into the public markets. Paying fewer commissions to the rest of Wall Street means more profits for Bankers Trust.[5]

For years Goldman, Sachs's name was synonymous with commercial paper. Founder Marcus Goldman walked the streets with the paper stuffed inside his stovepipe hat. It was Marcus who helped his clients bypass their bankers when they needed funds. They returned the favor by supporting Goldman when he branched out into the more lucrative underwriting business. Now the wheel is turning yet again. Today as much as $2 trillion in new commercial paper comes to market or is rolled over in a year, but this is no bonanza for Goldman or the rest of Wall Street. Corporate clients find it cheaper to issue paper on their own or in partnership with their regular bankers.

Goldman hasn't sat idly by. It has set out to dominate other niches. Goldman is big in commodities plus foreign exchange and shrewdly stayed in municipal bonds when many of its competitors were pulling out. Today Goldman ranks among the top oil traders in the world. If someone needs a tanker full of crude oil in a hurry, chances are they don't go to Exxon or Shell. They call Goldman first.

In a moment of rashness, *Institutional Investor,* the industry bible, dubbed the 1980s the era of the boutiques and speculated that the full-line firms would go the way of the dinosaurs.[6] Perhaps the sight of so many hotshots opting for their independence and becoming instant millionaires had overwhelmed the judgment of its editors.

The boutiques—sold on the slogan "our brains, your money"—proved less than irresistible. Far from being a threat, many of the boutiques would become the endangered species.

In hindsight, it's easy to see why. What many of the boutiques offered was advice on dealmaking in general and leveraged buyouts in particular. Their downfall illustrates how difficult it is to stake out and keep niches when the forces of change are at work. The more famous boutique builders—Wasserstein, Perella, Blackstone, Lodestar, and Wolfensohn—are still around but have suffered setbacks periodically. Their survival is due both to their own brilliance and to deep-pocketed Japanese investors—Nomura, Nikko, Yamaichi, and Fuji Bank respectively.[7]

When they were flush with funds, the Japanese poured a couple of billion dollars or more into alliances with U.S. firms. If some of this was dumb rather than smart money, it had plenty of company. In the 1980s, dozens of bankers in the United States put money and careers on the line by trying to match the prodigious accomplishments of two guys who had made it big on their own. Their names: William Simon and Peter Peterson.

If they wrote ballads about the making of money instead of love, "Simon's Song" would have been the hit of its era. Legend has it, Bill Simon came into the finance business because he lacked a hat. Fresh from college, Simon was seeking a job in textiles and was told he couldn't even have an interview without the appropriate headgear.

The hatless and irate Simon hotfooted it down to Wall Street, where he soon was a big-league trader in government securities at Salomon Brothers, a house noted for things other than its sartorial requirements. Simon parlayed that job into an appointment as Gerald Ford's Treasury secretary.

His days of power and prestige inside the Beltway were short in number. Simon appeared headed for the beach when Ford bowed out of Washington, leaving him stranded with nowhere to go. Salomon didn't want him back, or at least not at the level Simon thought his due. Almost in desperation, Simon teamed with a former tax accountant to launch leveraged buyouts with a bid for Gibson Greetings. Simon put $330,000 into the deal; sixteen months later, when Gibson again became public, he took out $70 million. On Wall Street, a folk hero was born.

Peter Peterson, too, had a humble beginning. This son of Greek immigrants, whose parents ran a small-town coffee shop, capped a career as a minor industrialist by becoming secretary of commerce in Richard Nixon's cabinet. From there he moved to Lehman Brothers as its chairman.

Lehman was long past its prime as a banking house, and Peterson did little to slow the decline. Ousted in a palace coup, Peterson, too, seemed washed up. However, in 1985 he teamed up with Stephen Schwarzman, a well-heeled and well-connected (Yale Skull and Bones) son of a Philadelphia dry-goods merchant, who knew something about dealing.[8] Together they formed the Blackstone Group as an independent merchant banker, using their connections to get funds from the rich and famous.

Blackstone prospered. Espousing the merits of relationship banking and shunning hostile deals, the pair expanded rapidly by adding the likes of Sony, Nestle, Union Carbide, and PepsiCo to their client list. Such a roster soon enabled Peterson and Schwarzman to award themselves $12 million apiece in annual compensation, before such a sum became commonplace on Wall Street.

These were the pacesetters the new boutique owners tried to emulate. Yet with few exceptions, these newcomers proved to be no more immune to the ills plaguing Wall Street than were the full-line firms they sought to replace.

If anyone seemed set to succeed as a boutique operator, it was Sheldon Gordon. A top gun at Lehman under Peterson, Gordon rounded up a group of colleagues and put himself into business. First he bought an insurance holding company, Stamford Capital, and then an old-line Wall Street firm known for its institutional research. His aim was to offer three lines of business, proprietary trading, investment banking, and asset management.

For a supposedly smart banker, Gordon's timing to launch such an ambitious business in the second half of the 1980s was horrendous. His awakening to the real facts of business life was abrupt. Soon Gordon was watching his firm disintegrate before his eyes. Dealmaking, Gordon confessed, was "as slow as I've seen it since I've been in the business."[9] At first, Gordon's strategy made sense. He would carve a niche by serving midsized companies in deals of less than $150 million. Gordon figured these would be too insignificant for the lions of the merger game.

Trouble was, when a financial drought comes even lions lose their dignity and fight for whatever scraps they can get. His dream shattered, Gordon sought refuge at Blackstone, where he heads its European operations.

The rich life has been less evident at most boutiques since the gloss went off dealmaking and leveraged buyouts. LBOs were the quintessence of Wall Street in the 1980s, full of hype and based upon dubious economic theory. Buyouts shot from barely $1 billion at the start of the decade to $60 billion in 1988. Two years later, the total was $4 billion at best.

This buyout business was erected upon two planks of dubious strength. First, the assumption that there is always another sucker waiting to be stiffed, and second, that the brains of Wall Street know more about interest repayments and corporate reorganization than those chosen by a company's shareholders to run the business. If the latter were true, how do you explain the sudden drop in buyout activity in the early 1990s? Jeremy C. Stein teaches at MIT's Sloan School of Management. "Surely," says Stein, tongue firmly in cheek, "the available supply of inefficient corporations and wayward managers did not dry up overnight."[10]

The answer, of course, is that as the decade progressed, the dealmakers and camp followers were skimming more of the cream and lessening the chances for success. Stein studied 124 deals spread across the decade. The default rate on the earlier ones ran around 2 percent but later jumped to over 24 percent. Stein cites a couple of reasons. Commercial bankers shortened the length of their loans, while the sundry advisors tripled the rate for their fees to around 6 percent of the value of the debt.

Few now argue that buyouts did much to enhance the competitiveness of the companies involved. In one aspect, Wall Street was right. For a while, there was always another set of shareholders waiting to buy the reorganized companies. The greater fools, however, were those among the LBO designers and boutique builders who figured the game would never end.

*   *   *

The story of Theodore J. Forstmann tells much about this era. Forstmann, with brother Nick and brother-in-law Brian Little, runs the boutique that carries their names.

Ted Forstmann had merged and acquired with the best and profited when dealmaking was in its infancy. Suddenly Forstmann went cold turkey. He even earned himself some notoriety with his diatribes against the excessive use of debt. His critics mocked Forstmann for raining on Wall Street's parade and said he was too chicken to keep pace with his arch-rival, Henry Kravis at Kohlberg Kravis Roberts.

Forstmann had the last laugh, even if it was a tad smaller than he expected. With Kravis stuck trying to unwind such ludicrously overleveraged deals as RJR Nabisco and Beatrice, Forstmann assembled billions in fresh funding. Among his new backers were the pension funds of such blue-chip firms as GE, IBM, and AT&T.

Setting out to make a comeback as a dealmaker in mid-1990, Forstmann bragged, "I am the only financial buyer in the country." Forstmann was more right than he knew when he added, "LBOs are dead along with KKR."[11]

The deal game was largely over, and with it the era of quick wealth for every dealmaking boutique builder no matter how limited in talent. Austerity was in. Banks hadn't the funds or no longer found it politically correct to back Wall Street's extravaganzas.

What the demise of so many boutiques shows is that it takes more than sheer brainpower and good connections to succeed. As *Institutional Investor* commented with more prescience than it had shown earlier, "The 90's will be the era of the big firm—one with deep pockets able to afford the technology needed to maintain and improve quantitative skills and to develop and provide a wide range of products."[12]

The few boutiques that do thrive as they survive are either cautious, like Forstmann Little, or veterans whose tendency to eschew glitz is only exceeded by their phobia of publicity. No point in telling others when you have established a profitable niche.

For example, look at the Allens. They took the modest fortune they made in the 1960s from backing long shots ($1 million invested in pill maker Syntex became $360 million) and turned it into a much larger one by keeping their focus narrow. Their family-run Allen and Company is closer to Hollywood than any other Wall Street house. It was the Allens who engineered Coca-Cola's purchase of Columbia Pictures and its later sale to Sony. This, in turn, put them in touch with Hollywood agent Michael Ovitz, who was part of the Sony team. Later, when Matsushita was negotiating for MCA, Ovitz brought in the Allens to help with that deal.

The head of the house today is Herbert A. Allen. A skilled raconteur, he lives at New York's Carlyle Hotel, where many of the world's powerful men keep apartments. "They are one of the few all-star merchant banks left," says Roberto C. Goizueta, chief executive at Coca-Cola.[13]

Such relationships translate over the years into substantial wealth, which is why, by some estimates, the Allens are members of the billionaire class.

Another reclusive old-line boutique is Lazard Frères. Lazard was banker to Harold Geneen in the heyday of his ITT empire building. Today the firm is strong in Paris, London, and New York and has a sizable stake in Mediobanca, Italy's leading merchant banker.

Lazard has deep roots, but the modern firm is largely the creation of Michel David-Weill, whose family has exercised control for four generations. *Financial World* once put David-Weill on its cover as the richest man on Wall Street, estimating his annual take at $125 million. That was in the days before people knew how much Michael Milken was making.

The hallmarks of Lazard's success: an aversion to rapid growth or trendy dealmaking and a liking for frugality. Its offices are among the dowdiest in Manhattan. Such conservatism may upset junior partners eager for instant wealth, but it keeps the firm from repeating the mistakes of other, more aggressive boutiques.

The boutiques' affinity for dealmaking has lost its allure in the 1990s. This is why none of the ones created in recent times came close to replacing the old-line firms, as many predicted they would. To be sure, Wasserstein, Perella is still in business, but then so is

First Boston. Both needed funding from foreigners, Japanese in the former's case, Swiss in the latter's.

What of Pete Peterson and Bill Simon nowadays? Both are prosperous, even if they do not cut quite the swath they once expected. With adroit timing, Peterson's Blackstone talked Nikko Securities, the large securities house, into buying a one-fifth stake for $100 million when the Japanese were flush with cash. (Simon, too, would have to tap deep Japanese pockets, in his case insurer Tokio Marine.) Thus armed, Blackstone featured prominently among deal-makers while the M&A boom lasted.

Of late, Blackstone's investments have taken on a riskier note. For example, Blackstone is now the nation's largest hotel franchiser. It acquired the principal assets of troubled Days Inn when it came out of bankruptcy,[14] the result of an earlier buyout.

As for Bill Simon, he is struggling. His attempts to repeat his success by turning around ailing S&Ls have faltered. Simon had plans for a fast cleanup and resale, but these came unstuck when Congress rewrote the rules.

Also, Simon has suffered through the breakup of two business partnerships and an estrangement from his wife after forty-one years of marriage.[15] In the midst of his woes, Simon confessed to a reporter that he had one final ambition. He dreamed of becoming a *taipan,* the dominant leader of a vast ocean-spanning trading conglomerate. The inspiration apparently came from reading the best-seller *Noble House.*

For sheer intrigue, few strategies rival what Morgan Stanley has done in building its own industrial empire. Earlier than most, the bankers at Morgan Stanley realized what might happen when the SEC changed the rules on underwritings and shelf registrations. How the fat fees would vanish as competition for underwriting business turned cutthroat.[16]

One of Morgan's solutions: buy controlling interests in a slew of industrial companies. Using its own funds plus others raised from private investors, banks, pension funds, and insurance companies,

Morgan Stanley by 1990 had acquired sizable and often controlling stakes in forty-two companies. The combined assets of these firms exceeded $25 billion and their interests ranged from textiles to packaging to communications. Also included among this hodge-podge was the Southern Pacific railroad, Ireland's Waterford Crystal and Glass, and the Seattle Mariners.

The emergence of Morgan Stanley and others on Wall Street as corporate owners raises many questions. Not the least of these is whether the firms knew what they are doing in tying up so much of their own money. After all, investment bankers, unlike commercial bankers, aren't taught how to lend money and get it back—not that the commercial bankers have learned the lesson well. And investment bankers don't have loan officers or operations people to deploy if their newly acquired companies run into trouble.

In its reports to stockholders, Morgan Stanley was less than frank about its intent. What began as "leveraged acquisitions" became over the years "a longer-term investment portfolio." Early on Morgan Stanley had reaped a massive gain—$124 million—by investing in tiny Cain Chemical and probably hoped its other investments would be as bountiful. The recession dashed that hope.

True, Morgan Stanley's bankers earned some of the most incredible returns ever seen on Wall Street. They also earned their firm the label of "brash dealmaker" from the *New York Times* when Morgan Stanley became ensnared in a series of lawsuits that blackened the firm's once-stellar reputation.

The troubles began when the economy faltered with the 1990s' recession and began dragging down the firm's highly leveraged group of companies. Irate investors pounded Morgan Stanley with lawsuits, claiming it had used insider information and manipulated deals to its own advantage. Its accusers, for instance, said Morgan Stanley had created conflicts of interest by transferring equity positions between funds under its management. Among those suing the firm were some wealthy Californians, plus Equitable Life Assurance and a mutual fund managed by Merrill Lynch.

To appreciate how lucrative this empire building and dealmaking became for Morgan Stanley, consider its involvement with Burlington Industries, the Greensboro, North Carolina, textile firm.

Morgan entered the scene in the spring of 1987 as a white knight, brought in by management to thwart an unwanted takeover by Asher Edelman, a sometime raider.

Morgan Stanley's solution was a $2.9 billion takeover funded almost entirely by junk bonds and bank loans. For putting up $46 million of its own money, Morgan Stanley gained control of the entire company. In the first fifty days, the banker received some $87 million in fees, largely as payment for advising Burlington on how to be acquired by Morgan Stanley. Those fees eventually would balloon to $176 million.

Some three and a half years later, Burlington was awash in red ink, its junk bonds unwanted. Burlington's former chief executive bitterly denounced another Morgan Stanley scheme that included gutting the firm's research operations while giving Morgan Stanley yet more fees.

Then too, there was Morgan's neat bailout plan. This involved selling its holdings to Burlington's employees through a stock option program. Shortly afterwards the stock market collapsed. The employees would have to wait years before their investment came back above water.

To be sure, when Morgan Stanley sold the shares it took a hit on their already diminished value. But for Morgan Stanley there were other compensations, such as the fees for setting up the ESOP. Morgan Stanley's bill for that task, as the *Wall Street Journal* pointed out, "was so rich that it equaled more than half of Morgan's third-quarter earnings in 1989."

No group had higher hopes for expanding into new markets than did the commercial banks. Their sorties into investment banking increased in the mid-1980s and followed a simple premise. They would learn the craft while following their big-time corporate customers around the globe. Deregulation was moving apace abroad, particularly in London. By going to Europe, the bankers figured they could test the waters while waiting for Congress to lift the Glass-Steagall regulations that separate commercial and investment banking activities at home. For Citicorp and other money center banks this was also an opportunity to catch up with European bankers such as Gut's Credit Suisse and Germany's Deutsche Bank or Britain's National Westminster, whose operations are less shackled by regulators. The Europeans have quite an advantage. In their domestic markets they can offer a complete range of banking services. In the United States, special exemptions to the rules also enable the foreigners to operate as both commercial and investment bankers. For example, a unit of NatWest used a loophole in the regulations to grab Drexel Burnham Lambert's retail operations.

Among the U.S. commercial bankers, no one tried harder, or with less success, to turn the dream into reality than Richard Flamson. As head of Los Angeles–based Security Pacific, Flamson launched a three-pronged strategy. His plan was to build upon his California base, offer nationwide services, and then become a global banker. No matter that the bank's asset base was, by world standards, quite small or that its customer list included few big names. What counts in California as much as it does in New York's financial circles is chutzpah, and Flamson had plenty of that.

Flamson demonstrated this when London threw open its financial markets to all comers during the Thatcher era of deregulation. Few bought in more fully than did Flamson to the idea that the British market would become the proverbial level playing field.

In the pursuit of efficiency, the Thatcher government showed few qualms about throwing the local financial firms to the wolves from abroad. This was the era of Big Bang—or Big Bust, as it later became—and the Thatcherites were determined to make London the financial capital of a unified Europe.

Enter Flamson. Carrying a briefcase stuffed with cash, Flamson bagged Hoare Govett, a crusty, old-line British broker-dealer, whose chairman was a close advisor to Prime Minister Margaret Thatcher. Hoare Govett had fiercely guarded its independence and had preserved an image of superior breeding but, as one local commentator put it, was about to lose both.[17]

Flamson wasn't known as a man who attended to details. He relished his reputation in banking circles as a painter of the big picture, proclaiming his commitment to "a philosophy of excellence in providing financial services worldwide." His canvas soon also included investment houses in Toronto and Melbourne.

The boldness of the moves might have paid off but for a surfeit of competition. Every other money center bank had also decided to act. With every whiff of speculation that Congress would lift Glass-Steagall, another commercial bank caught the global bug. Like lemmings, they were all jumping off the same cliff. Or more accurately, duplicating each other's services. For instance, in a two-year time span, the capitalization of the firms participating in London gilts—the British counterpart of U.S. Treasuries—shot from 50 million pounds to 680 million.[18] One year later, with margins vanishing, the capital had shrunk by a third, but not enough to forestall some terrible losses.

If the U.S. bankers believed they could use London as a testing ground, they were only partially right. London became like a laboratory for some Mendelian experiment gone badly awry. "When we ventured into new products, services, and geography we found ourselves with less than a competitive edge," said Robert H. Smith.[19] That was by way of explaining why in 1990 he replaced Flamson as chief executive and why the bank was disbanding its global merchant bank.

The immediate cost of Flamson's folly to Security Pacific: a write-off that ran into the hundreds of millions of dollars. In its weakened state the bank, far from becoming a world powerhouse, faded into obscurity, ending its days as a subsidiary of Bank of America.

In withdrawing, the U.S. bankers showed far less tenacity than their European, Japanese, or Arabian counterparts. Overall, the number of foreign banking organizations in London grew in the eighties by a quarter to almost a hundred, while those from the United States shrank by a fifth to fewer than sixty.[20]

For now there's no immediate prospect of Congress rescinding Glass-Steagall. Many of the commercial bankers have retreated to the sidelines. Chase Manhattan shut down its London equity operation after swallowing a $40 million loss. By 1990 Chemical Bank, which once trumpeted its intent to be a major player in global capital markets, had reduced its ambitions to regional banking. At Citicorp, Chairman John Reed was jettisoning one new venture after another in a desperate bid to keep the bank independent.

For Citicorp, all that could go wrong, did. None of the numerous strategies Citicorp adopted gave it the prominence it sought as an investment banker. The firm repeatedly changed its managers, and its executives in Europe, when they weren't being sacked, gained a reputation for arrogance and ineffectual control. The firm managed to lose $50 million in the tiny Irish market in rampant speculation and gutted Scrimgeour Vickers not long after overpaying for its purchase. Scrimgeour's investment operations in London and Hong Kong had been the toast of the industry before its acquisition by Citicorp. Finally, in an about-turn whose timing could hardly have been worse, Citicorp in the late 1980s set out to be, of all things, the lead player in leveraged buyouts.

Hardly a commercial bank hasn't had its setbacks, but that doesn't mean the turf wars won't continue.

From his Zurich office, Rainer Gut is preparing for a world where travel between Tokyo and New York takes a mere four hours and telephones will come with automatic language translation. In this world, Gut wants to ensure that no financial transaction is too big for Credit Suisse to handle. To this end, the Swiss bank has diversified and assembled pools of capital in various banks, in life insurance, and even in industrial-holdings companies. Gut's plan calls for First Boston to be a cornerstone of this global banking strategy.

The fortunes of First Boston have always had a tendency to veer to the extreme. Rising star of the late 1960s, moribund in the mid-1970s, the house was finally revived by a bagpipe-playing former president of Merrill Lynch. In one four-year span, First Boston saw its earnings soar fiftyfold, enough to briefly push it ahead even of Morgan Stanley.

What seemed certain to move First Boston far ahead of the competition was its alliance with Credit Suisse, inked just in time for the global boom in finance and the oil mergers. Those were heady times. For seventy-nine hours' work at the last minute in the Texaco–Getty Oil battle, First Boston once collected $10 million in fees, a bit more than $2,000 a minute.[21]

First Boston's subsequent follies, particularly in merchant banking and bridge loans financings, forced Gut to spend years retrenching and reorganizing. The mistakes committed by Credit Suisse and First Boston didn't differ markedly from those of their competitors, except perhaps in scale and frequency. Oddly, what compounded the errors was top management's timidity.

The Swiss worried about American sensibilities. After all, no country takes happily to foreigners owning a sizable stake in one of its better-known financial concerns, even if, in this case, it wasn't a controlling ownership. The hierarchy in Zurich feared offending the U.S. regulators by exerting pressure. For example, Gut and his colleagues made few attempts to disband the petty fiefdoms within the First Boston empire, even when these threatened to tear everything apart.

This hands-off approach encouraged rivalries and clashes. The backbiting between the London and New York operations became the talk of the trade. Staffers in London openly attacked their better-paid counterparts in New York, saying their incompetence was matched only by their arrogance.

Credit Suisse itself managed to avoid getting caught up in the trap that had Campeau's name emblazoned on it. "Believe me, we were asked in on three or four occasions," says a Credit Suisse man. "Not only asked in, pleaded with to get in because our name would be a star to add to the syndicate group. We were noticeable by our absence."

In fact, First Boston's participation as a Campeau fund-raiser was a major embarrassment for Gut since he was a director of both the Swiss commercial bank and the U.S. investment bank. But Credit Suisse at that point didn't have majority stakeholding in First Boston and didn't want to be accused by the Federal Reserve of overstepping its already privileged position in the New York banking firmament. So Gut had to bite his tongue, limiting himself to raised eyebrows and a few pointed questions as to whether the First Boston hotshots really knew what they were doing. That they didn't, as Gut suspected, became embarrassingly clear.

After the Campeau affair, Gut's patience finally ran out.

To stop the anarchy and prevent a possible plunge into bankruptcy, Gut sank nearly $300 million in fresh capital into First Boston. He also persuaded the regulators to bend the rules, allowing Credit Suisse to turn its minority holding into a majority stake in First Boston.

This gave Gut the power to make the changes a more courageous man would have ordered years earlier. Down went First Boston's bloated payroll and out went most of First Boston's top management. After banging together the heads of the remaining staffers, Gut set some much-needed ground rules. No more bridge loans by the New York office, nor acquisitions, and a strict limit on merchant banking. "There was some resistance to that," says a Credit Suisse banker privy to the change making. "The entrepreneurial types didn't like being told what to do." Some of those who survived speculated that if Gut had made any more cuts, he would have turned First Boston into a boutique.

First Boston isn't yet the powerhouse envisioned a few years earlier. Still, say this for Rainer Gut: He knows what it takes to survive.

CHAPTER ELEVEN

In the Winners' Circle

IF YOU THINK OF WALL STREET IN THE
manner of a Churchill Downs bettor, you get this early-morning line
on which houses are favored to make the winners' circle and which
are destined to be runners-up or also-rans.

FIRM FAVORITE: Goldman, Sachs will continue riding to victory
under its top jockey, the fiercely competitive, buttoned-down Stephen Friedman. Goldman espouses teamwork, not stars, and gets
corporate America's respect for its savvy advice. The best firm on the
Street in the 1980s, Goldman looks set to keep the crown this
decade.

SHOW AND PLACE: Morgan Stanley, Bankers Trust, and Bear,
Stearns are the likeliest contenders. These houses make a tough trio.
Well capitalized and with clear assessments of their missions, they
have learned to play the global game while dominating key niches.

MOST OVERWEIGHT: Shearson Lehman, tottering back from the
brink of bankruptcy, and Merrill Lynch, a still-troubled company.

DARK HORSES: Sandy Weill's Primerica and First Boston under

the leadership of Archibald Cox, Jr. Both have the courage needed to make a comeback. Also on this list must go Michel David-Weill's Lazard Frères. Lazard, in its quiet way, is always in the money.

STURDIEST OUTSIDERS: Boston-based Fidelity, whose interests are expanding beyond money management, and Tokyo's Nomura. The former is a private company; the latter just acts like one. Both exhibit strengths in their core businesses that will allow steady and possibly significant expansions into new ventures in the 1990s.

Let's study the field in greater detail and see why Goldman, Sachs stands out as the firm favorite.

Goldman is the industry's last major partnership, which accounts for much of its strength. The partners foster an ethos and philosophy geared to balancing short-term opportunism with long-term conservatism. An important part of Goldman's success comes from the inordinate amount of time partners spend making sure they attract the cream of the business school crop.

The Goldman philosophy, say its competitors, is very simple. It's "Did you win?" On occasion, Goldman, reportedly, will send as many as twenty managing directors to a meeting to convince an important client that it should do business with the firm.

At Goldman, "You're told to leave your personality at the door," says a headhunter. "A militaristic mind-set is an asset." Staffers receive clearly defined missions. Success brings bountiful rewards; failure means rapid demotion. Staffers are reviewed every six months and the 5 percent with the worst performance records get the chop.

The prospect of making partner at Goldman, Sachs is the golden carrot that keeps so many trying. Selection into this inner group can mean an immediate 10 percent increase in net worth for those smart enough to get the call. By one count, no fewer than forty of Goldman's partners ranked among the hundred highest-paid executives on Wall Street.[1]

One Goldman characteristic may come as a surprise to outsiders. The firm is opportunistic. It lets others, particularly Salomon or First Boston, take the lead in product development. Later, if a market looks promising and there's money to be made, Goldman muscles in quickly, if necessary reverse-engineering its competitors' products.

There are stains on the record, notably in the highly publicized sexual harassment and discrimination charges filed against the firm. The death of Robert Maxwell exposed Goldman's surprisingly close ties to the disgraced financier.[2]

As Goldman has grown, power has moved into the hands of a dozen or so partners who run the firm. The other partners are "simply extraordinarily well paid employees," says one ex-Goldman trader. Those outside the inner group, including longtime partners, grouse that they get to make few decisions.

Few firms, however, now boast better connections in Washington, D.C. Friedman had shared control as senior partner with Robert E. Rubin until Rubin gave up that lucrative job for the prestige of being President Bill Clinton's point man on economic affairs in the White House.

The challenge ahead for Friedman is to hold the firm's social fabric together and maintain the ethos while attracting the capital needed for expansion and the all-important trading for its own account. This won't be easy. Speculation is rampant that Goldman soon will issue shares to the public.

If any firm can claim to rival Goldman, Sachs, it is Morgan Stanley, which used the 1980s to become a battle-hardened warrior and a public company. "Morgan makes people believe this is a genteel firm when really they are vicious pirates," says an observer, who knows the firm well. "They are extremely aggressive."

Morgan Stanley is a tough competitor. Waspy pedigrees are still important, but less so. Competitors are rarely in doubt about Morgan Stanley's strengths in fixed-income and equity trading or in derivatives, which nowadays produce much of its profits.

Part of Morgan Stanley's strategy under Chairman Richard Fisher is to push development of its foreign business. As Fisher says, "The two hundred largest private pension funds have about 5.5 percent of their assets in nondollar investment. The right number is 30 percent."[3] Already the firm has branches in thirteen foreign cities, where it garners slightly over 40 percent of its revenues. There isn't yet much profit being made abroad, but Fisher wants to be in place as U.S. investors become more global in their own strategies.

Morgan Stanley went into the 1980s as a private firm and with a mere eighteen hundred employees, of whom barely fifty worked abroad. In those days Morgan Stanley freely confessed to clients that it knew nothing about foreign currencies, commodity trading, or high-yield debts. Its traders were only starting to get a handle on options, futures, and swaps. The firm's net income then was a modest $24 million and every penny of it garnered from serving its clients' needs rather than its own.[4]

Today, in an era of admittedly inflated figures, Morgan Stanley would reckon to net that amount every couple of weeks or so, and the bulk of its business comes by acting on its own behalf.

Of late, Morgan Stanley has gained a reputation as a political hotbed. In one showdown, investment banking lost out to trading. Some fifty investment bankers received pink slips only days before the Christmas 1991 holidays. Says a recruiter, "There's a feeling that Morgan Stanley is no longer the kind of place it used to be."

That Bankers Trust and Bear, Stearns are among the more successful Wall Street houses may surprise some people. The former is a relative newcomer to Wall Street; the latter is a management iconoclast. The strengths of both houses, nonetheless, are formidable.

In trade jargon, Bankers Trust is a *wholesale* bank. Since dumping its retail branches, Bankers Trust has moved away from traditional commercial banking to become a Wall Street house in all but name. With $70 billion or so in assets, the firm offers a challenge few can ignore.

In the 1980s, the firm was a major backer of leveraged deals, with mixed results. Today, the bulk of its assets and its profits are tied up in trading, often in the derivatives markets. As a big player in government securities and currencies, both for its own and for its customers' accounts, Bankers Trust is making a direct challenge for Wall Street's business.

Half its pretax profits already come from international operations. This makes the firm as well positioned as any to take advantage of Eastern Europe's return to capitalism. Bulgaria's cement industry is but one of many new clients.

At Bear, Stearns, Chairman Alan "Ace" Greenberg is a shrewd

trader and a traditionalist. He doesn't see the need for long-term strategies. "Forward planning in this business is a futility," insists Greenberg, who followed a long line of traders into the top spot. "We just hire good people and let them do their thing."

Early on, Greenberg set the tone in a memorandum to his fellow managers. In it, Greenberg said that if someone applies for a job with an MBA degree, "we will certainly not hold it against them, but we are really looking for people with PSD degrees. It stands for poor, smart and a deep desire to become rich."[5] The firm had a fling in investment banking, but lately has returned to basics with the stress on carefully hedged trading, mainly for its own account.

What of Merrill Lynch and Shearson Lehman? Both tried and, as we saw in the last chapter, failed to differing degrees in their quest to dominate in every investment area.

After its bridge loan fiascoes, Shearson is under new management. It faces the strictures of tight controls imposed by officials seconded from American Express who had limited prior knowledge of Wall Street's workings. For the early part of the 1990s, Shearson will be preoccupied with redefining its role. The odds are that American Express will make Shearson a public entity again or, failing that, sever its offspring into two or more independent and possibly freestanding companies. None is likely to be large or strong enough to generate excessive profits or excitement. Shearson appears destined to be an also-ran.

Merrill, too, soon will come under new leadership. Dan Tully, the present chairman, is a caretaker. In the wings, numerous heirs apparent are strutting their wares, trying to prove they have learned from past errors. The firm's admirers say Merrill has tightened its cost controls and has the heft to succeed. They point to the top positions Merrill holds in underwriting and in commission business. Merrill's dominance comes by default. Wilier competitors have found better uses for their funds than to fight over such marginally profitable businesses. Merrill, too, will follow rather than lead.

Among the dark horses in this race, two are mounting a comeback. At Primerica, Sandy Weill is building his second empire on Wall Street much the way he did his first—by buying beaten-down assets cheaply. After selling Shearson to American Express, Weill didn't survive the political intrigues at AmEx and spent a year or so raising funds for Carnegie Hall and plotting his return.

Already Weill has turned Primerica into a diversified finance company spanning consumer credit, insurance, and money management, the latter through Smith Barney. Primerica is a haven for former hotshots, attracting ex-Drexel employees plus many of Wall Street's more talented, but controversial, characters. As Jeffrey Lane, once Shearson's top numbers man and now working for Primerica, says, "Weill's great opportunities have come when there's blood in the streets."[6]

Also on the comeback trail is First Boston, which is starting to regain lost ground under Archibald Cox, an ardent long-distance cyclist and son of the Watergate prosecutor. Cox is determined to bang heads with Morgan Stanley to prove Morgan erred by not promoting him to be its chief executive. Cox had worked for Morgan Stanley for two decades. "Archie has a real vendetta against the Morgan Stanley guys," says a recruiter who works for him. "He feels he wasn't treated fairly and is hiring all his Morgan Stanley cronies." If Cox can indeed remake First Boston in the Morgan Stanley mold, he will be riding a winner.

Fidelity must rank as an intriguing long shot, if Wall Street is right about the importance of gathering and managing assets. In a decade, Fidelity scored a sevenfold increase in the value of funds under its management. These now top $140 billion, which puts Fidelity far ahead of its nearest rivals—Merrill, with $95 billion, and Dreyfus, with $70 billion.[7]

From this base, Fidelity is vigorously invading the turf of Wall Street's retail houses. Fidelity now mails its customers questionnaires that it uses to help them reallocate their assets for better returns. Traditionally, advice was something investors received from their brokers, not from their mutual fund managers.

As the largest discount brokerage after Schwab, Fidelity is hustling hard for individual clients. In 1992, Fidelity unveiled a software program that lets customers use their personal computers to track the markets and catch the financial news as it breaks.

These days Fidelity runs what amounts to its own mini–stock market. It handles all the trades and the paperwork for 180 small brokers and numerous other institutions as well as for its own fund managers. On most days, Fidelity handles transactions equal to about one-tenth of the Big Board's volume.

Chairman Edward C. "Ned" Johnson III, who succeeded his founding father, has pushed Fidelity into consumer credit cards and insurance. Johnson owns art galleries, a head-hunting firm, and started a car service when he couldn't hail a cab. He controls 47 percent of Fidelity's stock, with the rest held by employees, who must sell it back when they leave.

The changing fortunes of the Japanese add zest to this race. A few years back, the Japanese appeared likely to become formidable global competitors. By 1988, Nomura Securities had eclipsed Toyota as Japan's most profitable corporation. For a while its profits exceeded the combined earnings of Goldman, Salomon, Morgan Stanley, Dean Witter, and Bear, Stearns. Then the bubble burst. With its unsavory links to the Japanese mob publicly exposed, Nomura no longer looked quite so formidable. But don't count the firm out yet.

With more than five million domestic customers, $6 billion in cash, and two dozen offices in the United States and Europe, Nomura remains by far Japan's largest securities firm and a powerhouse, even if the glow is off the Tokyo stock market. Another plus: the firm had done little trading for its own account until government officials began suggesting Nomura support the local market. This shielded it from what otherwise would have been horrendous losses when the stock market began collapsing in 1991.

For the moment, the easy-money days in Tokyo are over. Investors are paranoid about stocks and the government may insist the brokers unfix their commission rates. The U.S. firms operating in Japan relish that thought. By fixing commission rates, the Japanese artfully limit how much market share the foreigners get. Unable to cut prices, the foreign firms have had to rely on their superior research to make gains in market share.

In a policy switch, Nomura's legion of brokers no longer pushes the hot stock tip of the week but promotes the idea of asset management, much as their counterparts do in the United States. With the Japanese saving their money at triple the rate of Americans, this promises to be a sound strategy.

How strong Nomura becomes depends, in part, on whether Japan bows to external lobbying and opens more of its domestic financial markets to foreigners. The U.S. securities firms in particular attracted a sizable following among Japanese institutions by predicting the Tokyo crash and have prospered in Nomura's backyard. Morgan Stanley, Salomon Brothers, and Goldman, Sachs all have a more profitable time in Tokyo than does Nomura in New York, a point that doesn't get widely publicized in the trade debates between the two countries. This perhaps explains why after the U.S. firms make confidential filings with the Tokyo Stock Exchange—as they are required to do periodically—their figures become common currency in Tokyo financial circles. In one six-month span in 1991, Goldman, Salomon, and Morgan Stanley raked in almost thirty-six billion yen in pretax profits on their Japanese operations.

The source of the U.S. profits is also contentious. Much of it has come from program trading. Salomon in particular was so successful that at one point graffiti started appearing in the Tokyo subway urging the Japanese not to do business with Salomon. The sight of foreigners exploiting the blowoff in their inflated markets both annoyed and embarrassed the Japanese.

The head of Salomon's Tokyo office and the man ultimately responsible for offending the Japanese, ironically, was none other than Deryck Maughan, the deputy Mr. Clean chosen by Warren Buffett to lead Salomon out of its scandal problems in New York. Under Maughan, Salomon's Tokyo office also was a key player in the trading of Japanese government securities.[8] In one auction at least, Salomon bid for one-fifth of all the paper, upstaging even Nomura.

Unlike the Americans in Tokyo, the Japanese securities firms in New York have yet to make any money worth bragging about. The learning curve is steep, and the process of buying their way in has proved costly, with much of the investment in the boutiques wasted. That said, Nomura and the other major Japanese houses are unlikely to retreat far. "We have to stay in New York. We have to become more global," says Koji Yoneyama, who heads the North American operations of Daiwa Securities, arch-rival to Nomura.

The Japanese regard New York as a laboratory, a place where they can learn how to manufacture the latest in financial instruments. Thus Daiwa and Nomura are slowly blossoming in mortgage-backed securities and other derivatives in New York. At home, Nomura is far more cautious, perhaps because critics in Tokyo believe program trading exaggerated the fall of the Tokyo stock market.

Still, the importance of finance is well recognized in Japan.

Among the central planners in Tokyo, financial services are viewed in much the same way steel, autos, and electronics were—essential for the national development. As they did in other industries, the Japanese are showing they will take setbacks and spend whatever it costs to become global players in finance. Hence all the foot dragging about opening the doors to foreigners. Even so the Japanese aren't taking anything for granted. Against the day when full-scale competition comes to Tokyo, Nomura is assembling its own *keiretsu*—a closely tied empire of companies whose interests span real estate, insurance, research, and advertising.

Meanwhile in the United States, advisors and consultants talk of the need for Wall Street to reinvent itself. The more eloquent talk of a metamorphosis, predicting a new Wall Street is about to emerge. There's speculation of strategic alliances, particularly among the midsized firms eager to find allies in foreign markets. Such partnerships between firms operating from different geographical bases could shore up weaknesses, say the consultants.

The appeal of the alliance idea among consultants probably explains why Kidder, Peabody's top gun, Michael Carpenter, a former consultant, tried that approach. Before he came to Wall Street, Carpenter was with the Boston Consulting Group. In mid-1992, when rumors swirled about Kidder's future, he went to see Sandy Weill, his counterpart at Primerica, and proposed such an alliance. "I'll never do that again," a chagrined Carpenter later told colleagues.

Weill didn't reject the idea, and there was a chance some arrangement might have worked. General Electric would have welcomed a chance to bail out of its investment in Kidder. Here was a sensible solution. Kidder's banking and derivatives operations would have dovetailed into Primerica's Smith Barney, which concentrates on managing money for wealthy individuals.

Then Carpenter explained his proposal to various Kidder people. "It had seemed all right on paper," Carpenter later confessed, "but then it all burst apart when people saw what would happen to their departments." That's feudalism at work.

Modern-day feudalism, as we saw earlier, flourishes and explains why management restructuring by the likes of the Merrills and the Shearsons can become an exercise in futility and frustration. Power in the hands of the barons ensures weak central management. No one, lord or vassal, wants to move from a hot department to a cold one for the possible future good of the whole house. Personal sacrifice has its limits among the million-dollar-income crowd.

Look what happened at Kidder. These barons weren't about to let the king trade away their hegemony, even if Kidder may be too weak to survive without GE's support.

"We don't make alliances in this business," says James Hanbury, an analyst who spends his days studying Wall Street. "Look at every successful company—Goldman, Morgan Stanley, Warburg, or J. P. Morgan—they never buy anybody. They don't believe in alliances or in having 5 percent of anybody. They do it themselves. The most important thing you have is your culture and your managerial skill. If you make alliances and acquisitions, you dilute them."

Listen to Oppenheimer's Nate Gantcher, who, perhaps because he runs a midsized company, ranks among the more pragmatic of his peers. He contends that with all its problems, Wall Street will not change much. "I don't think there's going to be much consolidation," says Gantcher.

So what is Wall Street's future when the reluctance to change runs so deep in its culture?

Nate Gantcher doesn't respond immediately when asked that question. "What you have to do," he says after a moment of careful thought, "is to make a little bit of money in the tough times and be there in the good times." Gantcher pauses again and then adds with a wistful note in his voice, "The saddest thing is not being there for the good times."

Chances are many won't be. Their Wall Street is dying.

NOTES

Chapter One: Bear Trap

1. James Srodes, "Curmudgeon in Winter," *Financial World,* November 28, 1989, p. 82.

2. Anthony Bianco, "What's Behind the Profit Squeeze at Salomon," *Business Week,* April 20, 1987, p. 72.

3. Ford S. Worthy, "What We Learned from the '87 Crash," *Fortune,* October 5, 1992, p. 101.

4. Paul Volcker, "Reflections of a Central Banker," *Wall Street Journal,* October 16, 1990, p. 26.

5. Alvin Toffler, *Power Shift* (New York: Bantam Books), p. 57.

6. Phillip L. Zweig, "NYSE Chairman John Phelan," *Financial World,* December 29, 1987, p. 22.

7. Mitchell Pacelle, "Skyline Turning Hollow Near Wall Street," *Wall Street Journal,* June 11, 1992, p. 2.

8. Neil Barsky, "Back from the Dead," *Wall Street Journal,* July 6, 1992, p. 1.

Chapter Two: The Winds of Change

1. Robert J. Cole, "Small Investors Stoic While Institutions Bargain Hard," *New York Times,* May 2, 1975, p. 45.

2. William C. Freund, "Brokerage Services," Working Papers No. 99, August 1, 1991, Pace University, New York.

3. Eileen Shanahan, "SEC Study Says Stock Exchange Is Remiss in Guarding Investors," *New York Times,* July 18, 1963, p. 1.

4. Cole, op. cit.

5. Securities Industry Association, *Trends* vol. 8, no. 7, December 6, 1982.

6. Ann-Marie Meulendyke, *U.S. Monetary Policy and Financial Markets* (Federal Reserve Bank of New York), p. 82.

7. Samuel L. Hayes III and Philip M. Hubbard, *Investment Banking: A Tale of Three Cities* (Boston: Harvard Business School Press, 1990), p. 37.

8. Darrell Delamaide, *Debt Shock* (New York: Doubleday, 1984), p. 40.

9. Jacques Attali, *A Man of Influence: The Extraordinary Career of S. G. Warburg* (Bethesda: Adler & Adler, 1987), p. 258.

10. Richard D. Lyons, "Pension Reform Is Signed by Ford," *New York Times,* September 3, 1974, p. 1.

11. Moira Johnston, *Takeover: The New Wall Street Warriors* (New York: Arbor House, 1986), p. 68.

12. John Brooks, *The Takeover Game* (New York: Truman Talley Books, 1987), p. 107.

13. Roy C. Smith, *The Global Bankers* (New York: Truman Talley Books, 1989), p. 164.

14. *Securities Industry Association 1992 Fact Book,* p. 15. In the United States the value of public corporate financings had stood at $138 billion in 1985. From that point on the leverage craze took over, creating a debt explosion in all financial markets.

15. Thomas L. Friedman, "Investment Banks' New Day," *New York Times,* March 11, 1982, p. D1.

16. Walter Guzzardi, Jr., "The Bomb IBM Dropped on Wall Street," *Fortune,* November 19, 1979, p. 52. Frederick Whittemore, renowned head of Morgan Stanley's syndicate department, would say later, "I participated in that decision—a watershed decision—and I thought we were right, but obviously we were wrong." *Institutional Investor,* 20th Anniversary Issue, June 1987, p. 48.

17. Paul Hoffman, *Dealmakers: Inside the World of Investment Banking* (New York: Doubleday, 1984), p. 34.

18. William Power, "Merrill Strengthens Underwriting Lead," *Wall Street Journal,* October 1, 1991, p. C1.

19. Federal Reserve Bank of New York memorandum, March 20, 1992.

20. Speech to New York State Bankers' Association, January 30, 1992. A wise man, Corrigan volunteered to quit before disaster struck, tendering his resignation from the New York Fed, effective in the summer of 1993.

Chapter Three: A Question of Ethics

1. Norman Jonas and Joan Berger, "Do All These Deals Help or Hurt the U.S. Economy," *Business Week,* November 24, 1986, p. 88.

2. "Surviving the Drexel Whirlwind," *Economist,* March 24, 1990, p. 69.

3. Walter Adams and James W. Brock, *Dangerous Pursuits: Mergers and Acquisitions in the Age of Wall Street* (New York: Pantheon Books, 1989), p. 150.

4. Robert G. Eccles and Dwight B. Crane, *Doing Deals* (Boston: Harvard Business School Press), p. 221.

5. New York Stock Exchange memorandum no. 91-8, March 18, 1991.

6. Michael Siconolfi, "Under Pressure," *Wall Street Journal,* July 14, 1992, p. 1.

7. Michael Siconolfi, "Appeals Court Says Merrill Must Pay," *Wall Street Journal,* June 18, 1990, p. C13.

8. Ann-Marie Meulendyke, *U.S. Monetary Policy and Financial Markets* (Federal Reserve Bank of New York, 1989), p. 49.

9. Lowell L. Bryan, *Bankrupt* (New York: HarperBusiness, 1991), p. 158.

10. Meulendyke, op. cit., p. 51.

11. Martin Mayer, *The Greatest-Ever Bank Robbery* (New York: Scribner's, 1990), p. 90.

12. "International Finance Survey," *Economist,* April 27, 1991, p. 23.

13. "Round Two: The FDIC vs. Milken," *Business Week,* April 1, 1991, p. 69.

14. Paul Volcker, "Reflections of a Central Banker," *Wall Street Journal,* October 16, 1990, p. A26.

15. Resolution Trust Corporation letter to Congressman Edward Markey, March 6, 1992.

16. Stratford P. Sherman, "Bankruptcy's Spreading Blight," *Fortune,* June 3, 1991, p. 123.

17. Richard S. Teitelbaum, "LBOs Really Didn't Pay, Say the Chiefs," *Fortune,* August 26, 1991, p. 73.

18. William Power and Michael Siconolfi, "Wall Street's Slide Could Last Two More Years," *Wall Street Journal,* November 5, 1990, p. C1.

19. Michael Siconolfi, "Goldman Sachs Is Earnings King on Wall Street," *Wall Street Journal,* September 22, 1992, p. C1.

20. Eccles and Crane, op. cit., p. 66.

21. Securities Industry Association, 1992 Fact Book.

22. John Marcomb, Jr., "Welcome to Hauppauge," *Forbes,* October 30, 1989, p. 149.

23. Samuel L. Hayes III and Philip M. Hubbard, *Investment Banking: A Tale of Three Cities* (Boston: Harvard Business School Press, 1990), p. 58.

24. Kidder, Peabody Quantitative Research Group.

25. Ron Chernow, "Bank Reform?" *Wall Street Journal,* April 19, 1991, p. A14.

26. Fran Hawthorne, "Who's In Charge Here?" *Institutional Investor,* September 1990, p. 63.

27. Volcker, op. cit.

28. Keith Stock, "Regulations Drive Lending to Non-Banks," *Wall Street Journal,* July 30, 1992, p. A14.

Chapter Four: Michael Milken's Legacy

1. Securities Industry Association, *Trends* vol. 18, no. 3, May 8, 1992.

2. "The Wisdom of Salomon?" *Fortune,* April 11, 1988, p. 31.

3. "Mergers That Worked," *Fortune,* April 30, 1984, p. 270. In fairness, *Fortune* appeared to be having second thoughts two weeks later when it published Monica Jo Williams's "Shearson Bites Off a Mouthful with Lehman," *Fortune,* May 14, 1984, p. 129.

4. Anthony Bianco, "American Business Has a New Kingpin: The Investment Banker," *Business Week,* November 24, 1986, p. 80.

5. Joshua Mendes, "Getting the Most from Brokers," *Fortune 1992 Investor's Guide,* p. 184.

6. Terence P. Paré, "Tough Birds That Quack like Banks," *Fortune,* March 11, 1991, p. 79.

7. James A. White, "AMR's High-Flying Money Fund," *Wall Street Journal*, October 18, 1991, p. C1.

8. Michael R. Sesit, "Free-for-all," *Wall Street Journal*, March 25, 1991, p. 1.

9. John Meehan, "Mighty Morgan," *Business Week*, December 23, 1991, p. 64.

10. Allan Sloan and Howard Rudnitsky, "Taking In Each Other's Laundry," *Forbes*, November 19, 1984. Through the years, these reporters covered the power and the foibles of the Milken money machine as well as anyone. Among their other stories that served as sources for this narrative are: "Red Faces at Morgan Stanley," *Forbes*, July 29, 1985, p. 43; "A One-Man Revolution," *Forbes*, August 25, 1986, p. 34; "A Chat with Michael Milken," *Forbes*, July 13, 1987, p. 248.

11. English playwright John Osborne, in his memoirs *Almost a Gentleman* (Faber), frequently claims the quote originates with St. Augustine. *Economist*, November 23, 1991, p. 100.

12. Ida Picker, "The Big Bet," *Investment Dealers' Digest*, June 1, 1987, p. 16.

13. Miriam Bensman, "Weighing the Risks," *Investment Dealers' Digest*, August 20, 1990, p. 24.

14. The exploits of Credit Suisse and First Boston fascinate the media. Prominent among the many stories consulted for this narrative are: Anthony Bianco, "First Boston's Daring Bid to Grab Center Stage," *Business Week*, November 17, 1986; Carol J. Loomis, "The Biggest, Looniest Deal Ever," *Fortune*, June 18, 1990, p. 48; Ron Cooper, "Gut's Gang of Four," *Euromoney*, November 1990, p. 94; "As Many Names as a Russian Novel," *Economist*, November 3, 1990, p. 90; Kurt Eichenwald, "A Global Push by Credit Suisse," *New York Times*, November 11, 1990, p. D1.

15. James W. Michaels and Phyllis Berman, "My Story—Michael Milken," *Forbes*, March 16, 1992, p. 78.

16. *The Oxford Dictionary of Quotations*, 2d ed. (London: Oxford University Press).

17. Ron Chernow, letter to the editor, *Economist,* May 25, 1991, p. 8.

18. Richard L. Stern, "The World as Milken Sees It," *Forbes,* August 25, 1986, p. 40.

19. James W. Michaels, "History Lesson," *Forbes,* December 24, 1990, p. 38.

20. William Power and Nicholas Bray, "Dillon Read Seeks," *Wall Street Journal,* November 13, 1991, p. C1.

Chapter Five: At the Closing Bell

1. Craig Torres and Kenneth H. Bacon, "Wall Street Fire," *Wall Street Journal,* December 28, 1990, p. 15.

2. William E. Sheeline, "Who Needs the Stock Exchange?" *Fortune,* November 19, 1990, p. 119.

3. Speech to New York Financial Writers Association, March 12, 1991.

4. Speech to Financial Executives Institute, October 1, 1991.

5. Letter from James E. Buck, senior vice president, New York Stock Exchange, to the Securities and Exchange Commission, January 7, 1991.

6. Eileen Shanahan, "S.E.C. Study Says Stock Exchange Is Remiss in Guarding Investors," *New York Times,* July 18, 1963, p. 1.

7. Robert Steiner and Kevin G. Salwen, "Stock Specialists Often Keep Best Quotes," *Wall Street Journal,* May 8, 1992, p. C1.

8. *Securities Industry Association 1992 Fact Book,* p. 12.

9. "Specialists: Special at Exactly What?" *Fortune,* February 1, 1988, p. 22.

10. Even the NASDAQ boasts 6.1 percent of its listings come from abroad versus 4.6 percent on the NYSE, 6.7 percent on the Tokyo, and 22.7 percent on the London. "Trading Around the Clock," background paper, Congress of the United States, Office of Technology Assessment, July 1990, p. 30.

11. "Troubles in the Swiss Alps," *Economist,* February 15, 1992, p. 89.

12. Anne Newman, "Global Trading via NASDAQ System to Start," *Wall Street Journal,* January 10, 1992, p. C1. In fact, the launch of NASDAQ International took several months and trading didn't begin until early in 1992.

13. Speech to Securities Industry Association, New York, April 9, 1991.

14. Dana L. Thomas, *The Plungers and the Peacocks* (New York: Putnam, 1967, 1989), p. 69.

15. Neil Barsky, "Big Board, Amex Discuss Sharing a New Home," *Wall Street Journal,* June 12, 1992, p. C1.

Chapter Six: Weird Products for a Wired World

1. William Power and Craig Torres, "Stocks Drop as Salomon Clerk Errs," *Wall Street Journal,* March 26, 1992, p. C1.

2. William Glasgall, "Swap Fever: Big Money, Big Risks," *Business Week,* June 1, 1992, p. 102.

3. "Derivatives," *Economist,* May 16, 1992, p. 136.

4. Michael Liebowitz, "The Reincarnation of Richard Sandor," *Investment Dealers' Digest,* May 4, 1992, p. 26.

5. Barbara Donnelly and Craig Torres, "Sluggish Wall Street Is Rushing into Derivatives," *Wall Street Journal,* November 30, 1990, p. C1.

6. Carol J. Loomis, "A Whole New Way to Run a Bank," *Fortune,* September 7, 1992, p. 76.

7. Speech to New York State Bankers' Association, January 30, 1992.

8. Steven Lipin, "J. P. Morgan Had $50 Million in Losses," *Wall Street Journal,* March 10, 1992, p. A4.

9. Michael R. Sesit, "Chase Is Hiring Options Broker," *Wall Street Journal,* March 12, 1992, p. C1.

10. Salomon Inc. 1991 Annual Report to Shareholders.

11. Craig Torres, "Salomon Raises Its Bets," *Wall Street Journal,* June 2, 1992, p. C1.

12. Hearings before the House of Representatives' Subcommittee on Telecommunications and Finance of the Committee on Energy and Commerce, July 27, 1989.

13. "Coming to Terms with Futures," *Economist,* November 23, 1991, p. 85.

14. Stanley W. Angrist, "The Big Money Gives Futures a Whirl," *Wall Street Journal,* May 11, 1992, p. C1.

15. Hearings before the House of Representatives' Subcommittee on Telecommunications and Finance of the Committee on Energy and Commerce, October 25, 1989.

16. William Shepherd, "A Securities Roundtable," *Global Finance,* May 1991, p. 59.

Chapter Seven: Into the Private World of the Program Traders

1. Gregg A. Jarrell, "En-Nobelling Financial Economics," *Wall Street Journal,* October 17, 1990, p. A14.

2. Randall Smith, "Flood in Chicago Waters Down Trading," *Wall Street Journal,* April 14, 1992, p. C1.

3. Barbara Donnelly, "Goldman Pitches Commodity Futures," *Wall Street Journal,* July 22, 1991, p. C1.

4. Josef Lakonishok, Andrei Schleifer, and Robert W. Vishny, "The Structure and Performance of the Money Management Industry," *Brookings Papers on Economic Activity* (Washington, D.C.: Brookings Institution, 1982), pp. 339–91.

5. Speech to Financial Executives Institute, October 1, 1991.

6. Richard A. Booth, "In Defense of Program Trading," *Wall Street Journal,* April 1, 1992, p. A16.

7. Meulendyke, op. cit., p. 49.

8. Robert E. Litan, "The Frank M. Engle Lecture in Economic Security," American College, Bryn Mawr, Pa., April 30, 1991.

9. Bryan, op. cit., p. 156.

10. Glasgall, op. cit.

11. Litan, op. cit.

Chapter Eight: The Nelson Gambit Goes Awry

1. Craig Torres, "Dangerous Deals," *Wall Street Journal,* June 18, 1991, p. 1.

2. Charles McCoy, "Bad Bets," *Wall Street Journal,* August 9, 1991, p. A1.

3. Litan, op. cit.

4. "High-Yield Bonds," General Accounting Office, General Government Division, GAO/GGD 89-48, March 2, 1989.

5. Alan Murray, "Salomon Scandal Calls for Auction Overhaul," *Wall Street Journal,* August 26, 1991, p. 1.

6. William Simon, "Don't Let Salomon Doom T-Bonds," *Wall Street Journal,* March 30, 1992.

7. Mark C. Hansen, "Public Sympathy for Milken," *Wall Street Journal,* August 8, 1991, p. A12.

8. Speech to the American Council of Life Insurance, Washington, D.C., November 11, 1991.

9. Jonathan Macey, "The SEC Dinosaur Expands Its Turf," *Wall Street Journal,* January 29, 1992, p. A12.

10. Carol J. Loomis, "How Bankers Trust Lied About $80 Million," *Fortune,* September 7, 1992, p. 78.

11. *Report of the Presidential Task Force on Market Mechanisms* (Washington, D.C.: U.S. Government Printing Office, January 1988), p. 55.

12. David A. Vise and Steve Coll, *Eagle on the Street* (New York: Charles Schribner's Sons, 1991), p. 119.

13. Securities and Exchange Commission Release No. 34-30920.

14. Kevin G. Salwen and Sandra Block, "CFTC Gets in Habit of Rejecting Advice," *Wall Street Journal*, May 12, 1992, p. C1.

15. Speech to the Securities Industry Association, Boca Raton, Florida, December 3, 1992.

Chapter Nine: The Ripple Effect

1. Neil Barsky, "New York Commodity Exchanges Spurn New Jersey Offer," *Wall Street Journal*, November 7, 1990, p. A5.

2. Michael E. Porter, *The Competitive Advantage of Nations* (New York: The Free Press, 1990), p. 155.

3. "Managers Ranked by Tax-exempt Assets," *Pensions and Investments*, May 21, 1990, p. 3.

4. Myron Magnet, "The Money Society," *Fortune*, July 6, 1987, p. 26.

5. Dennis Levine with William Hoffer, *Inside Out* (New York: G. P. Putnam, 1991), p. 89.

6. James Sterngold, "Under Indictment," *New York Times*, December 22, 1988, p. D5.

7. Irving Kristol, "How to Restructure Wall Street," *Wall Street Journal*, November 1, 1991, p. A14.

8. Michael Siconolfi and Robert Johnson, "Broker Grandmother Accused," *Wall Street Journal*, August 29, 1991, p. C1.

9. Jon Nordheimer, "Whiz-Kid Broker's Downfall," *New York Times*, February 24, 1986, p. D1.

10. Michael Siconolfi, "Arbitrators Rule," *Wall Street Journal*, March 4, 1992, p. C1.

11. William Power, "Broker's Case Shows Justice Can Be Slow," *Wall Street Journal*, April 12, 1991, p. C1.

12. Milo Geyelin and Ann Hagedorn, "Moran Founder Indicted," *Wall Street Journal,* June 27, 1991, p. C1.

13. Carol J. Loomis, "Have You Been Cold-Called?" *Fortune,* December 16, 1991, p. 109.

14. John R. Dorfman, "Analyst Cheered Cascade, but Sold Stock," *Wall Street Journal,* March 11, 1992, p. C1.

15. Barbara Donnelly, "Small Investors' Hunger for CMOs Scares Pros," *Wall Street Journal,* November 11, 1991, p. C1.

16. Leah Nathans Spiro, "George Ball Finally Falls," *Business Week,* February 25, 1991, p. 42. See also Michael Siconolfi, "Prudential Is Told to Pay," *Wall Street Journal,* April 14, 1992.

17. Kevin G. Salwen, "Investors May Get Some SEC Help," *Wall Street Journal,* February 26, 1991, p. C16.

18. Michael Siconolfi and Kevin G. Salwen, "Investor Group Assails Roll-ups," *Wall Street Journal,* March 22, 1991, p. C8.

19. Steven Lipin and William Power, "Derivatives Draw Warnings," *Wall Street Journal,* March 25, 1992, p. C1.

20. Michael Siconolfi, "Morgan Stanley Told to Pay $48 Million," *Wall Street Journal,* May 11, 1992, p. C13.

21. Jonathan Clements, "Two States Sue," *Wall Street Journal,* November 9, 1990, p. C1.

22. Speech to the AIMSE Conference, Boca Raton, Fla., April 28, 1992.

23. Terence P. Paré, "How Schwab Wins Investors," *Fortune,* June 1, 1992, p. 52. See also George Anders, "PCs Bring Savvy to Mutual-Fund Reps," *Wall Street Journal,* November 11, 1992, p. B5.

24. James W. White, "Schwab Aims Its Discounts," *Wall Street Journal,* September 30, 1991, p. C1.

25. William Power, "Peter Lynch's Advice," *Wall Street Journal,* December 3, 1992, p. C1.

26. Lakonishok, Schleifer, and Vishny, op. cit.

27. Jonathan Charkham, *Creative Tension?* (London: National Association of Pension Funds, 1990).

28. "Safer Than It Looks," *Economist,* August 4, 1990, p. 63.

29. Craig Torres, "Heard on the Street," *Wall Street Journal,* January 10, 1992, p. C2.

30. Robert Jeffrey, "The Folly of Market Timing," *Harvard Business Review,* July-August 1984.

31. "A Survey of Capitalism," *Economist,* May 5, 1990, p. 8.

Chapter Ten: Strategies for Survivors

1. Among those who have traced the Merrill Lynch saga over the years are: Stratford P. Sherman, "Merrill Lynch's Not-So-Thundering Recovery Plan," *Fortune,* August 6, 1984, p. 75; Brett Duval Fromson, "Merrill Lynch: The Stumbling Herd," *Fortune,* June 20, 1988, p. 44; Richard Behar, "Can Merrill Catch Up?" *Forbes,* June 1, 1987, p. 39.

2. George Ball's rise and fall was widely chronicled in the media. In addition to personal interviews, this narrative draws upon "Not So Prudent," *Economist,* August 31, 1991, p. 60, and Leah Nathans Spiro, "George Ball Finally Falls," *Business Week,* February 25, 1991, p. 42.

3. Thomas O'Donnell, "The Tube, the Card, the Ticker and Jim Robinson," *Forbes,* May 25, 1981, p. 100.

4. Michael Siconolfi, "Dean Witter Proves an Asset to Sears, Confounding Pundits," *Wall Street Journal,* March 15, 1991, p. A1. See also "Sears Roebuck's Decision to Shed Dean Witter Could Spur a Trend," *Wall Street Journal,* September 30, 1992, p. C1.

5. Julie Rohrer, "Bankers Trust Goes Its Own Way," *Institutional Investor,* March 1990, p. 65.

6. "Brains versus Brawn," *Institutional Investor,* May 1988, p. 156.

7. Wasserstein, Perella and Company, for example, agreed to pay $18.5 million to assuage irate investors of Interco. This, as the *Wall Street*

Journal noted (May 11, 1992, p. A5), was three times larger than its fees for advising Interco to resist a takeover by loading up with debt. Interco later went into bankruptcy.

8. Randall Smith, "Self-Promoters," *Wall Street Journal,* October 24, 1990, p. A1.

9. Michael Siconolfi, "Stamford Capital's Investment Boutique," *Wall Street Journal,* June 27, 1990, p. C17.

10. Jeremy Stein, "What Went Wrong with the LBO Boom," *Wall Street Journal,* June 19, 1991, p. 18.

11. Stephen Taub, "Ted Forstmann's Last Laugh," *FW,* June 12, 1990, p. 14.

12. Julie Rohrer, "Money Management Powerhouses," *Institutional Investor,* January 1990, p. 44.

13. Leah Nathans Spiro, "Schmoozing All the Way to the Bank," *Business Week,* December 24, 1990, p. 68.

14. Randall Smith, "Blackstone Firm to Close Deal," *Wall Street Journal,* January 31, 1992, p. A9, and Kevin Helliker, "Weak Links," May 26, 1992, p. A1.

15. Tom Herman and George Anders, "Simon Breaks Up Partnership," *Wall Street Journal,* October 10, 1991, p. C1. See also, in *Forbes,* Thomas Bancroft, "Simon Stumbles," August 5, 1991, p. 40, and John H. Taylor, "When Friends Fall Out," March 16, 1992, p. 42.

16. Morgan Stanley's empire building has received close attention over the years. This account draws from numerous sources, including: Carol J. Loomis, "The New J. P. Morgans," *Fortune,* February 29, 1988, p. 44; Matthew Schifrin, "Bull in Morgan's China Shop," *Forbes,* February 19, 1990, p. 94; Alison Leigh Cowan, "A Brash Deal Maker," *New York Times,* August 31, 1990, p. D1; George Anders, "Captive Client," *Wall Street Journal,* December 14, 1990, p. 1, and "Morgan Stanley Faces More Suits," *Wall Street Journal,* January 30, 1991, p. C1.

17. *Investment Dealers' Digest,* May 30, 1988, p. 23.

18. Booz, Allen and Hamilton.

19. G. Christian Hill, "Security Pacific Will Post Loss of up to $360 Million," *Wall Street Journal*, December 11, 1990, p. A3.

20. Noel Alexander Associates.

21. Ken Auletta, *Greed and Glory on Wall Street* (New York: Random House, 1986), p. 237.

Chapter Eleven: In the Winners' Circle

1. Stephen Taub and David Carey, "Wall Street's New Austerity," *FW*, July 21, 1992, p. 36.

2. "MCC Moved in a Mysterious Way," *Economist*, December 21, 1991–January 3, 1992.

3. Craig Torres, "Morgan Stanley Is Betting on Big Overseas Growth," *Wall Street Journal*, June 21, 1992, p. C1.

4. Morgan Stanley and Company annual reports.

5. *Investment Dealers' Digest*, August 14, 1989, p. 16.

6. "People," *Institutional Investor*, March 1990, p. 14.

7. Lipper Analytical Services.

8. "Capital Markets Survey," *Economist*, July 21, 1990, p. 18.

G L O S S A R Y

Financial terminology changes almost as rapidly as the financial markets invent new products and ways of selling them. These are some of the current definitions for terms used by Wall Streeters that sometimes confuse outsiders.*

Agent: an individual or firm authorized by another person, called the principal, to act in the latter's behalf in transactions involving a third party. Assumes no risk, acts as a broker, and collects a commission.

Arbitrage: a strategy aimed at profiting from price differences when the same security, currency, or commodity is traded in two or more markets. Involves simultaneous purchase and sale in the different markets.

---

*Based loosely upon numerous sources, including *The Investor's Dictionary*, by Jerry M. Rosenberg (John Wiley & Sons, 1986); *Barron's Dictionary of Finance and Investment Terms*, by John Downes and Jordan Elliot Goodman (Barron's Educational Series, 1985); *Coopers & Lybrand Guide to Financial Instruments*; and *Securitization of Credit*, by James A. Rosenthal and Juan M. Ocampo [John Wiley & Sons, 1988].

Back office: operations department at financial institutions for handling record keeping, quotation, and communication systems plus regulatory compliance requirements.

Bankers: traditional separation of roles is fading.

—*Commercial bankers* are still primarily in the loan business, but several now also underwrite various securities and operate brokerages.

—*Investment bankers* are Wall Street's upper crust, who underwrite securities and use their own funds to facilitate trading. They also make bridge loans.

—*Merchant bankers* is historically a European term for a select bank with close ties to a limited but important set of clients. In the United States, the term became fashionable in the takeover era, but now it's a generic term synonymous with investment bankers.

—*Universal bankers* is a European term for commercial banks that also offer customers a full range of investment banking and brokerage services.

Basis point: a measure for interest-rate quotations with one basis point equaling 0.01 percent of a yield. Thus a move from 3.50 to 4 percent equals 50 basis points.

Bear trap: technically, what happens when a declining stock attracts heavy selling and then rebounds in price. In this book, *bear trap* refers to the misguided management actions taken in the financial arena by overly bullish executives.

Bell: signal that opens and closes trading on major exchanges.

Big Bang: deregulation of Britain's financial markets in 1986, when barriers between certain financial institutions were lifted and fixed commission structures were eliminated.

Big Board: nickname for the New York Stock Exchange.

Block: an institutional trade of a security amounting to at least 10,000 shares or bonds worth $200,000.

Boiler room: office for high-pressure telephone selling of speculative securities.

Bonds: the interest-bearing certificates of debt that obligate the issuer to repay the principal amount at a specified time. They now come in many varieties. For example:

—*Eurobonds* are an important source of capital for multinational corporations and foreign governments. They're sold to investors outside the country in whose currency they are denominated.

—*Sushi bonds* are issued in Eurocurrencies by Japanese borrowers and placed in the Euromarket, while *Samurai bonds* are issued in Japan by a non-Japanese firm in yen.

—*Junk bonds* carry speculative credit ratings and typically offer high interest rates to compensate for the possibility of default.

—*Yankee bonds* are denominated in dollars, issued in the United States by foreign firms.

—*Zero coupon bonds* are issued at steep discounts to their face value, which is paid on maturity, and don't offer periodic interest payments.

Boutique: a small financial institution that specializes by offering a limited range of investment advice and services. Usually caters to large investors and frequently acts as a principal.

Bridge loan: used in takeovers as interim financing, with the funds supplied to the acquisitor by investment or commercial bankers. Numerous bridge loans collapsed when bankers miscalculated the mathematics of their deals.

Broker-dealer: any Wall Street firm offering both commission- and fee-based services.

Brokers and Brokerages: act as agents and don't put their own funds at risk as principals, unlike investment dealers. Brokers are intermediaries between buyers and sellers and collect commissions. The term describes either the firm or its registered representatives who deal with customers. Brokerage services include advising on trades, asset management, tax shelters, and financial planning. Discount brokers charge low commissions but offer limited services.

Certificate of deposit (CD): an interest-bearing receipt payable to the depositor for funds deposited with a bank.

Collateralized mortgage obligation (CMO): a security backed by pooled mortgages. Each pool is divided into segments or tranches that mature sequentially. For each tranche a separate class of CMO is created, offering interest payments pegged to risk and duration. Introduced by Freddie Mac in 1983.

Commission: fee paid to a broker for executing a trade.

Credit securitization: the packaging, underwriting, and selling of loans and other receivables in the form of securities. Started in the 1960s with mortgages and now includes auto loans, credit cards, and trade receivables.

Derivatives: Broadly, a financial instrument derived from another. Includes futures, warrants, swaps, and literally dozens of other products. Widely used in hedging.

Erisa (Employee Retirement Income Safety Act of 1974): protects workers' interests in private pension and welfare plans and sets guidelines for the management of pension funds. Signed by President Ford on Labor Day 1974 and shifted power away from Wall Street.

Eurocurrencies: funds retained on deposit and circulated among banks and financial firms by corporations and national governments away from their home countries. Mostly used for short-term transactions. Some securities are issued in Eurodollars with a promise to pay interest in dollars deposited in foreign bank accounts.

Financial institution: here used broadly to cover all entities whose business involves collecting funds from the public and participating in the investment process.

Financial market: broadly covers any transaction involving capital and credit and breaks into at least five categories, whose boundaries aren't always clear.

—*Primary* market (for financial securities) involves the underwriting by investment bankers and the distribution of stocks, bonds, and other instruments to investors.

—*Secondary* market is the exchanging of those securities by the original and subsequent investors, with brokers acting as intermediaries. Transactions are processed via public exchanges such as the NYSE.

—*Upstairs* *market* is where securities transactions are completed within a brokerage and without using a stock exchange.

—*Over-the-counter* *market* is where securities that are not listed on traditional exchanges trade through a sophisticated computer network. The largest OTC market is the publicly run NASDAQ, but increasingly other private OTC markets are emerging for institutional trading in derivatives, synthetics, and swaps.

—*Third* *market* operates electronically, away from and in competition with the public exchanges, for the trading of both exchange-listed and OTC securities. Patronized by brokers and institutions seeking to lower execution costs.

—*Fourth* *market* eliminates Wall Street middlemen and commissions with institutional investors trading among themselves from their own inventories of securities.

Front running: an illegal practice used by professional traders acting on information not yet transmitted over the exchange tape about large forthcoming share transactions. Often involves option trading.

Futures contract: an exchange-traded agreement for the purchase or sale of financial instruments, indexes, or commodities at a predetermined date and price. Its value, however, is assessed daily.

Glass-Steagall Act of 1933: barred commercial banks from the underwriting and commission trading of most securities. The segmentation of the financial industry is fast being eroded, with commercial banks owning discount brokers, selling mutual funds, and, in some cases, underwriting stocks.

Guaranteed investment certificate (GIC): public bonds that typically promise a fixed rate of return for relatively short periods of time—three to ten years. Marketed by insurance companies.

Haircut: jargon for the formulas used in calculating net capital required for regulatory purposes by a broker-dealer. The worth of the securities held in the firm's inventory is reduced by their inherent risk, with equities typically having a 30 percent haircut and cash-equivalent government securities, zero.

Hedging: strategies used to offset investment risk caused by movements in interest rates, currencies, and commodities. Short selling and option trading are typical hedges. A perfect hedge eliminates the possibility of future gain or loss.

Index funds: mutual funds that invest in a portfolio of stocks to mirror either the whole market or a particular segment (health care, oils, etc.).

Indexes: measure value changes in groupings of stocks. Investors increasingly buy indexes or contracts based upon indexes rather than assembling portfolios of individual stocks in an attempt to match market performance and reduce risk and trading costs. Indexes now number in the thousands and are custom designed on computers.

Information vendors: the suppliers of current prices and other statistics for a variety of securities. Their information lessens Wall Street's importance for institutional traders.

Institutional investors: a confusing term that embraces everyone trading securities except individuals. Institutions such as mutual funds, banks, insurers, unions, pension and college endowment funds are Wall Street's main clients. But each Wall Street house is also an institutional customer of its competitors, since brokers and investment dealers constantly trade securities with each other.

Interest Equalization Tax: a 15 percent levy imposed by the Kennedy administration on foreign borrowers in the U.S. capital markets. Instead of reducing the U.S. balance of payments, as intended, it spurred development of the Euromarket as a serious competitor for Wall Street.

Investment banker/dealer: the title is often interchangeable, although technically bankers underwrite securities and dealers trade them. In practice, any firm that puts its capital at risk while underwriting and serving as intermediary between an issuer of securities and investors. Most carry large inventories of securities and trade both for their own and their customers' accounts. Most also operate commission-based brokerages and their own mutual funds.

Leveraged buyout: takeover of a company, usually by management, using borrowed funds. Loans are secured by the company's assets and repaid out of its cash flow.

May Day: May 1, 1975, the date when fixed minimum commissions were terminated in the United States.

Money center banks: large commercial banks headquartered in the world's leading financial centers, whose global interests usually encompass some investment dealing and brokerage business.

Mortgage-backed or Pass-through security: part of the trend of turning fixed loans into tradable securities. Typically, the principal and interest payments from homeowners are passed from the banks or savings and loans originating the mortgages through quasi-governmental agencies that, with Wall Street's help, pool and repackage them in the form of securities. Investors receive payments out of the interest and principal on the underlying mortgages.

NASDAQ: market founded in 1971 to offer computerized trading in small-cap companies, eliminating the need for a trading floor. Now the fastest-growing stock market, with over 5,000 listings. Owned and operated under SEC supervision by the National Association of Securities Dealers, a trade body.

Options: a contract giving its owner the right, but not the obligation, to buy (call) or sell (put) a specified item at a fixed price during a specified period. The buyer pays a nonrefundable fee (the premium) to the seller (known as the writer).

Principal: buys and sells for own account at own risk.

Private placement: sale of securities or other investments directly to a limited number of investors.

Program trading: originally involved buying or selling a basket of stocks that roughly corresponded to the leading stocks in the S&P 500 index and buying or selling an offsetting amount of stock index futures. If gains on one leg of the transaction offset losses on the other, the trade is profitable. Now the term includes all manner of index trades and swaps, with much of the trading done privately away from exchanges.

Quants: the computer whizzes who manufacture artificial and complex securities from the component parts of several financial instruments.

Regulation Q: Federal Reserve Board ceiling on the rates that banks and other savings institutions could pay on savings and other time deposits. Phased out in mid-1980s.

Repurchase agreement (Repo): Wall Street dealers' method of financing inventories of Treasury bills, notes, and bonds. The seller agrees to repurchase securities at an agreed price at a stated time (often as short as twenty-four hours). The borrowing charge is less than on a collateralized bank loan.

Shelf registration: the SEC's Rule 415, which allows a corporation to preregister securities, which it will issue and market in batches at future dates.

Soft dollars: the agency business that institutional investors assign to brokers in return for advisory services and computer and communications equipment, for which they would otherwise pay cash.

Specialist: member of a stock exchange who maintains a fair and orderly market in one or more securities in return for trading privileges.

Swap: basically, the exchange of one financial instrument for another. Typically involves the swapping of the characteristics (e.g., fixed or variable interest rate and currency denomination) of one debt instrument for those of another. Swaps permit borrowers to enhance their offerings and lower their costs. Holders can face increased risks in a daisy chain of swapped instruments if the credit worthiness of the counterparties alters.

Synthetic instrument: Any financial instrument artificially crafted out of another. For example, what's created in a swap. Typically complex and created by computer.

Underwriting: the basic business of investment bankers, who raise capital for issuers. The bankers' profits are the spread, or difference, between what the issuer receives and what the investor pays for new securities. A *bought deal* is when an underwriter commits to buy the entire issue.

Wall Street: the generic name used here for members of the financial community with offices and operations in Manhattan who raise and sell capital and securities for others. Members wear many hats and carry out varying functions as they serve institutional and individual clients. Few have offices on the Street itself.

Warrants: issued with a corporate debt instrument, but are traded separately and allow the holder to buy within a set time frame a specified amount of the issuer's common shares at a predetermined price.

INDEX